# THE
# WICHITA DIVIDE

## ALSO BY STEPHEN SINGULAR

# THE
# WICHITA DIVIDE

The Murder of Dr. George Tiller and
the Battle over Abortion

## STEPHEN SINGULAR

St. Martin's Press 🞢 New York

www.stmartins.com

Library of Congress Cataloging-in-Publication Data

Singular, Stephen.
   The Wichita divide : the murder of Dr. George Tiller and the battle over abortion / Stephen Singular. — 1st ed.
         p.   cm.
   ISBN 978-0-312-62505-4 (hardback)
   1. Abortion—Moral and ethical aspects—United States.   2. Tiller, George, 1941–2009.   3. Physicians—Kansas—Wichita.   4. Murder victims—Kansas—Wichita.   5. Roeder, Scott.   6. Pro-life movement—United States—Case studies.   7. Pro-choice movement—United States—Case studies.   I. Title.
   HQ767.5.U5S545 2011
   364.152'3092—dc22

                                                                2010042132


First Edition: April 2011

10   9   8   7   6   5   4   3   2   1

*To Lindsey Roeder*

# CONTENTS

# THE
# WICHITA DIVIDE

# PROLOGUE

After waiting forty minutes in the lobby of the Sedgwick County Detention Facility in Wichita to meet the accused killer Scott Roeder, I thought he'd changed his mind and was stiffing me. This did not make me happy. Six weeks earlier, I'd written him asking to be put on his visiting list, which is under the complete control of those who are locked up. If they don't want to talk with you, you don't get into the jail. Roeder quickly mailed back a letter saying that he'd go through the process of adding me to his list. To be safe, I made a series of calls to the facility to find out if I was, in fact, an approved visitor. Jail personnel said they couldn't give out that information unless I came there in person and showed them a photo ID. I was five hundred miles away in Denver and didn't want to drive to south central Kansas unless I was absolutely sure I could see the prisoner.

"We can't help you with that," the man at the jail had said. "It violates procedures."

I asked to speak with his superior and then asked *him* to give me a break.

When he waffled slightly, I knew I was making headway. He peeked at the list and my name was on it. If I showed up at the jail on Tuesday at nine a.m., I'd be able to spend as much as an hour with the man charged with entering Wichita's Reformation Lutheran Church seven

Sunday mornings ago and placing a gun barrel directly against the forehead of Dr. George Tiller, America's most controversial abortion provider. The local district attorney's office contended that Roeder had killed the physician with one shot and then committed aggravated assault against two church ushers who'd tried to stop him from fleeing the crime scene.

In a sense Dr. Tiller's death had ended thirty-five years of bitter history over abortion in Wichita, but in another sense his death had only deepened the bitterness around the issue that had divided the country for more than three decades. Abortion was just one front in the new civil war the United States had been fighting throughout those decades—a battle that by spring 2009 seemed to be growing every day. Following the inauguration of President Barack Obama several months ago, protests against the new leader and racial violence had been spreading; this would only intensify as the weather grew hotter. Since Obama had taken office, threats against him were up 400 percent and ten political murders had erupted around the nation. I'd driven across two states to meet with one of the foot soldiers in this conflict, because he was eager to speak with me, or at least that's what his letter had said.

I was now in Wichita on a July day that would reach 104 degrees. As the clock on the wall behind the guard's desk approached 9:45, I was getting edgier by the second and more annoyed that Roeder wasn't responding.

Every Tuesday, he got one hour to speak to outsiders. Two of his strongest anti-abortion supporters from the Kansas City area, Anthony Leake and Eugene Frye, had been advising him and he'd probably decided to see them today instead of me. For years Leake, according to *The Kansas City Star*, had "vocally supported the killing of abortion doctors" and both men had been counseling Roeder about finding him a lawyer sympathetic to their cause. They hoped to hire an attorney who'd use the "necessity defense"—the legal argument that killing an abortion doctor was a lesser offense than abortion itself.

As I fidgeted and glanced at the clock, a stream of youngish women checked in at the front desk with the female officer on duty. Several were dressed provocatively and had on more than enough perfume, something I'd observed in every jail I'd been in from Long Island to San Diego. The women wanted the men inside to see and smell what they were missing. After a few minutes, all the women's names had been called and they were led through a side door into the room holding their husbands or boyfriends (none of these inmates was being held in maximum security, as Roeder was). Twice, I'd left my seat and walked to the front desk to ask about my situation. Twice, the officer in charge had told me to sit down and be patient. What had I expected driving out here? Why did I think that the alleged gunman would keep this appointment? He had nothing to gain from speaking with me, and it was going to be a very long ride home.

As I stood for the third time, the phone rang on the guard's desk and she picked it up.

"Who's here to see Roeder?" she asked.

I charged toward her.

"Get onto that elevator"—she pointed toward a far wall—"and go to the second floor. They'll take care of you up there."

The only thing on my person other than my clothes, I told her, was my car key because I didn't want to set off any metal detectors.

"Should I leave the key with you?" I said.

She smiled the smile of all people who are bored with their jobs, have a little authority, and are looking for amusement.

"That isn't necessary," she replied. "But try not to shoot or stab anyone with it."

When I got off the elevator and stepped into the second-floor lobby, it was empty and dark. I stood there for a few moments, confused. Had I followed her directions correctly? Was this would-be comedian playing a trick on me?

An armed guard arrived with a magnetic wand and told me to take off my shoes, which I did. I handed him the key. He scanned me and the detector went off three times in a row—loudly—which baffled both of us. I must have been edgier than I realized, giving off a very heavy vibe.

"You got any metal inside of you from surgery?" he said.

I shook my head.

"Any screws in there holding stuff together?"

"No."

"That's really weird."

He shrugged and scanned me again. This time it was silent.

He escorted me into a tiny room divided in half by a smudged, thick glass wall; on either side of the glass were a chair, a small counter, and a beaten-up telephone. After leaving me alone and closing the door, the guard stood directly behind me and stared in through a small open-ing, hovering about four feet over my shoulder. With a nightstick, a flash-light, or some other hard object, he banged on the door every few seconds just to let me know he was still there—an unnerving sound.

The door on the other side of the glass burst open and Roeder rushed in, wearing a bright red jumpsuit. With a huge grin enlivening his face, he bounded over to me and reached for his phone, while I picked up mine. We stared at each other, about eighteen inches apart. Like all prisoners, he was quite pale, and much larger than I'd anticipated, with a balding, dome-shaped head.

"Hiya, Steve!" he boomed. "How are ya!"

Fine, I said, as his exuberance reached me through the glass. Was he in one of those manic phases his ex-wife, Lindsey, had warned me about? Or was this how he greeted everyone? Without a wall between us, I'm sure he'd have given me a two-fisted handshake or clapped me on the back. However much we try to imagine what other people are like from reading about them or seeing their image on television, we're always wrong. Nothing matches coming face-to-face with a jailed stranger.

"You drove all the way from Denver?"

I nodded.

"I was born in Denver, but we moved to Kansas when I was very young. Why did you come here? What are you interested in? What do you want to talk to me about?"

I always preferred to be the one asking the questions, but in this game there are no rules.

Twenty-five years ago, I explained, a liberal Jewish Denver radio personality named Alan Berg had been assassinated by a small band of neo-Nazis from the Northwest, called the Order, who'd committed nearly 250 other crimes. Ever since then, I'd been writing about people who embraced very strong (I avoided the word "fanatical") political or religious beliefs and acted them out in criminal behavior. I was aware that Roeder, like the men in the Order, believed that he was one of God's "Chosen People." They all thought of themselves as the "real" Jews of biblical history, while every other group making this claim was an impostor.

"I heard about that case," he said, shooting me another grin.

Of course he'd heard of it. Everybody in the circles he'd traveled in had heard about it and some of them had been celebrating Berg's murder for the past quarter century.

"I'm glad you came to see me."

The guard banged the door again, sounding like gunfire, causing both of us to flinch and glance around. Roeder leaned in closer and said he was certain that prison employees in another part of the jail were listening in on our phones. But one day we'd be able to talk without this piece of glass between us and then he'd open up and tell me what he really knew about underground plans for more violence against the government or other targets.

He launched into a list of the problems caused by his arrest following Tiller's death last May 31. Roeder badly needed a high-fiber diet, but they served only low-fiber food at the jail, and that was messing up his digestive tract and bathroom habits. He had to eat at least 2,000 calories a day to keep his large body going, but they were giving him a meager 1,200. It was too cold in his cell to sleep through the night, even though he had on long underwear beneath his jumpsuit, and he needed his sleep apnea machine. The other inmates weren't as friendly as he'd expected, but at least he was off suicide watch and out of solitary confinement, able to mingle with the general prison population. He'd met one man who shared his religious convictions and they were studying the Bible together.

"Jail is hard, man," he said. "Too hard. I don't mind prison so much, but I can't stand being in jail. I'm gonna go on trial in about a month and then they'll send me to prison and that will be much better. The only thing worse than jail is a mental hospital. I was in there once and I'm never going back."

As a teenager, he'd been diagnosed with schizophrenia and put on mood-altering drugs, which he'd hated and vowed not to take again. He'd kept that vow. When I brought this up, he insisted that he'd never been mentally ill and had stopped taking recreational drugs decades ago, in his twenties.

"When something like this happens," he said, "people always go back and bring up things from your past. They like to talk with your ex-wife and get all her opinions. You can imagine what she'd tell the media about me. I'm not schizophrenic."

As he talked, he never stopped moving, bobbing and weaving in front of me, hunching his shoulders and laughing, exuding energy and friendliness. He reminded me of some of the Kansas farm kids I'd grown up with—big-boned, lumbering good ol' boys who were a little more calculating than they appeared.

The longer he complained about conditions at the jail, the more I was struck by his demeanor. Despite all the grumbling about the food and the temperature, he seemed happy behind bars. Most people serving time deny doing the crime they've been charged with, offer excuses for their actions, or try to fool you about their motives. They're depressed or angry. The fifty-one-year-old Roeder made no attempt to hide that he'd been locked up for shooting Dr. George Tiller a month and a half earlier, nor did he try to deny that he was about to be convicted of the first-degree murder and sent to prison, possibly for the rest of his life. He didn't just look at peace; he looked proud of himself.

When I asked him about Tiller's death, he said, "My only regret is that I didn't do this sooner."

Right after the killing, Sedgwick County District Attorney Nola Foulston had announced that this would not be a death penalty case because it didn't meet several criteria including murdering a minor or killing for money, and it wasn't a homicide involving sex or multiple victims.

Did Roeder realize that back in the 1990s Kansas had reinstated capital punishment and if convicted he could have faced lethal injection?

"That never crossed my mind," he said. "What Tiller was doing was wrong, even though it wasn't illegal. When something is morally wrong, even if it's legal, it violates God's law. God's law is always more important than man's law."

He paused, made eye contact with me through the glass, and forcefully stated, "I stopped abortion in Wichita."

It took a few moments for the full weight of those five words to sink in, given the history of the city's involvement with the issue since the mid-1970s.

"I've heard," he went on, "that since this happened three women have changed their minds and decided not to get an abortion, because Tiller isn't around anymore."

He smiled and said, "Wichita is no longer the abortion capital of the world."

He conveyed no emotion at all about Dr. Tiller's death—a void where one might have expected rage or anxiety or fear about his legal fate. Nothing was there, and that was the most unsettling thing about him. He seemed to have released his own personal stress over the abortion issue, and could at last relax.

I asked if this was true.

"Yes," he said. "I'm more relaxed now and so is Wichita."

The guard banged the door, making us cringe.

We stared at each other and he repeated how glad he was that I'd driven out to see him. He hoped we could meet again.

In twenty-five years of writing about domestic terrorism, I'd never been this close to a terrorist before—or to the civil war unfolding in my own backyard. When I'd begun tracking this war back in 1984, it had existed only at the fringes of America: nine white men out in the Idaho woods, filled with hatred and committed to murdering a talk show host. Now it permeated our entire society, in our media, politics, culture, and religion. The mind-set of "us against them" had become not just normalized, but the pathway to great acclaim and success. The mainstreaming of hate and the glorification of this divisive mentality was perhaps the biggest—and most deadly—change in the United States in my lifetime.

The first American Civil War lasted about four years before the North won its victory in 1865 and began the path toward ending slavery. This second one has gone on for about forty years now, with no end in sight. The new millennium, which many had felt would usher in a time of healing and unity, has seen this war spread and intensify; some called it a fight for the soul of the nation. Ever since Alan Berg was gunned down in his driveway, I'd been traveling around the Midwest and West bumping into this same story over and over again, and every time I found it, it was bigger and more disturbing.

At Wichita's Reformation Lutheran Church on May 31, 2009, something larger than a single murder was unleashed. Tiller's demise was the start of a homicide investigation—but also the culmination of a struggle whose chief battleground was in the American heartland, in Kansas, dead center in the first War Between the States. In 1861, Kansas had come into being as a "free state" to stop the spread of slavery in neighboring Missouri. The phrase "Bleeding Kansas" was coined after the 1856 killing of five pro-slavery Southerners in the Kansas territory at the hands of the anti-slavery leader John Brown and his supporters, in response to a pro-slavery raid on the "free soil" town of Lawrence. In 1859, Brown led his infamous attack on the federal armory at Harpers Ferry, West Virginia, where seven more people lost their lives. Brown was later caught, tried for treason, and hung in Charles Town, Virginia, a catalyst for the Civil War, which began two years later.

Topeka, thirty miles from my hometown, was the site of the landmark 1954 civil rights case, *Brown v. Board of Education*, which led to the racial integration of American schools. In the 1970s, the University of Kansas, where I'd attended college, had seen a citizen shot dead in the street over protests against the Vietnam War, and during the past three decades Kansas had been the most contested turf in the nation's fight over women's reproductive rights, with 2,700 arrests of abortion protesters in Wichita in 1991. More recently, parts of the Kansas legislature had tried to stop the teaching of evolution in public classrooms, and in 2004, Thomas Frank's book *What's the Matter with Kansas?* had made the Sunflower State the front line of America's cultural combat. Wichita in particular had become the dividing line between two visions of the United States, two views of God, and two radically different perceptions about what women can and cannot do with their own bodies.

With one shot to Dr. Tiller's forehead inside a house of worship, the battle in Kansas had gone from protest to political assassination. No place was safe anymore; no sanctuaries remained for escaping this conflict. The new war was everywhere.

# ON THE FRINGES

# I

What George Tiller remembered most about his father, he once said, was the admiration and respect, even love, he had received as a community physician. Born in Wichita in 1941, George spent his boyhood tagging along with his dad, Jack, who served patients around town or at his office near East Kellogg Street, a major business artery running through the city. The youngster liked to carry Dr. Tiller's black bag and watch him practice medicine, not just with instruments and pills, but with the manner and words required for someone who was ill or nearing death. His father had a general medical practice, delivering babies, performing major surgeries, and treating people with heart attacks and strokes.

"There was a very special and unique and very warm, close relationship between my father and his patients," Tiller recalled. "I liked that. I continued to see this doctor/patient relationship through high school and through college, and I decided that's what I wanted to do."

What could be better than making a living helping people who really needed you and playing a vital role in the health of your community? As a teenager, George swam competitively and played other sports, but he never lost his early ambition to enter medicine. After high school, he attended the University of Kansas in Lawrence on a swimming scholarship and earned the nickname "Tuna," while taking a degree in zoology.

Following his graduation from the KU School of Medicine, he wanted to set up a practice in dermatology. It was a safe, lucrative, and fairly predictable field; dermatologists rarely got called into emergency rooms or worked late at night. George had been raised to pursue a secure career and taught the conservative Republican values of his family. After getting his MD, he joined the Naval Aerospace Medical Institute Flight Surgeon School and was on a tour of duty as a surgeon in 1970 the day the call came in.

His father, a trained pilot, was flying his family to British Columbia in a small turboprop airplane, when the craft smashed into a hillside in Yellowstone National Park. George's father, mother, sister, and brother-in-law were all killed. The Navy gave the young doctor a humanitarian discharge and he and his wife, Jeanne, returned to Wichita to take care of his ailing grandmother and to adopt his deceased sister's one-year-old son. With these affairs in order, he stopped by one morning at the office where his father had worked for decades, now kept open by nurses.

"On September 21, 1970," he recollected, "I spent my first day in my dad's office, and there were just dozens of people flooding in there. They said, 'You've got to stay and take care of us. There's nobody else to take care of us.' At that time, there was competition for physicians, not competition for patients. So there was nobody else to absorb this practice."

While agreeing to treat them, he explained that this was only a temporary arrangement. He'd stay for a year at the most, before moving on and pursuing his dermatology career probably outside of Kansas. But the patients kept coming, urging him not to shut down. They admired and respected him, just as they had his father, and he was becoming attached to them. He liked the routine of going to work at this familiar office each day and having a general practice—a year passed and he didn't leave Wichita. He was delivering babies and taking care of stroke patients, heart attack victims, and those with diabetes. To his surprise, he was drawn to family medicine because, he said, people "depended on you for their health care, not only for themselves, but for the rest of their families—their grandmothers and grandfathers. And being a member of that extended family, for the health care provider, was fascinating and engaging. It was exactly what I wanted to do."

As his female patients grew more comfortable with him, they shared stories and medical secrets. Back in the 1950s, women in Wichita had started coming to his father for abortions and Jack Tiller had performed them, at a time when this was illegal and dangerous for a physician. He'd taken the risk after refusing to help a patient who'd later died during her botched attempt to end her pregnancy through an unqualified abortionist. Very quietly, he'd become the local, healthy alternative to backstreet abortions; as his underground reputation spread, so did the gratitude women around town felt for him.

George Tiller had been practicing medicine for several years when the U.S. Supreme Court issued its landmark 1973 *Roe v. Wade* decision, making abortion legal. The patient and her doctor were now the sole decision makers regarding pregnancy. With the law in place, a new generation of females approached Dr. Tiller and asked him to carry on his father's practice. He begged off: this wasn't his mission or, for that matter, what he'd been trained to do. Still they kept asking. Some were desperate for help and others reminded him of the woman who'd died after his father had refused her treatment, their stories building up and carrying an emotional impact. Eventually, he said yes, and his immersion into this nearly unmapped medical field began. Unwanted pregnancies were a far more complex medical, and social, challenge than he'd ever realized.

Many years later, Tiller told the Feminist Majority Foundation about his early years in his profession:

"One of the first people who taught me about the devastation that can occur in a family as a result of alcoholism, drug addiction was Haddie Mueller. She's been dead for about thirty years now. But she was one of my father's patients, and she did have three terminations of pregnancy before it was legal. And she explained all of those things to me. She explained about poverty, and she explained about abuse, and she explained about alcoholism and drug addiction and how it impacted negatively the family. So, I am a woman-educated physician in every aspect of my understanding about abortion and about responsibility of women in the family, both socially and financially."

After performing his first few abortions at a prominent nearby hospital, Wesley Medical Center, Tiller learned he was good at this work. He found it to be an important service, and very rewarding to help women go through what was usually a traumatic experience, both before and after their operations.

If he was kind with his patients, he could be demanding of his staff and a bit vain, especially when he was drinking. No one at work was allowed to call him "George," only "Doctor Tiller." He drove a red Corvette he named Igor and wore a full-length mink coat around Wichita. He was curt with the nurses and assistants whom he felt were less than diligent. More than once he was heard shouting in the Wesley hallways at someone who wanted to cut a procedural corner or go home early. Medicine, he reminded them brusquely, wasn't a nine-to-five job, but a calling.

Like his father, he was learning things he'd never been taught in medical school. He was known for repeating a series of pet sayings, and two of them were:

"The woman's body is smarter than the doctor."

"I want to make the world better, one woman at a time."

Occasionally, after a patient's operation, he and his wife invited her into his home to recuperate. Some stayed for weeks. He expected other medical personnel to treat the women as he did, and his feelings became stronger as his practice expanded, and the controversy around his work grew. You were either loyal to him and his staff—"Team Tiller"—or you didn't belong in his clinic. He began recruiting and hiring mostly females, who called themselves "the sisterhood," and their mission was larger than abortion.

"We have made higher education [for some women] possible," he once said. "We have helped correct some of the results of rape and incest. We have helped battered women escape to a safer life. We have made recovery from chemical dependency possible. We have helped women and families struggle to save their unwell, unborn child a lifetime of pain."

Tiller offered abortions for about one-fourth the price ($250 as compared to $1,000) that other places were charging. And there was an ever-growing demand; *Roe v. Wade* had made public a practice that had earlier been handled in secrecy, and the United States would soon see about a million abortions a year nationwide. In 1975, Tiller hung a portrait of his father in his office, rechristened Women's Health Care Services. Patients from across the country heard about him and the word spread—a first-rate abortion doctor out in Kansas was willing to take on the most difficult medical challenges facing pregnant women: undeveloped fetuses; fetuses with cancer; disfigured infants; and genetic dysfunctions. But as talk of his skills grew, so did a different kind of word-of-mouth. By 1975, his clinic was attracting its first protesters, changing the atmosphere not just in his office but throughout Wichita, a small city proud of its history and heritage, not at all the sort of place that went looking for controversy or notoriety.

In 1541, Francisco Vasquez de Coronado, searching for the mythical "golden cities of Quivira," had ventured into what would become south central Kansas. He didn't find any gold, but met up with the Wichita Indian tribe, living for centuries in grass huts on this flat and fertile landscape. Coronado moved on, and three hundred years later the first white settlers arrived, trapping and trading goods with the Wichita. The pioneer Jesse Chisholm lent his name to the famous trail that sent six million cattle north from Texas to Kansas between 1860 and the late 1880s. After the Civil War, the Wichita were "removed" to Indian Territory and whites took hold along the banks of the Arkansas River, naming their settlement after the indigenous tribe.

In 1900, Wichita achieved fame, or infamy, when Carrie Nation of the Woman's Christian Temperance Union took her crusade against alcohol to the fledgling city. On the night of December 26, she went to every bar in Wichita and demanded they shut themselves down. That didn't happen, so the next day she charged into the crowded Carey House tavern and smashed up the place with a pool ball and a rock.

People later said that while all of the bars had upset her, the John Noble painting *Cleopatra at the Roman Bath* displayed inside the Carey House had pushed her over the edge.

In 1914, oil was found near Wichita and the money from this discovery provided the funds for local entrepreneurs to invest in another budding industry. In 1917, America's first mass-produced airplane, the Cessna Comet, was manufactured in Wichita, followed by the founding of Learjet, Beechcraft, and Boeing. The city became a test center for new aviation, and dubbed itself the "Air Capital of the World." The region had a knack for innovation and in 1932, the Wichita orchestra leader Gage Brewer helped bring the electric guitar into the world of concertgoing.

During World War II, a significant part of the domestic war effort was centered in Wichita, as Boeing was converted into a manufacturing base for U.S. military bombers, its factories running twenty-four hours a day. Money flowed into the city and nearly any adult could walk into one of these businesses and get a decent-paying job. Movie theaters, dance halls, and restaurants never closed, so that people leaving their shift in the middle of the night had places to unwind. By 1945, 4.2 bombers were being produced each day in Wichita. Following the war, the city became home to a number of successful start-ups: Pizza Hut, White Castle, Mentholatum, Taco Tico, Coleman, and Koch (oil and gas) Industries, the nation's second-largest privately held company. It was a modest, Republican town, yet had a strong union presence because of its thriving aircraft industry.

It was also a town that prided itself on its openness, friendliness, and affordability (in March 2010, NBC's *Today Show* named it one of the top five most affordable cities in America). Whenever you pass through the tight airport security in order to fly out of Wichita, the armed guards inspecting your photo ID thank you for your cooperation and call you by your first name. It's also a place where the Christian religion is pervasive and important in ways that would be difficult to overstate, ways that go beyond doctrine and theology. It's no coincidence that the two most famous local crimes—involving the BTK serial killer and the murder of Dr. George Tiller—both involved churches. Dennis Rader, aka BTK, lived in tiny Park City, a few miles north of Wichita, and as you drive into that village from the east on Sixty-first Street, you pass the Park City Baptist Church, the Park City Christian Church, the Church of the Nazarene, and the Calvary Temple Assembly of God, all within a few hundred yards of one another. Rader, who killed at least ten people starting in 1974, was president of his congregation at Christ Lutheran Church, just outside Park City. After murdering one victim, he carried her into the sanctuary of his church around midnight and took elaborate photos of her body in bondage. It was inconceivable to anyone in his congregation, and especially to Pastor Michael Clark, that Rader could have done these things, but in the summer of 2005 he confessed to all of them on live national television.

This kind of thing just wasn't supposed to happen in or near Wichita, Kansas, which in 1945 had been given the Grand Award from the National Safety Council for being the safest city in America. It won the same award in 1958, 1959, and 1960. How could it have been terrorized by a serial killer who'd maddened and eluded the Wichita Police Department, and the entire community, for more than thirty years?

Part of the answer was trust, and a great desire among the local population to think the best of others, even strangers. If this was true in general, it became ever truer inside the churches of Wichita and the surrounding area. Growing up in rural Kansas myself, I never heard people debate the finer points of their faith. They went to church because they wanted to be inspired by a sermon, to be connected to a realm beyond the mundane and the physical, and because it provided a special environment for them to show their care, even their love, for their neighbors. It was safe to open up a little more here, to throw back your head and sing hymns loudly, or to reveal your heart. On Sunday mornings, the sanctuary was a place of refuge from a more difficult or dangerous outside world.


A hundred years after its founding, even a place as bedrock conservative as Wichita was being shaped by new social forces. Between 1950 and

1970, the city's black population nearly doubled, from 5 percent to 9.7 percent. Change and division were coming to the nation everywhere and in the early 1970s a race riot broke out in the halls of Wichita's West High. During a meeting to discuss the violence, an African-American student confronted a white teacher and asked if she'd marry a black man. "She said she wouldn't do this because of the effect on the children," recalls the Wichita author Robert Beattie, who attended West High in the seventies and was injured in the riot. "Back then, in that time and place—Wichita in 1972—that was all that needed to be said. The children would have had great difficulty being accepted by either racial group."

A few years after the West High riot, nuns began showing up at Dr. Tiller's clinic, sent there by the Catholic Church. They were polite but intent on making a statement about Catholicism's view of abortion, which they considered an affront to both God and humanity. The nuns were about to find a lot of allies. As the evangelical movement swept across the country in the 1970s, millions of Americans reported having born-again Christian experiences, and this number would continue to grow. The official 2004 U.S. survey of religion and politics identified the evangelical percentage of the American population at 26.3 percent, or nearly 70 million people, while Roman Catholics were 22 percent and mainline Protestants made up 16 percent.

When the evangelical movement took off in the early 1970s, I was living in New Jersey and around a number of people who were deeply involved in it. Many were either too young to have lived through the social unrest of the 1960s or had felt alienated and left behind by the cultural upheaval of that decade. They wanted a countermovement of their own and were eager to join something larger than themselves, something they perceived as historically rooted and fundamentally good. If they were initially reacting to the student protests against the Vietnam War, sexual liberation, gay liberation, and the rise of feminism, they were also trying to define themselves and their beliefs in a country that had suddenly changed. The Jesus Movement, as those I knew called it, helped them feel connected to others and to core values of love, forgiveness, and filling their lives with a higher sense of purpose. It would take a while for these movements to turn fully political.

Many evangelicals felt that abortion, like homosexuality, was a mortal sin that would destroy the nation from within and had to be stopped. Politics and religion came together over the issues of human sexuality and reproduction, and doctors who performed abortions were now public enemies in ways Jack Tiller could never have imagined. Instead of being admired and revered in his hometown like his father, George Tiller's name had begun seeping out into Wichita's institutions in a very nasty and very public way. Protesters waved signs in front of his clinic, threats were phoned in to his business, and children in local middle schools took up a chant that had nothing to do with class pride or team sports: "Tiller, Tiller, the baby killer."

His life was going to impact total strangers, drawn into the same war he now found himself trapped in.

# II

Scott Roeder's father, John, had what some have described as a schizophrenic or manic personality. In a good mood, he told jokes, tanned
himself to improve his appearance, dressed better, spent money freely
on himself and others, and was fun to be around. Then he'd withdraw
and become inactive and downbeat. That made it difficult for him to
keep a steady job, so he worked on and off in Topeka, Kansas, where he
and his wife, Doris, had three children: Denise, David, and Scott
(John and Doris divorced in Scott's adolescence). In high school in the
early 1970s, Scott displayed some of the behavioral patterns of his father. He also began experimenting with illegal drugs. When his parents found out about this, they sent him to a mental hospital, and he
was diagnosed with the early signs of schizophrenia. Years later, Roeder
said that he'd hated being in a mental ward because they'd bound him
up in a garment, like a straitjacket, and given him medications like
Thorazine, leaving him feeling "loopy" and "very weird." As soon as he
left the ward, he vowed never to go back and stopped taking his meds.
All those problems were behind him now, he believed, and he was as
normal as anyone.

The Roeders were a warm, large family that celebrated together at
Christmas parties, Super Bowl gatherings, and Easter egg hunts. They
weren't a politically or religiously strident clan, and nobody talked much

about the mood swings that affected John and may have touched other members of the household. In the best tradition of Midwestern silence and stoicism, that wasn't something to dwell on. While Topeka had one of the finest psychiatric hospitals in the nation, at the Menninger Clinic, and while many Kansans were proud of the institution and felt that it did a lot of good for others, that didn't always mean members of their own family needed to go there. Depression and mental instability could be handled oneself, along with life's other challenges and hardships.

When Lindsey Roberts met Scott at a friend's home in December 1983, she didn't doubt his stability. Outgoing, considerate, polite, and fun-loving, he had ambitions to go into life insurance. He liked to party, but in a moderate way, and didn't have strong feelings about social issues. That was fine with Lindsey, because she didn't either. Scott was tall and broad-shouldered, with a large, roundish face, a full head of dark, wavy hair, and energy in his stride. He and Lindsey agreed that they'd seemed fated to meet and fall in love. She'd grown up less than an hour's drive from Topeka, in the Kansas City, Kansas, suburb of Overland Park. She and Scott both had grandparents who'd run restaurants in Kansas City, both had flirted with becoming Mormons before moving on, and they had common friends and interests.

They dated for three years before they were married in a church in 1986, yet neither was a member of any congregation. The couple spent their honeymoon at an elegant downtown Kansas City hotel and dined that first night at an expensive Italian restaurant.

"Everything," Lindsey recalls, "was so good back then, so simple."

Not entirely simple. She'd earned a college degree in elementary education, but soon became pregnant. A sonogram showed two umbilical cords, which might have suggested that she was carrying twins, and a protein test was needed to see if the fetus had a serious genetic defect. If the test came back positive, her physician suggested that she might want to consider an abortion. Scott didn't go with her to these doctor appointments, but Lindsey wasn't particularly worried about bringing the subject of abortion to his attention, since it had never been a controversial issue between them. They were, if anything, casually pro-choice. She had to wait two grueling weeks to learn about the test results, which in the end were negative.

She gave birth to a healthy son, Nicholas, and became a stay-at-home mom. Money was tight, even though they were living with her family in a small home in Overland Park, an arrangement Scott despised. His plans to enter the life insurance business hadn't developed and he'd been moving from job to job: Kansas City Power & Light, K-Mart, and the Darling Envelope Company. He had been very attentive to his wife during her pregnancy, sitting beside her throughout the twenty-six hours of labor, and he doted on his newborn son. For the next two years, Lindsey raised Nicholas and took care of her dying mother, while her spouse felt increasing pressure to generate more income. She found work as a telemarketer from their home, and was soon making more money than her husband. At times he seemed manic—hyperactive and not eating or sleeping at all, then crashing and nodding off on the couch. He had sleep apnea and might doze off in the middle of the afternoon. One day she came home to find him passed out in the living room, as their toddler was about to walk out the front door, toward the traffic outside their house. He wasn't the same man he'd been when they'd gotten married—especially after his born-again Christian conversion.

Lindsey watched him sit hour after hour before the TV and stare at Pat Robertson's *700 Club* or at a Texas televangelist named Robert Tilton, who sold believers a "miracle link" piece of cloth that would bring them miracles if they'd mail the cloth back to him to display on his altar. Lindsey felt dismay and anger when her husband sent an entire paycheck to Tilton, who was later exposed by Diane Sawyer as a fraud. At first, the only thing the couple fought about was finances. When things got tough, Scott's father, John, slipped Lindsey some money behind his son's back so she could buy necessary things for the family, and for Nicholas in particular. He was smitten by his grandson. One day in 1991, Scott learned of a seminar in the Kansas City area about how to avoid paying federal and state income taxes because (those running the seminar contended) the Sixteenth Amendment to the U.S. Constitution was never actually ratified. He went to the event and was told that collecting these taxes was illegal in America. He drove home and informed Lindsey that he'd found the solution to all their troubles: from now on, they wouldn't be handing any more money over to the state or federal government.

"Things," says Lindsey, "were never the same."

When she tried to talk to her husband about this strategy and to steer him away from the anti-tax movement, he had a favorite word for her.

"He always called me ignorant," she says. " 'You're ignorant about what the government is doing to us,' he'd tell me, 'and ignorant about the tax situation in America. You should read up on it. You should study the Constitution. I'll give you some material to educate you. You should watch some videos about this and listen to certain radio programs. You should find out what's really going on. Then you wouldn't be so ignorant.' "

All of this was hard for Lindsey to hear, she says, "Because I was the one with the college degree."

She didn't like fighting, especially in front of others, and tried to keep the peace inside their small house. When she spoke with members of Scott's family in Topeka about the direction his life was taking, they didn't know what to say or do. He was just going through a phase that would soon end, they'd suggest; he'd always been high-strung and would straighten himself out. He needed to find a job and stick with it. These responses didn't satisfy Lindsey, who wondered if the current troubles were related to Scott's mental health diagnosis as a teenager. Was he schizophrenic? Should he be seeing a psychiatrist? Or be on medication? He'd hated those meds and made that very clear to her every time the subject came up. There wasn't anything wrong with him, he said, Lindsey was just "ignorant" of what was happening to America. No matter what he did with *his* income, she fired back, she was going to keep paying federal and state taxes on her earnings.

Scott wasn't the only one she was concerned about. If her husband got into legal trouble, she'd have to raise their son alone. All of this conflict was already starting to have an impact on Nicholas. At school activities and Cub Scout meetings, Scott approached other parents and talked to them about taxes and religion. Lindsey was a Scout den mother and it was embarrassing to bring Nick to these public functions, where the boy watched his father harangue others about the evils of the American government. Why was his dad acting that way?

Of all the people in Scott's family, Lindsey had the strongest bond with his father, so she contacted him. John had observed his son drifting away from his responsibilities as a husband and a father, while drifting toward fringe politics and religion. What he needed was a wake-up call, so John suggested that Lindsey toss Scott out of the house, let him think about his behavior and appreciate what he had at home. That would turn him around. She took the advice.

Living on his own, Scott hooked up with an older woman in Independence, Missouri, just outside of Kansas City, who only furthered his view about taxes. Through her and other contacts, he began meeting people in other protest movements that were critical of the U.S. government.

One day he came back home to Lindsey with a girlfriend who was as erratic and politically extreme as he was. To Lindsey's chagrin, the two of them began kissing and fondling each other in front of her and her son. Scott showed Nicholas, age five, images of aborted fetuses, the evils of abortion now one of his strongest-held views.

Lindsey watched in horror—before hustling them out of the house.

"You just can't do this to a five-year-old," she says. "Scott and I had so many arguments at that time about abortion and other adult topics that you don't bring up with a child."

Her choices were painful. She could keep trying to help her husband, but he'd shown no desire to help himself. If she filed for a divorce, the couple would likely end up with joint custody of Nicholas. Since meeting the girlfriend, Lindsey knew she couldn't allow her son to be alone with his father, not to mention the extremists he had begun associating with. If Nicholas left the house with his father for a joint custody visit, he might not come back, she worried, or he could be harmed. She'd never forgotten the day her husband had fallen asleep on the sofa, with their young child headed out the front door into traffic. What if the couple ran off to another state and took Nick with them? Lindsey had already taught her son a secret password so that if somebody came to pick him up at school or a friend's house and didn't know that word, Nick must refuse to get into the car.

After weighing her options, Lindsey asked her husband to return home; she recommitted herself to repairing the marriage for the sake of their son. Scott agreed, and he was soon back on the couch watching anti-government videos, imploring her to "get educated" and stop being so ignorant. In high school, he'd used recreational drugs for escape. Now religion and politics helped him cope.

He wasn't the only one having trouble adjusting to a changing America.

# III

In the mid-1980s, Dr. Tiller hit bottom. As a churchgoing registered Republican who belonged to the oldest country club in Wichita, he wasn't raised to be a political activist. He was a man who liked corny jokes, mystery novels, floppy hats, Elvis Presley, Johnny Cash, James Bond, ice cream, and rooting for his beloved Jayhawks up in Lawrence. He loved swimming and playing with his four children. His decision to perform abortions wasn't an ideological one, but it put him at odds with certain members of his community and with elements of his faith (although a significant majority of Americans, and of Kansans, about 75 percent, supported a woman's right to choose).

The problem wasn't that he was doing something illegal; between 1973 and 1992, Kansas placed no restrictions on abortions or when they could be done. The problem was how deeply abortion disturbed some of his fellow citizens. The first church Tiller and his family attended in Wichita asked him to leave because of the feelings his presence had stirred within the congregation, so they'd moved on to Reformation Lutheran Church on the well-heeled northeast side of town.

Tiller attempted to fit in to Wichita. He served as staff president at Wesley Medical Center (the two other major local hospitals, St. Francis and St. Joseph, were Catholic and refused to perform abortions).

He was medical director of the Women's Alcohol Treatment Services at the Sedgwick County Health Department. He lectured widely about abortion to medical groups, promoting new scientific breakthroughs and backing stem cell research, which the anti-abortionists opposed. But he eventually stopped trying to explain himself and his work to the local and national media, an unproductive drain on his time.

Like Lindsey Roeder, he was faced with a challenging set of options. His medical practice and expertise in reproductive health were growing by the week. His commitment to helping women at the most vulnerable time of their lives gave him a great sense of purpose, and he was certain that his work saved lives. According to the World Health Organization, there are 19 million unsafe or illegal abortions a year, which kill 70,000 women. Unicef reports that unsafe abortions cause 4 percent of deaths among pregnant women in Africa, 6 percent in Asia, and 12 percent in Latin America and the Caribbean. At his clinic, Tiller was building a body of knowledge about severe pregnancy problems that was unparalleled in the United States, if not in the world. He'd evolved into an expert in diagnosing fetuses with spina bifida, hydrocephalus, fused legs, and deadly chromosomal abnormalities. The walls at Women's Health Care Services were becoming lined with letters of gratitude from women across the country, thanking Tiller and his staff for being there for them during a crisis. His career was extremely fulfilling, in addition to being lucrative.

But starting in 1975, protesters began showing up in front of his clinic, and they were no longer a group of meek nuns there on behalf of the Catholic Church. These demonstrators were more likely associated with evangelical Christianity and they carried grotesque signs showing aborted fetuses and denouncing Tiller as a murderer. Threats to himself, his family, and his employees had become routine.

What could a doctor do in these circumstances?

"There are pivotal patients in everyone's practice," he once said to the Feminist Majority Foundation, when showing the audience photos of some females he'd treated. "This girl on my left is nine and a half years old. She came from Southern California with her mother and her aunt for a termination of pregnancy. I told them . . . she was too far along, and I couldn't help. There were some stories in the newspaper about Dr. Tiller is getting ready to kill babies for a nine-year-old . . . I was trying to explain to my daughters, who were ten and nine at the time, about why I had planned to do this procedure . . . I was about thirty seconds into explaining about this [when] Jennifer said, 'Daddy, a ten-year-old girl, a nine-year-old girl shouldn't be pregnant, and simply not by her father or her grandfather or her uncle.'

"One of the things that my father taught me was that to be credible in medicine, you must require for your patients the same care that you would require for your family. I made a decision that if my nine- and ten-year-old daughters at that time were in that situation, I would do the procedure. I did it for this girl. It turned out marvelously. There were no problems, no complications. And I made that decision at that time that I was going to help as many people as I possibly could . . . If a woman was or a girl was able to get pregnant, we should be able to do a termination of pregnancy."

If he couldn't walk away from his work or from the expanding number of women who came to his clinic, he needed to adapt to the contempt of those around him. Some days, adapting was easier than others.

In 1984, he was pulled over for driving under the influence of alcohol and he also had substance abuse issues. The Kansas State Board of Healing Arts, a medical regulation body, told him to seek treatment and he did. One of his best friends was Don Arnold, who'd come to Wichita from Saskatchewan and started the first substance abuse treatment program in rural Kansas. Arnold helped him get clean and Tiller later served on the Kansas Medical Society's impaired physicians committee and supported Alcoholics Anonymous.

His abuse problems, he claimed, had nothing to do with being under constant assault by abortion foes, but many doubted that. The pressures were everywhere: he was in life-and-death situations with his patients all day at work, and life-and-death situations when he left the office and rode home in his car (security professionals advised him always to drive in the far right-hand lane, because that lessened the number of angles he could be attacked from). His only escape was relaxing with his wife, Jeanne, and with his four children and friends. They helped him kick the addictive habits, but Tiller's challenges were just beginning.

He wasn't the only doctor in America facing this kind of pressure. Those who performed abortions, especially complicated late-term abortions, made up a small and select group of physicians. One was Warren Hern, a couple of years older than Tiller and also born in Kansas, but his family had soon moved to the Denver suburbs. After graduating from the University of Colorado School of Medicine in 1965, Hern did an internship in the Panama Canal Zone, served as a doctor in Brazil for the Peace Corps, and worked in the Family Planning Division of the Office of Economic Opportunity in Washington, D.C., as part of the nation's "War on Poverty." With each job, his political consciousness and commitment to human rights, including women's rights, had deepened. Neither Tiller nor Hern had ever imagined becoming an abortion specialist, but *Roe v. Wade* changed everything.

Hern did his first abortion in the early 1970s and later wrote that the patient was "a 17-year-old high school student who told me . . . before the operation that she wanted to be a doctor and an anesthesiologist. I was terrified, and so was she. She cried after the operation for sadness and relief. Her tears and the immensity of the moment brought my tears. I had helped her change her life. I was relieved that this young woman was safe to go on with her dreams. I felt I had found a new definition of the idea of medicine as an act of compassion and love for one's fellow human beings."

Dr. Hern, unlike Tiller, was a born political and medical activist. He spoke widely and wrote at length about his work as an abortion provider, one of several ways in which the two men were opposites. Hern became a pioneer in the abortion technique known as D & E (dilation and evacuation). In the 1970s, a pregnant woman's cervix was manually dilated the day before an abortion, which created the risk of tearing or perforating her uterus. Once dilation was complete, the fetus and placenta were removed from the uterine wall and suctioned out by a vacuum. Dr. Hern and others began using laminaria sticks—sterilized stalks of seaweed—instead of manual dilation. After the sticks were inserted, they absorbed water, slowly expanded, and opened the cervix in a more gradual way.

"A protocol I have adapted from the Japanese experience . . ." Dr. Hern wrote in 1994 in a chapter of the book *Gynecology and Obstetrics*, "uses serial multiple laminaria treatments over 2 days. Under this protocol, one or more laminaria are placed in the cervix on day 1. They are removed and replaced by a larger number on day 2, and the uterus is evacuated with forceps on day 3 under paracervical block amnesia."

Dr. Hern was as concerned with a woman's mental state during an abortion as he was with the details of the medical procedure. For this reason, he opposed women being given a general anesthetic for the operation and losing consciousness.

"The use of general anesthesia," he wrote, "eliminates physician-patient interaction during the abortion and insulates the physician from the patient's emotional experience. This loss is a serious problem for physicians, and may make it extremely difficult for them to relate to the emotional problems encountered by abortion patients. It does nothing to enhance the physician's empathy for the patient's dilemma or the physician's understanding of the importance of the experience to the patient."

In time, three doctors from across America were rotated into Tiller's clinic from week to week to assist at WHCS, sleeping on a pullout sofa in a waiting room and using a shower in the basement. On Wednesday through Friday, WHCS performed first-trimester abortions, usually about fifty a week, and most were without complications. Women seeking late abortions, after the twenty-second week of pregnancy, arrived in Wichita on Sunday nights. Some were called "maternal-indication patients," whose own physical health was at risk if their pregnancies were brought to term. Others, called "fetal-indication patients," had babies that could not survive outside the womb without facing extreme medical complications and ongoing treatment. A third segment, by far the most controversial one, were women who suffered from depression and believed that giving birth would be too psychologically damaging—to both mother and child.

The late-term patients came to the clinic on Monday mornings and were shown a video of Dr. Tiller describing what they were about to experience. Then he took them through a group therapy session based on one offered by Alcoholics Anonymous. Some women openly talked about what had brought them to WHCS, while others sat quietly and listened or gave in to their feelings of pain and fear. On Tuesday, the patients came back to the clinic, where their fetuses were usually injected with digoxin and within a few hours were dead. The women were counseled again about what they'd just done, and then their cervixes were dilated so they could begin the process of miscarrying. After they'd started labor during the next several days, they went back to WHCS and discharged the fetus. Occasionally, patients wanted photos taken of their babies or to have them baptized by the resident chaplain or to be buried in tiny caskets. Others were cremated. WHCS accommodated their wishes and did whatever made the women most comfortable.

By the time Dr. Hern had opened the first private abortion clinic in Boulder, Colorado, in 1975, he was a veteran of political struggles. He and Tiller became close friends through their shared profession, despite their many differences. Tiller embodied Midwestern politeness and tried to avoid controversy, even if that wasn't possible for someone in his position. Hern's natural inclination was to fight the battle head-on.

"If George took Saint Francis of Assisi for his role model as a doctor," says Hern, "I took Machiavelli. If I have to choose between being loved and being feared, I'll take being feared because that can be more effective. George would go outside on a cold day at his clinic and offer the abortion protesters standing there some hot cider. I'd do the same thing, but put laxative in their drinks."

The men also worked in opposing environments. Wichita was conservative, with a huge Republican and Christian base. Boulder was known for its diversity and its own brand of political awareness. Women's rights were supported inside the city limits and at the University of Colorado, which would make a difference in the coming abortion war. When Hern first went to work in Boulder, a local group calling itself the Fight the Abortion Clinic Committee demanded that the city council shut down the clinic because it was "a clear and present danger" to community health. The clinic was only a block away from a public high school and a Catholic school and Hern was "corrupting the youth" of Boulder. The Colorado Board of Health backed Hern, as did the Boulder County Medical Society and Boulder Community Hospital medical staff. Now that he could legally perform abortions, his problems really began.

First he was picketed. Then the Boulder Valley Right-to-Life Committee sent out lurid anti-abortion brochures to every household in the county. Then came the late-night calls and threats to his home. He bought a rifle and kept it by his bed. Then came the calls of "murderer" each morning when he arrived at his office. Unlike Tiller, who remained silent and attempted to avoid the spotlight, Hern spoke out at abortion rallies, finding it "exhilarating" to shout over the protesters. He produced a steady outpouring of written materials, published everywhere from *The Colorado Statesman* to *The New York Times*, and they provided a running history of the abortion movement from someone on the front lines. By the mid-1970s, he'd drawn the condemnation of the Catholic Church.

In an editorial in *The Denver Post* in 1975, Father Virgil Blum wrote, "Have Dr. Hern and his profession grown so callous, has the mass of abortions, the literally millions of deaths, benumbed their sense of proportion to such that they can no longer ask, 'What is it that we are doing?' . . . The German program of mass euthanasia began with simple steps, backed by the intelligentsia and medical profession: the idea of useless lives . . . the convenience of society over the sanctity of human life; and once that sanctity was lost, once human life was held to be of relative value, there really could be no limit."

In the pages of the *Post*, Hern took on Father Blum and his church.

He called out the priest for writing about " 'Dr. Hern's enthusiastic applause for abortion.' I do not applaud fear, ignorance, unwanted pregnancy, or abortion. I take no cheer from human tragedy, no warmth from another's discomfort. These are difficult, painful problems which can be met with understanding, care, love, competence and a forthright willingness to help people do what they feel is best for themselves and their future . . . Those who have treated women near death from illegal abortion know that the alternatives to safe legal abortion are very unsatisfactory, indeed. We can deal with the world as it is or we can attempt to deal with it as it never will be. If we choose the latter course, who pays the price of our delusion?"

The seventies were mere prelude for the looming abortion war. On November 5, 1980, one day after his election, President Ronald Reagan held his first press conference, announcing that he intended to "make abortion illegal." Two days after that, Senator Strom Thurmond appeared on *The Today Show* and said that he'd seek the death penalty for abortion doctors. Ten weeks later, following his inauguration, Reagan invited leaders of the anti-abortion movement into the Oval Office and asked them what they all hoped to accomplish together. On Inauguration Day, the new secretary of health and human services, Richard Schweiker, spoke at an anti-abortion rally and said that he represented a "pro-life" administration. Reagan then instituted a "gag rule," declaring that workers at family planning clinics receiving federal funds could not speak to women about abortion, even if their lives were in danger from pregnancy. The president also opposed sex education and stem cell research.

"After [Reagan] took office," wrote Dr. Hern, "and lent the power of the Presidency to the anti-abortion fanatics, the violent attacks on clinics increased dramatically. Threats on my life and harassment of all kinds increased."

Between 1977 and 1981, there were 69 violent or aggressive incidents against abortion clinics. From 1981 to 1988, 780 violent or aggressive acts were reported against these medical offices. In 1988 Reverend Pat Robertson ran for president, and on the campaign trail in New

Hampshire he said that Planned Parenthood, a consistent supporter of women's rights, was using abortion to develop a "master race."

The day after he made this statement, five shots from a high-powered rifle were fired through the front windows and into the waiting room of Dr. Hern's clinic, just missing an employee. The physician immediately called a press conference and offered a $5,000 reward for information leading to the arrest of the shooter.

# IV

In 1986, Dr. Tiller's office was anonymously pipe-bombed, affecting about two-thirds of the building. Nobody was hurt, but the explosion caused $100,000 in damages. Instead of rethinking his abortion practice or taking a vacation to get away from the destruction, Tiller (like Hern) became more resolute and defiant, now advertising his services nationwide. Behind his wire-rimmed glasses, mop haircut, bland expression, and efforts to maintain his politeness, he was fierce in his convictions. Three days after the bombing, he planted a sign outside his office.

"Hell no!" it proclaimed. "We won't go!"

He put up $10,000 as a reward, but nobody ever collected on it. He installed gates, fencing, floodlights, metal detectors, and bulletproof glass.

"And I said, 'No, this stuff isn't going to happen again in Wichita,' " he recalled years later. "Well, I was wrong. We began to have people arrested outside our office. The clinic was blocked. People couldn't get in. Federal marshals finally had to take over. After six weeks, they had to take over the clinic. And things got back to relatively normal."

He wore a bulletproof vest to work, bought an armored SUV to get to and from the office (costing another $100,000), varied his route to the clinic, drove in the right-hand lane, and brought armed guards onto his staff. He hired high-powered attorneys and began donating money to the state's top-ranking pro-choice politicians, eventually forming a political action committee that he named ProKanDo. Yet he did little in the realm of public relations, even when abortion foes put up billboards and "wanted" posters of him around town asking, "Is Tiller Above the Law?" One heard grumbling in Wichita, from his own supporters, that he didn't do enough to promote himself in the community or media, or enough to let the city and region know that he didn't just perform abortions.

When patients were referred to Tiller by physicians nationwide, they were fully questioned by his staff to determine if they truly wanted to end their pregnancies. His clinic had seen hundreds of cases where potential patients had been screened and the women had changed their minds. Tiller helped these mothers put their babies up for adoption, but only if the newborns were going to a pro-choice family. He didn't publicize this adoption service or that nearly every day he confronted extreme medical problems with women who had nowhere else to go.

"The wife of one of my closest friends got pregnant," says the Wichita native and author Robert Beattie, "and there were serious complications. They went in to see Dr. Tiller and learned that their baby wasn't developing a head. They needed to abort the fetus, and as they walked into his clinic, protesters came up and screamed at them, calling them murderers and baby killers."

Tiller was much less concerned with Wichita's perception of him than with the science being developed inside Women's Health Care Services, and with keeping up morale at the office. He wasn't the only one targeted by anti-abortion activists. Pictures of his employees were hung on telephone poles, next to images of aborted fetuses. Abortion foes got the home addresses of his staff and rode through their neighborhoods with bullhorns, denouncing Tiller and those who worked for him. Each weekday morning, employees attempted to ignore the verbal abuse from protesters greeting them at WHCS. Some had their own brand of defiance, goosing the accelerator when driving past the demonstrators, to show that they weren't intimidated. In time, their names, phone numbers, and addresses would all be made public.

Tiller handed out staff bonuses, which he called "combat pay." He gave pep talks and passed around buttons that read, "Attitude Is Everything." He created plaques for the "Freedom Fighters" who worked at WHCS.

"The only requirement for evil to triumph," he told them, "is for good people to do nothing."

The protesters sent pregnant women into Tiller's office "under cover." Their job was to look for and find evidence that WHCS had violated some procedure or law—anything that could be used against Tiller in court and cause him to lose his medical license. When that failed, they harassed and boycotted the vendors who showed up at the office—an effective ploy, because these businesses didn't want to end up on an anti-abortion flyer or, in later years, on a Web site. Tiller's employees could no longer get a pizza or a bouquet of flowers delivered at work, and even one garbage pick-up service refused to come to WHCS.

In spite of the constant verbal abuse and almost a thousand clinic bombings that occurred throughout the United States in the 1980s and early '90s, somehow no human beings were physically harmed. Animals were a different matter.

Dr. LeRoy Carhart, a retired U.S. Air Force officer and a Republican like Tiller, was one of three abortion providers in Nebraska. On September 6, 1991, the state legislature passed the Nebraska Parental Notification Law, making it mandatory for minors to tell parents or guardians if they intended to get an abortion. That same day arsonists set fire to Carhart's home, barn, two other buildings, and his vehicles, killing a pair of family pets and seventeen horses. No one was ever prosecuted for the fire, but the next morning Carhart received a note claiming responsibility for the destruction and comparing the deaths of the animals to the "murder of children." Like Tiller and Hern, Carhart was not easily intimidated. Before the fire, his surgical practice had not focused on abortion—now he began doing them full-time. He'd eventually travel to Wichita and work every third week in Tiller's clinic.

If the doctors themselves escaped physical harm, it may have been because of a sense, among abortion opponents, that legal abortion's days were numbered. In 1988, Randall Terry had started Operation

Rescue, an innovative and aggressive anti-abortion group which conducted a number of successful demonstrations at that summer's Democratic Convention in Atlanta. These helped bolster their fund-raising,
giving hope to pro-lifers. The conservative-leaning Supreme Court
justices Sandra Day O'Connor, Anthony Kennedy, and David Souter,
they assumed, would work to overturn *Roe v. Wade*. And finally, Ronald Reagan was in the White House, about to be succeeded by another
anti-abortion Republican: George H.W. Bush.

The best days for the anti-abortion movement were just ahead.

# V

By the start of the 1990s, Scott Roeder and his anti-government friends in Kansas City were one piece of a growing ideological rebellion in America that still remained on the fringes. Some opposed abortion, others vilified homosexuality, and still others were against the mixing of the races. Many evangelicals believed that the human race was in its "Last Days," the Second Coming of Christ was imminent, and when He arrived, the nations of the world would be swept away in a cleansing fire. Those who'd already achieved salvation through a personal relationship with Jesus would ascend to heaven, while everyone else would be left behind in the mass destruction of earth. These rebellious segments touched one another and shared certain views, and that closeness would only increase with the arrival of the Internet.

The apocalyptic visionaries and prophets of doom usually had several beliefs in common: America had gone tragically awry with the sexual and racial liberation movements of the 1960s; our state and federal governments not only couldn't be trusted to fix the country, but were major problems themselves; evil had been set loose within the nation and was spreading throughout schools, churches, and other public institutions. Evil was a tangible force—embodied by gay men and women, by those on spiritual paths different from fundamentalist Christianity, by people embracing liberal or progressive politics, and

by abortion doctors or women who wanted to control their own reproduction. Because evil was a concrete thing and some individuals so
clearly represented it, they should be removed by any means necessary.

None of this, of course, was entirely new. Coming of age in rural
Kansas in the 1950s and '60s, I remember the prevailing racism: the un-
written law in our small town was "No niggers inside the city limits after
sundown." At fifteen, I worked at my father's lumberyard alongside
truckers, carpenters, farmers, and hired hands. One summer afternoon,
an older employee and I made a delivery out into the countryside and de-
toured to a large white farmhouse at the base of a valley, surrounded by
cottonwood trees. A rough-looking, uneducated man thirty years my senior, he went into the house and came back half an hour later, explaining
to me that he'd been meeting with other "Minutemen," a white supremacist vigilante group on alert in case of a race riot or some other uprising
in Kansas City or Topeka. His group was well armed and prepared for
battle.

My father had been a bombardier pilot in World War Two a few
years before I was born. His plane was shot down over Europe, instantly
killing three of the nine crew members, but he parachuted out, was
picked up by German soldiers, and was transported in a wheelbarrow to
a prison camp. For about a year in 1944–45, he was a POW under the
Nazis. As a boy, I tried asking him questions about the war, things like
"Why would a whole country go crazy and act the way Germany did?
How could the Nazis do those things to Jews? Why didn't somebody
stop them?" He wouldn't respond, but just get up and leave the room.
World War Two was over for him and should be left in the past—a very
Midwestern response to painful memories—yet parts of the war were
still visible in our home. His hands wouldn't stop shaking, he couldn't
sleep, and he was constantly hungry and claustrophobic, flailing his
arms in the backseat of a car hard enough to hurt another passenger.

He'd never hated regular German citizens, he once told me, and
hadn't taken any pleasure in dropping bombs on them. It was a brutal
job that had to be done to put down a worldwide scourge, and once it
was finished he wanted it behind him. My father refused to talk about

his POW experience, so I stopped probing him, but that only made me more curious.

For my part, I tried to keep at bay the racism and religious bigotry around me, and to escape my father's highly visible anxiety, by burying myself in music, specifically black music, the soundtrack of my life. The jazz and blues of Duke Ellington, Ella Fitzgerald, Billie Holiday, Count Basie, B.B. King, Muddy Waters, Ray Charles, Etta James, Howlin' Wolf, Aretha Franklin, and James Brown convinced me that the "Minutemen" were wrong, when almost nothing else in my environment did. Blacks may not have been allowed in town after sunset, but nighttime radio signals reached into my bedroom from Chicago and Denver, from Canada and New Orleans, and those blue notes hinted at a much larger world not so shaped by anger and fear. That essential conflict—between love for family and shame for the sins of my culture—couldn't be reconciled, but the music was a window into something that offered hope.

In my twenties, I moved to New York City, where I became a journalist and an avid student of the conditions that had created the Third Reich. At age thirty, I moved from New York to Denver, and on the day I arrived in September 1981, the week of Yom Kippur, I heard a Jewish radio talk show host demanding on the air that listeners call in and talk about their hidden, or not-so-hidden, anti-Semitism; maybe speaking openly about these things would help release uncomfortable feelings and get rid of some of the prejudice. Hearing this man on radio for the first time was haunting for me and that experience would only grow in future years. A wildly provocative ex-lawyer and ex-alcoholic from Chicago, Alan Berg and talk radio were just starting to explode throughout the country. As he became more popular, white supremacist and anti-Semitic groups were studying a blood-soaked manifesto called *The Turner Diaries*, a fantasy novel about a white power revolution—led by a cell known as the Order—that rolled across the United States and purged the nation of minorities, gays, feminists, liberal judges, physicians who gave women abortions, and Jews.

In the early 1980s, a band of extremists began attending the church on the Aryan Nations compound outside Hayden Lake, Idaho, where they heard one hate-filled anti-Semitic sermon after another. They believed in Identity Christianity, which held that the Anglo-Saxon tribes that had settled Europe and America were the real descendants of the Jews of the Old Testament, and all others were frauds. In the fall of 1983, they went into the woods, swore an oath of loyalty to one another, and decided to act out the novel. Based on the sermons and their beliefs, they identified their first target, and on June 18, 1984, four men traveled to Denver and gunned down Berg in his driveway, shooting him twelve times in the face and torso at point-blank range.

Soon after the murder, I found myself standing in front of the Aryan Nations compound, researching a book about the assassinated talk show host and those who'd killed him. The compound was sealed off by a chain-link fence and had a watchtower, armed guards, a rifle range, German shepherds, and Doberman pinschers. On a wooden shed were two words painted in red and blue letters: "Whites Only." The rifle range held Stars of David, used for target practice, and the inhabitants inside the fence called these twenty acres of land the "Heavenly Reich" or "God's Country." Richard Butler, who ran the compound and preached the sermons that had motivated the men in the Order, claimed that he had nothing to do with Berg's death. He was just practicing his right to free speech under the First Amendment.

Like Dr. Tiller, Dr. Hern, and so many others, I too was being drawn into the war infecting my country. When it became known in neo-Nazi circles that I was writing a book about Berg and his killers, I received threats and was informed by associates of the Order that I (as a white man) was betraying my race. Some told me I was in danger, and this brought on nightmares of jack-booted thugs kicking in my front door and taking me away. By the time the book was complete, I wasn't sleeping enough, drank too much, was in the middle of a painful divorce, and was having the kind of meltdown that no escape—whether through music or otherwise—could dampen. The book had brought on all the unexamined feelings, especially about my father, that I'd never confronted or felt, until now. I needed a healing that went beyond politics.

The second civil war that had started tugging at the seams of America about a hundred years after the first one wasn't a war between the states, or about anything as concrete as the emancipation of slaves. It was a much more subtle struggle between different perceptions and ideologies, different states of mind. The core issues were intensely private, personal, painful, and emotional, and spoke to very different views of the American future, as the conflict gradually moved away from the fringes and into the mainstream. After the Berg book, I never wanted to touch this subject again.

# VI

In 1991, the nation's most rabid anti-abortion organization, Operation Rescue, led by Randall Terry, picked Wichita for its largest event ever. Terry had selected the city for one overriding reason: George Tiller worked there. Yet Wichita was not their first choice. In October 1990, Terry had come to Boulder and prayed outside Dr. Hern's office for the physician's death (in 1993, Terry would appear on a Christian Broadcasting Network program and invite radio listeners to assassinate Dr. Hern). Before the so-called Summer of Mercy, Operation Rescue protesters met with a Boulder SWAT team officer named Jerry Hoover, who told them that Dr. Hern had the backing of the community. Long known for its activism, Boulder in the 1980s had passed a "bubble law," making it illegal for abortion protesters to get closer than eight feet from women entering clinics.

A group of prominent local citizens from the University of Colorado and elsewhere rallied behind Dr. Hern and women's reproductive rights, signing a petition that declared, "We will not accept terrorism in our state."

The police also gave the physician an assist.

"Jerry Hoover explained to Operation Rescue," says Dr. Hern, "that many people in Boulder didn't like them and it was going to be bad for them here. If they tried anything at my clinic, the police were going to have a hundred officers on hand. My office would resemble an armed camp and I'd go on television and say very bad things about them. It's okay to protest abortion, but if they made threats against us, I was going to tell them to go fuck themselves. So they changed their mind."

And turned to Wichita. It had long been called the birthplace of the nation's aircraft industry, but was about to become better known as the abortion, or anti-abortion, capital of the United States.

Seven years earlier, Terry had begun his crusade in Binghamton, New York, a college town near the Pennsylvania border, by protesting the local abortion clinic. His wife, Cindy, couldn't conceive, so she stood with her husband outside Binghamton's Southern Tier clinic, begging women going in for abortions to change their minds and let her adopt their baby. By that fall, the clinic was receiving bomb threats.

Terry's background was remarkably similar to many other leaders of the anti-abortion movement: he was a white male who as a teenager had been drawn to drugs. He wanted to escape a drunken father who'd beaten him, and he liked to fantasize about becoming a rock star. He was a seeker, on a quest for meaning and purpose, and he had a born-again Christian experience in his early twenties. As a street-corner preacher, he witnessed to others, even when he worked at McDonald's. Not long after his conversion, a minister laid hands on the young man and consecrated him to go out and serve God in some special way. What could he possibly do to fulfill such a grand and noble mission?

One day, according to James Risen and Judy L. Thomas, authors of *The Wrath of Angels*, an account of the anti-abortion movement, Terry began to weep uncontrollably and had a vision in which God chose him to do something extraordinary—something that wouldn't merely affect individual lives, but alter and improve the course of human history. His purpose had suddenly become clear: protecting unborn children and stopping abortion in America. God had declared that abortion was murder. At least 50 million babies had died in the abortion holocaust, according to those in Terry's movement, making it a far worse atrocity than the concentration camps of World War Two (Terry's followers sometimes referred to themselves as "survivors of the holocaust" that had begun on January 22, 1973, the day the Supreme Court ruled on *Roe v. Wade*). In their eyes, abortion was simply evil and had to be halted by any means at hand.

No other political or religious issue unleashed more heated rhetoric or more grandiose dreams—or more hatred of the women who actively supported abortion. It was the dividing line in a war between the sexes.

"I despise feminism," Terry once said, "because it is out to destroy . . . the Christian heritage of motherhood and what it means to be alive."

Another abortion leader, Joseph Scheidler, described his ambitions more bluntly, "We take away their [the feminists'] right to fornicate."

The fight was primal, and the protests against *Roe v. Wade* had started right after the Supreme Court decision came down. Justice Harry Blackmun, who'd written the opinion, received tens of thousands of pieces of hate mail and countless death threats, and was shot at in 1985—the first and only Supreme Court justice to have that distinction. Between 1983 and 1985, the anti-abortion movement bombed 319 medical clinics; at that time about 1.5 million women a year were getting abortions. In 1988, Randall Terry launched Operation Rescue with a protest in New York City and co-opted the civil disobedience strategies used so effectively by the Democratic left a few decades earlier in the civil rights movement. They disrupted everyday life (traffic and business) and got arrested in order to draw attention to their cause. Until now, the right and particularly the religious right had never attempted anything like this, but in Atlanta, during the 1988 Democratic Convention, Terry-led forces lay down in the crowded streets, crawled through the legs of police officers, and generated havoc. Twelve hundred people were arrested, including their leader.

Like many others jailed for their anti-abortion convictions, Terry closely identified with Saint Paul in the Bible, who'd had a blinding, transforming vision on the road to Damascus and was incarcerated for promoting the new religion called Christianity. The original evangelist, Paul spent his time in prison writing epistles that became part of the New Testament. In sacrificing his freedom for God's law when he was certain that man's law was wrong, Paul was destined to become the patron saint of the anti-abortion movement.

The Atlanta protests were followed by similar ones in Los Angeles in 1989. Demonstrators were injured and the city conveyed the clear message that the movement wasn't welcome there. By the summer of 1991, Operation Rescue hadn't launched a major event for a couple of years and was faltering, with a splintered leadership (Randall Terry and Keith Tucci now both led the group). The organization was looking for an infusion of energy and a revitalization of its message. They needed to put a human face on their enemy. The place was Wichita and the face was George Tiller's.

Come to Kansas, Terry wrote to Operation Rescue members before launching the Summer of Mercy in 1991, because "Our God is the God of Second Chances . . . God is doing something here we have never seen before, but always hoped and prayed for. Now it seems God is answering our prayers. He's giving us another chance."

"The nation's most notorious killer," Keith Tucci wrote when recruiting troops, "practices his demonic trade in Wichita, killing babies until 'birth.' George (Killer) Tiller advertises nationally and internationally to solicit women in the second and third trimesters [of pregnancy]."

The Operation Rescue faithful answered the call and began flocking to Kansas. The "Summer of Mercy" started on July 15, as hundred-degree heat settled onto Wichita, the sunlight and humidity quickly soaking anyone who stepped outside. Into this furnace came thousands of pilgrims from across America committed to ending abortion, with thousands more about to join them, alarming the municipal government and nearly overwhelming the Wichita Police Department. Protesters kicked off the event by gathering en masse on business streets and singing "He's Got the Whole World in His Hands" and "Jesus Loves the Little Children." Hoping to avoid trouble, city officials decided to accommodate the visitors, and Tiller himself agreed to shut down his clinic for a week. The other four local abortion clinics did the same.

"Wichita didn't yet understand," says Julie Burkhart, who later worked with Tiller and ran his political action committee, "that these people were not reasonable. If you gave the protesters an inch, they took a mile."

Even though it was closed, demonstrators gathered outside Tiller's office, a low cement structure just off Kellogg, a major highway through Wichita. An American flag flew above the clinic and floodlights, a locked gate, and chain-link fence stood at the rear, with electronic surveillance cameras recording everyone who came near. The windows had been covered with bricks and no sign out front announced the nature of the business going on inside Women's Health Care Services, which looked as bland as possible. Even the address numbers on the face of the building had been partially scraped off. The Wichita police brass believed that closing Tiller's office and the other clinics would defuse the situation, but it only emboldened Operation Rescue. As Terry proclaimed victory for his troops—who'd now turned Wichita into an "abortion-free city"—thousands more protesters heard the news and headed for south central Kansas.

During its first week, the Summer of Mercy remained mostly peaceful, with the WPD closely watching the protesters and waiting for them to leave town. When that didn't happen, the cops moved in on Tiller's clinic, determined to reopen it. As the heat gathered and thickened on the streets, the police came in patrol cars and on horseback, nightsticks at the ready, meeting resistance on every inch of the searing pavement. Across the sidewalk outside Tiller's office and on the small strip of asphalt running alongside it, protesters lay down and refused to move. When the police showed up at WHCS one morning at six a.m., the anti-abortion forces were already standing seven deep in front of them, waiting to get arrested.

As Terry had hoped, Operation Rescue found a few sympathizers among local law enforcement (some of the cops had relatives participating in the Summer of Mercy and protesting at Tiller's clinic). Mayor Bob Knight had anti-abortion leanings and Police Chief Rick Stone was a moderate. What Terry hadn't envisioned was encountering the wrath of Wichita's U.S. District Judge Patrick Kelly, outraged over the Summer of Mercy. He was committed to keeping Tiller's clinic open and ordered protesters to stop blocking the clinic WHCS or face a $25,000 penalty for the first offense and twice that for the second.

When presented with a copy of Kelly's order, Terry threw it on the ground.

"We fear God, the supreme judge of the world," he said, "more than we fear a federal judge."

Kelly arrested Terry and jailed him for eight days, sending in federal marshals to keep WHCS in operation.

With more and more anti-abortion evangelicals arriving in Wichita and occupying the streets outside his clinic, Tiller returned to work in a specially armored Chevy Suburban. On July 30, two weeks into the Summer of Mercy, scores of protesters pressed into the WHCS driveway and shoved two dozen marshals and police officers into a fence. By sunset that evening, more than 200 people had been arrested. When Tiller came to his office on August 2, another 100 blocked his entry, including Randall Terry. Freed from jail, he strolled up to the physician's open car window.

"You can laugh now," Terry told him, "but you'll pay someday."

"Too bad," the doctor shot back, "your mother's abortion failed."

By noon, another 124 people had been arrested at the clinic, but returning home at night was no reprieve for Tiller. For six straight weeks that summer, protesters camped on the dirt road outside his country home and constantly yelled at his wife, children, and friends as they came and went. Before the event was finished, it would generate 2,700 arrests.

At the height of the protest, Kansas's Republican governor, Joan Finney, traveled to Wichita and offered her backing to the anti-abortion movement, as the Reverends Pat Robertson and Jerry Falwell had done earlier in Atlanta.

"I am pro-life," Governor Finney told an adoring crowd. "My hope and prayer is that Wichita's expression of support for the right to life for unborn babies will be peaceful, prayerful, and united in purpose. I commend you for the orderly manner in which you have conducted the demonstration."

# VII

On August 5, sixty-three more protesters were arrested at Tiller's clinic and Judge Kelly reached his breaking point. When he ordered Operation Rescue to post a $100,000 "peace bond" for any damages caused, a thousand more abortion foes gathered outside WHCS to chant slogans and block the entrance. Federal marshals moved them aside so that patients could come in for medical care. Terry didn't want to go back to jail, so he decided to go over Judge Kelly's head and appeal to a higher authority. He traveled to Kennebunkport, Maine, President George H. W. Bush's summer home, thinking that Bush would back him. The president refused to see him, but Terry was about to get a boost from U.S. Attorney General Richard Thornburgh. The U.S. Department of Justice, without consulting the White House or the president, filed an amicus brief on behalf of the protesters, calling for Judge Kelly's most recent order to be overturned.

"I am disgusted with this move by the U.S.," Judge Kelly told a federal lawyer, "and that it would put its imprimatur on this conduct. I will ask you to please report that to the attorney general personally."

Kelly then did something sitting judges almost never do, appearing on national television on ABC's *Nightline* to vent his feelings. The Department of Justice, he said, had given protesters a "license to mayhem" in Wichita. Without his injunctions, there would be "blood in the streets."

The Tenth U.S. Circuit Court of Appeals overturned Kelly's injunction and chided him for speaking out on TV. He soon received three hundred hate calls and had to be protected by U.S. marshals after a protester jumped him during an evening walk near his home. The situation had become too hot for Terry in Wichita, so he skipped the rest of the Summer of Mercy, fearful of getting arrested again. He looked on from afar as a fifteen-year-old girl, along with her five brothers and sisters (one age ten), sat down in front of cars trying to enter Tiller's clinic. Fortunately, none was hurt. On August 20, thirty protesters charged WHCS and tried to scale the six-foot-high fence. They were arrested, sending Judge Kelly into another outburst.

"It is war," he thundered from the bench, ordering $10,000 fines for Operation Rescue leaders and $500 fines a day for the next ten days.

In late August, pro-choice activists, who'd been caught off guard by the size and strength of the Summer of Mercy, held their own rally downtown. Five thousand people came out to hear speeches by Eleanor Smeal, head of the Feminist Majority Foundation, Patricia Ireland of the National Organization for Women, and Kate Michelman of the National Abortion Rights Action League.

"Randall Terry, go to jail!" the crowd shouted. "We're pro-choice and we'll prevail!"

Wichita was now the base to two angry, committed constituencies at odds in the city streets. Their outrage had culminated in front of Dr. Tiller's clinic, the first act of a drama that would shape Kansas politics for the next two decades.

On August 25, 1991, as the Summer of Mercy came to a close, 25,000 people joined prayers and voices at the football stadium at Wichita State University.

"We submit today that we will not rest," Reverend Pat Robertson told the cheering audience, "until every baby in the United States of America is safe in his mother's womb. We will not rest until the land we love so much is truly, once again, one nation under God."

A plane flew over the stadium, with a trailing banner that read, "Go home! Wichita is pro-choice!"

The crowd looked up at the sky, rose together as one, and began to chant, "We *are* home! We *are* home!"

In the weeks following the Summer of Mercy, the anti-abortion group Kansans for Life saw its mailing list grow by ten thousand names. A grassroots uprising was emerging from the protests, as those who'd gone to jail for their beliefs now entered mainstream politics. In 1992 in Sedgwick County, where Wichita is located, 19 percent of the new precinct committee members had arrest records from the Summer of Mercy. That year Republicans won the state legislature, and their victory in 1994 would be larger still. Many of the new legislators began to agitate and organize for changing the state's abortion laws. Since *Roe v. Wade* twenty years earlier, Kansas had made no alterations to its abortion statute. That was about to change, presenting Tiller with problems he'd never faced before.

Nobody knew, but the Summer of Mercy was the crescendo for the anti-abortion movement in terms of organized protests. No future demonstration would be nearly as big, as unified, or as successful at focusing the public and media on this single issue. The Democrat Bill Clinton, who strongly supported abortion rights, was about to win the White House, and the conservative Supreme Court justices David Souter, Anthony Kennedy, and Sandra Day O'Connor had not sided with the anti-abortion forces in the relevant cases that came before them. *Roe v. Wade* had not been overturned. States could try to modify their own laws regarding late-term abortion, but for those who opposed all abortions, like Randall Terry, hope was vanishing that they could end the practice by lobbying politicians or lying down in the streets. It was time to consider alternatives.

For Dr. Tiller, a certain kind of hope was also disappearing. He'd spent his adult life in the Republican Party, committed to the economic and political values it had once represented. But it wasn't the same party he'd known in the past. In the summer of 1992, the former President Nixon speechwriter Pat Buchanan had used the Republican Convention in Houston to deliver a prime-time televised address on his favorite subject: America's "cultural war." Buchanan spoke heatedly about the moral battle being waged in the country and the critical need to win it. Both moderate Republicans and Democrats watched Buchanan in Houston, shocked at his vitriol and at the importance he'd assumed within his party. He was anything but a fringe player inside the GOP.

Gary Bauer had been President Reagan's undersecretary of education from 1982 to 1987. He defined the battle for the nation's soul this way: "We are engaged in a social, political, and cultural war. There's a lot of talk in America about pluralism. But the bottom line is somebody's values will prevail. And the winner gets the right to teach our children what to believe."

One year after the Summer of Mercy, Tiller dropped his politeness, and his feelings about the new GOP finally erupted, when four protesters came to his clinic and chained themselves to a gate. Sprinting out from his office in a white lab coat, he rushed up to the gate and jerked a microphone from the hand of a startled TV camera operator covering the event.

"This right here," he said, pointing at a protester, "represents what the Republican Party is all about now. They have been taken over by religious fanatics like this man right here who wants to deprive citizens of the United States of their religious freedoms."

As he headed back toward his office, a demonstrator jammed an anti-abortion poster in his face.

"Why don't you stick that," Tiller said, "someplace where the sun doesn't shine?"

He had far more to worry about than protesters' signs.

Six weeks into Bill Clinton's presidency, a young man named Michael Griffin spotted David Gunn, an abortion doctor in Pensacola, Florida, pulling into a gas station and approached him at a pump. Early in 1993, someone in Pensacola had created an effigy of Dr. Gunn with Genesis 9:6—"Whosoever shed man's blood, by man shall his blood be shed"— hanging from its neck. When Griffin asked Gunn to identify himself, the physician stared back and told him to leave. Before walking off, Griffin announced that the Lord was giving Dr. Gunn one more chance to change his ways. Griffin then stood up during a service at his church, Whitfield Assembly of God, and asked if the congregation agreed with him that David Gunn should get saved and stop killing babies. Worshippers nodded and prayed for Dr. Gunn's soul.

Three days later, as Gunn stepped from his car at Pensacola's Women's Medical Services clinic, Griffin shot and killed the doctor with three .38-caliber bullets in his back. The next morning, Congress asked the FBI to launch an investigation into the murder, while anti-abortionists celebrated the death. One celebrant was the Floridian Paul Hill, who at seventeen had assaulted his father and caused his parents, who hoped he'd get treatment for his drug abuse, to file charges against him. The young man soon had a born-again Christian experience, but held such virulent anti-abortion views that his own Presbyterian church excommunicated him. Hill attended Michael Griffin's murder trial as a show of support for the assassin, and protested the verdict when Griffin got life without parole.

Dr. John Britton, who replaced Gunn at the Pensacola clinic, wore a bulletproof vest and carried a pistol to work. Abortion protesters made an "Unwanted" poster of him and left a pamphlet on his front stoop with a headline reading, "What Would You Do if You Had Five Minutes to Live?"

Some in the anti-abortion movement had moved far beyond civil disobedience, and Scott Roeder was moving with them.

# VIII

In the early 1990s, after Roeder came back home to live with his wife and son, he decided to take over the family's finances as "the man of the house." Like many other anti-abortionists, he was familiar with and greatly admired the writings of Saint Paul. One New Testament Epistle written by Saint Paul read, "Wives, be subject to your husbands, as to the Lord. For the husband is the head of the wife as Christ is the head of the church, his body, and is himself its Savior. As the church is subject to Christ, so let wives also be subject in everything to their husbands." For Roeder, being the man of the house did not mean holding a steady job, but learning more about how to evade paying taxes. The more of this information he absorbed, the more stressed he became, and the more verbally and emotionally abusive he was toward Lindsey and his young son. When he spanked Nick, he held him up in the air by the arms, and one time when he was finished, he dropped the boy on the floor.

"If you ever do that again," Lindsey told him, "I'm calling the police."

Despite this behavior, Roeder's relationship with the child was complex and poignant, no doubt the deepest emotional connection in his life. It's too simple to say that he loved Nicholas and more accurate to say that he tried to love him in the only way he knew how. Roeder desperately wanted his son to understand who he was and why he believed what he did. It never seemed to occur to him that a six- or seven-year-old didn't see the world in adult terms and looked to him for other kinds of support.

Lindsey ran the family and tried not to be overwhelmed. She had a serious heart condition, which prevented her from having another child and required expensive medication, and she diligently navigated her son through boyhood with a troubled father. They still lived in the same small house with her aging dad—a volatile mix. She'd used her elementary education degree to become a teacher and then director of a child care center at Knox Presbyterian Church in Overland Park. Things hadn't turned out at all as she'd hoped when marrying Scott, but she was determined to make the best of it and protect Nicholas, which meant avoiding political or religious discussions with her husband. Like most Kansans, and most Americans, she believed that a woman had the right to decide what to do with her own body, but was careful not to say this directly to her husband. One day she was teaching preschoolers when an enraged mother stormed into her classroom, picked up her child, and threw the youngster against a metal cabinet.

"I should have had an abortion when I could have!" the woman shouted.

Lindsey recoiled.

"Later on," she says, "when I'd had a chance to think about it, I felt that the woman was probably right. I told Scott about what I'd seen and said that not everyone was cut out to be a parent, but that only made him angrier."

His anger was evolving into action. In the spring of 1994, he began associating with members of local militia movements who were stockpiling firearms. The year before, the FBI had entered the Branch Davidian compound in Waco, Texas, to end a standoff between the sect's leader, David Koresh, and the authorities. The buildings erupted into flames, killing seventy-six people inside the compound and spreading paranoia among the anti-government groups. That paranoia reached into the Roeder household and came out in Scott's ramblings and other behaviors. He wouldn't drink tap water anymore, because it was laced with fluoride that would give him cancer; he insisted on buying bottled water instead. He had to have pricey vitamin B tablets and garlic pills, which smelled bad, to ward off other diseases being spread by the government. And he had to be prepared if his enemies came after him. As the man of the house, he'd recently forgotten to pay the bill for Lindsey's heart medicine, putting her health at risk. After getting her next paycheck, she gave him some money and told him to go pick up her drugs. He came back with a gun instead.

She thought about kicking him out again, but faced the same dilemma as before: while her husband was clearly becoming more radical, he hadn't broken any laws or physically abused his family members, at least not to the point of criminal activity. Despite his verbal assaults on Lindsey and his tirades about abortion, he had a gentler side. He made a point of taking bugs out of the house and letting them live in a natural environment, rather than killing them. Many who worked with or befriended Roeder were struck by his kindness and willingness to help. He may have been associated with people on the far right holding viciously racist views, but he didn't feel he was racist and was sensitive about being perceived that way. Violence was wrong, he often told people, no matter how deeply one felt about an issue. Still, if the couple divorced, he'd get a joint custody arrangement with Nicholas, and Scott was no longer just potentially dangerous, but armed. Wasn't it safer to have him inside the house, where she could keep an eye on him?

He had an old, flimsy-looking Bible he carried around and quoted from. One day he and Lindsey got into an argument because he didn't think she was obeying him as much as she should—or as much as he thought the Scriptures instructed her to. He liked to tell their friends that she was an atheist, even though she regularly attended church services at Knox Presbyterian. There were a lot of things she wanted to say to him about women's rights and her own political convictions, but she'd held back for the sake of her marriage and son. As the argument heated up, she grabbed the old Bible and hurled it at him.

"Stop twisting the word of God!" she shouted.

"You could have hurt me," he said, shocked at what his wife had done.

The couple moved to the brink of another separation, but once again she let him stay.

Scott was convinced that the FBI or ATF had tapped their phones and was monitoring his words and movements. Lindsey doubted this was true, but hoped it was. Sometimes, she picked up the receiver, imagined that someone really was listening, and said aloud that her husband was out of control and needed to be stopped before it was too late. Nobody responded to her pleas. Instead, she received calls from Scott's political and religious allies at all hours of the day.

"After speaking with me," she says, "most of these people realized that I wasn't the person my husband had told them I was. I wasn't a monster. They were calling because they were worried that he might try to kill me. They said that he was upset with me for not believing as he did or allowing him to be the head of household or man of the house. I was warned repeatedly that he had a rifle with a long-range sight on it. I tried to talk about this with some of his family members, but they didn't want to hear it."

When Scott asked if he could bring home a couple of his buddies to live with them, Lindsey said no. He was increasingly manic—not sleeping or eating much, and reading more about the coming End Times, when the earth would reach a devastating climax and only those saved by Jesus would escape into heaven. The fire at Waco had put the far-right extremists on alert and convinced many that the Apocalypse was at hand. Roeder was expanding his contacts inside that underground, associating with Mark Koernke, a prominent Michigan militia activist who in 2001 would be sentenced to three to seven years for resisting arrest and assaulting the police. Roeder had hooked up with the Unorganized Kansas Militia, led by Morris Wilson and now conducting maneuvers in the woods. Some of its members were connected with Terry Nichols, who'd joined forces with Timothy McVeigh, and in the spring of 1995, the word moving through the Midwest's radical circles was that "Timmy V was gonna go smoke some Okies."

McVeigh and Nichols had met in the late 1980s in army basic training.

Both were angered by the 1992 FBI standoff with Randy Weaver at Ruby Ridge, Idaho, which had left Weaver's son, Sammy, dead. They were further outraged the next year by the siege at Waco. McVeigh had visited the Branch Davidian compound during the standoff and after seventy-six people had lost their lives. Like the men who'd murdered Alan Berg, McVeigh was very familiar with the violent fantasy novel *The Turner Diaries*, peddling it at gun shows. One chapter outlined how a truck holding a homemade bomb was detonated in front of FBI head-quarters in Washington at 9:15 on a weekday morning. Seven hundred people died in the fictional carnage.

"It is a heavy burden of responsibility for us to bear," said the book's protagonist, Earl Turner, "since most of the victims of our bomb were only pawns who were no more committed to the sick philosophy or the racially destructive goals of the System than we are. But there is no way we can destroy the System without hurting many thousands of in-nocent people. . . . And if we don't destroy the System before it de-stroys us . . . our whole race will die."

On September 30, 1994, Nichols went to the Mid-Kansas Coop in McPherson and bought forty 50-pound bags of ammonium nitrate fertili-zer, a vast amount by the standards of local famers. He bought one more bag for good measure. On April 14, 1995, McVeigh paid for a room at the Dreamland Motel in Junction City in eastern Kansas. Using the alias Robert D. Kling he rented a Ryder truck, and on April 16 he and Nichols drove to Oklahoma City and planted a getaway car a few blocks from the Alfred P. Murrah Federal Building. They went back to Herington, Kan-sas, and loaded the Ryder truck with fertilizer, fuses, and other bomb-making materials. On April 19, McVeigh exploded the truck outside the Murrah building and killed 168 men, women, and children.

At McVeigh's 1997 federal trial in Denver, the witness Charles Farley testified that he saw several men near the loaded Ryder truck outside Junction City on April 18, 1995. Farley confirmed a photo of one man, later identified as Morris Wilson, the Kansas militia leader and acquain-tance of Scott Roeder.

"I remember watching the Oklahoma City bombing that morning

on TV," says Lindsey. "When I realized it was connected to Waco, I was scared to death. Scott was always ranting and raving about what had happened there."

By the time of the bombing, Roeder had moved out again and was living with an anti-government couple in Kansas City. He'd taken everything with him: the family car, their money, and any hope of reconciliation. One day a woman called Lindsey and said she was going to steal Roeder away from his wife.

"You can have him," Lindsey replied.

It had been increasingly painful for her to watch him suffer the past few years, to see his alienation and paranoia growing, and not be able to stop this. One night in February 1995, two months before the Oklahoma City bombing, Lindsey, Nick, and Scott attended a "Blue and Gold" Cub Scout banquet. Scott stared at the other couples, watching the fathers interacting with their young sons, laughing and enjoying each other. Wasn't that what he wanted? What was more important than being close to the boy in the years when he was small and just learning about life and needed a father's guidance? The men and women in the room looked happy to be married and raising kids together. He'd had this once, but thrown it away because of his religious and political convictions. The banquet left him shaken.

"Afterwards," says Lindsey, "he was very despondent. I heard how depressed he was from the wife of the couple he'd been living with. She told me that he had a girlfriend who was pregnant and this woman wanted to get an abortion. The baby wasn't Scott's, but had been fathered by the woman's husband, who wanted her to get an abortion. Scott was so down about this that he was thinking of committing suicide."

The girlfriend had made three separate appointments with doctors to get an abortion, and later told Lindsey that one of them was George Tiller. Three times Roeder had talked her out of going through with this, and she eventually had the child.

"The day after the banquet," says Lindsey, "Scott called and told me, 'I can't believe I've messed things up so badly. Look at what I've done to our marriage,' and then he quoted something from the Bible."

Worried about what Scott might do to himself, Lindsey called his sister, Denise, in Topeka, and explained that he was coming out of a manic phase and crashing into a depression. He needed help. Denise drove to Kansas City, took him back to Topeka, and checked him into a hospital. Doctors put him on medication and wanted to treat him, but he bolted the next morning, threw away his meds, and never returned to the hospital.

"The medication," Lindsey says, "made him feel weird, just as it had in high school. After this episode, he went back to Kansas City, ignored his depression, and got more involved with the militia."

This time he gravitated toward the "Freemen" movement based in eastern Montana, which claimed sovereignty from government jurisdiction, laws, regulations, and taxes. The Freemen were an ideological offshoot of the Posse Comitatus, which had arisen in the Midwest during the mid-1980s farm depression (and from the earlier Minutemen). They believed that God had given them—as white sovereign property owners in Montana—this western land, which they had to defend from other races coming across the border from Mexico. In March 1996, FBI agents and local law enforcement surrounded their 960-acre "Justus Township" compound. After an eighty-one-day standoff, the Freemen peacefully surrendered, with fourteen of them facing criminal charges relating to financial scams and threatening the life of a federal judge.

In April 1996, Roeder was stopped in Topeka after Shawnee County sheriff's deputies pulled him over for driving with an improper license plate. It read, "Sovereign private property. Immunity declared by law. Non-commercial American," and it connected him with the Freemen. In his car, officers found a fuse cord, a blasting cap, ammunition, a one-pound can of gunpowder, and two 9-volt batteries wired to trigger a bomb, which he'd intended to detonate at night at an empty abortion clinic. He was charged with one count of criminal use of explosives, failure to carry a Kansas registration or liability insurance, and driving on a suspended license. After his arrest, no one in his family offered to bail him out, as his father was convinced that jail would finally give Scott a chance to learn from his mistakes.

Following his conviction, Roeder was sentenced to twenty-four months of probation and ordered to dissociate himself from all anti-government groups advocating violence. Because of his arrest, he'd become visible to those who monitor groups on the extreme right, like Topeka's Suzanne James. She tracked right-wing radicals moving around eastern Kansas, and felt that for decades the state had been far too friendly to such activists—one in particular.

In 1954, a Mississippian named Fred Phelps was driving through Topeka when his car had a flat tire. As Phelps later told the story, this occurred right as the Supreme Court's landmark *Brown v. Board of Education* decision was being handed down, leading to the racial integration of American schools. Because the board of education in this case was located in Topeka, Phelps felt this was his sort of town, and he decided to stay. In 1962, he earned a law degree from Topeka's Washburn University, and his first major cases were based on supporting civil rights for African-Americans. He won enough of these to earn an award from the NAACP branch of Bonner Springs, Missouri.

Though Phelps fought for the cause of civil rights, his tolerance didn't extend to homosexuals. In November 1955, dissatisfied with the other religious services he'd found in Topeka and eager to express his own views from the pulpit, he founded the Westboro Baptist Church in the Kansas state capital. At Westboro Baptist, he'd eventually begin promoting slogans such as "God Hates Fags" and "Thank God for Dead Soldiers"—after the U.S. Army had adopted its "Don't Ask, Don't Tell" policy regarding gays in the military. He was also brutally anti-Semitic, and the Anti-Defamation League cited him for numerous comments, including something he'd once said about General Wesley Clark:

"Clark is a Jew . . . Beware! Jews killed the Lord Jesus, and their own prophets, and have persecuted us; and they please not God, and are contrary to all men . . ."

In July 1979, Phelps had been permanently disbarred from practicing law in Kansas, but continued working as an attorney in federal court and spreading his message. His church was made up mostly of extended family, and he sent them out to protest the funerals of U.S. soldiers who'd died in combat—another way of denouncing gays who'd served in the military. Today, a sign above Westboro Baptist Church reads, "God Hates America." Most of the local population tried to ignore Phelps and his church, tucked away in a quiet residential neighborhood a few miles from downtown. But not everyone.

Suzanne James was an Iowa native who moved to Topeka and joined a pharmaceutical company. After her parents were killed in one of the biggest murder cases in the city's history, she began learning about victims' rights, or the lack of them, and was hired as the Shawnee County director of victims' services. In the mid-1990s, she began tracking militia groups and other extremists who lived or passed through Topeka, eastern Kansas, and Missouri. After identifying leaders and members of hate groups, she gave their names to the Southern Poverty Law Center in Mobile, Alabama, which monitored these organizations nationwide. James was convinced that Topeka's decades-long tolerance of—or indifference to—Fred Phelps and his Westboro Baptist Church hadn't just altered the Kansas capital, or the atmosphere of eastern Kansas, but had made this landscape more attractive to dangerous people associated with fringe groups that demonized gays, minorities, and abortion doctors.

"Phelps desensitized the whole community to hatred and hateful activities," says James, "and that's part of the backdrop of Dr. Tiller's story in Kansas. Topeka has been far too tolerant of hate speech for far too long. For years, I believed that the local cops had a no-arrest policy toward the Phelps family because they were afraid of being sued by them. Phelps and his people are bullies and they enjoy making you a public target and then watching you squirm. The way to deal with them is to not allow yourself to be bullied, but to bully them right back. Topekans are way too polite and too reluctant to stand up against the Phelpses, but I'm not."

As director of victims' services, James openly criticized the Phelps family and its church. They retaliated by sending out faxes to offices across Topeka denouncing her as the Shawnee County district attorney's "whore."

"I filed charges against one of their teenagers for harassment," she says, "after he started yelling at me on the street, 'There goes the DA's whore!' I went straight to the police and the Phelpses stopped bothering me. Some places in America would have run Fred Phelps out of town a long time ago, but not here. Not Kansas. Not Topeka. Go over to the state capitol building and take a good look at that picture of John Brown. That's the image they're promoting. The fanatic with the gun in one hand and a Bible in the other."

In 1996, after Roeder was arrested, James attended one of his court appearances to get a sense of who he was:

"Red flags were everywhere. He was a big imposing guy and I was struck by his manner. He didn't rant and rave in court, the way some people do, but was very insistent and intense. His intensity was scary.

"What it all comes down to with a lot of these men is the issue of power and control. What really drives the abortion debate is that men feel they've lost control of women. And in fact, they have. Women are now free to make their own decisions about how they want to live their lives. Because of this, some white, heterosexual males in our society have a feeling of *false* disenfranchisement and alienation . . .

"I've tracked a number of these men with extreme views and they share certain characteristics. They're overly aggressive, prone to physical violence, and have run-ins with the law. Some have domestic violence backgrounds or problems paying their bills. Others are not that stable to begin with. Schizophrenics, for example, tend to become obsessed with things and make them larger than they are. By associating with movements that are racist, misogynistic, homophobic, and anti-government, these men can rationalize their feelings by blaming everything on blacks, Jews, women, and the government. They're angry to begin with, and these groups furnish them with an endless supply of scapegoats. The more they listen to the rhetoric, the more upset they get and the more they need an escape valve."

# IX

While incarcerated, Roeder imitated his biblical hero Paul and began composing a series of letters. Many were written to his nine-year-old son, and they captured his affection for the boy and his desire to convey to him why he believed and acted as he did. The letters assumed that a child would not only understand the complex legal and religious issues the inmate was raising, but would agree with his point of view. It was the same style Roeder later used in virtually every conversation with adults, including strangers, almost as if he were talking to himself. On May 3, 1996, he wrote Nick how proud he was of him for helping his grandfather put new siding on their house and new caulking on the windows. After asking for a picture of the siding he acknowledged that he'd been stopped by the police for having a "perfectly legal" license plate.

"I'm in jail in Topeka now," he told the youngster, "but that doesn't mean I've done anything wrong."

He'd studied common law, he explained, which said that for a crime to be committed there had to be a damaged party. Because none existed in his case, he hadn't broken the law, but he had joined a long list of distinguished people who'd been unfairly locked up. Half of the New Testament had been written by Paul from prison, and it was now God's purpose for Roeder to be behind bars:

"Romans 8:28 says 'All things happen for the good of those that love the Lord, who are called according to His purpose.' Sometimes we can't see what God's purpose is in our circumstances, or situations, but we just have to trust the Lord it is for the best."

In closing, his tone shifted and became more fatherly and heartfelt. He said how much he missed his son, praised him for being such a good boy, and wanted to see him soon: "I LOVE YOU!!! Your Daddy."

A few weeks later, he wrote Lindsey that his father had recently come to the jail for a visit and told him that Nick was confused by what had happened to Roeder:

"The way Dad put it, he might be afraid of me. He said that you said he doesn't talk much about it."

Nick's confusion and silence about his dad were just beginning. In the future, as Roeder's behavior became more challenging to everyone in his family, that silence would deepen as he tried to make sense of the man. Like others, Nick would eventually wonder what he could have done differently or better with his father.

In the letter, the inmate launched into a defense of himself, imploring Lindsey to make certain that the boy understood that Roeder had intended to hurt no one, desperately wanting his son to know he wasn't violent. After admitting to Lindsey that she might not accept as true all the things he said about himself, he wanted her to "tell Nick what my intentions were, because I think he'd be more able to believe it if it were coming from you."

He apologized for all the problems his arrest had created for her, their son, and her dad, but one day all of them would understand his choices, when he was finally able to tell the truth. In signing off, he didn't tell Lindsey that he loved her.

The Kansas Court of Appeals overturned Roeder's conviction, ruling that the police had conducted an illegal search when seizing evidence from his car. But while on probation, he'd disobeyed the judge's orders and continued associating with anti-government groups. His probation was revoked and he was sent back to jail for failing to pay Social Security taxes.

With Roeder behind bars, Lindsey now filed for divorce, confident that she'd win sole custody of Nicholas and remove him from his father's influence. She did, in fact, win, Scott was ordered to pay $134 a month in child support, and Lindsey had discretion over when Roeder saw the boy. She was present during many of their visits, but couldn't always control what her ex-husband talked about on these occasions.

"When Nick was ten," she says, "the three of us were shopping at a mall. We went into a Radio Shack and Scott came up to Nick and put his hand on his shoulder. He said that he'd plant a bomb at Planned Parenthood at night so that no one would get hurt. Nick looked up at him and reminded him that when he was a small child, his dad would never hurt a bird or a bug. He wouldn't step on an ant or a spider. Nick didn't understand why Scott wanted to blow up a building.

"Later on, when Nick was in the bathtub, he said to me, 'My dad is just like the bomber at Oklahoma City.' I didn't know what to tell him."

As Lindsey raised her son alone, Scott bounced back and forth among his contacts in various movements in Topeka and Kansas City, about to meet someone he regarded as a hero and possibly a love interest.

# X

Shelley Shannon was thirteen and living in Wisconsin in 1969 when her parents got divorced. A few years later, as a high school junior, she became pregnant and gave birth to a girl named Angela. The two moved to Washington State, where Shelley had a born-again experience and began receiving apocalyptic literature from the "Last Days Ministries" in Texas. She came across a manual published by the Army of God, the most extreme and secretive anti-abortion group in the country. The booklet had bomb-making instructions of the kind McVeigh and Nichols had employed in Oklahoma City. During the Summer of Mercy, an AOG manual had surfaced in Wichita and echoed Genesis 9:6:

"We, the remnant of God-fearing men and women of the United States of Amerika, do officially declare war on the entire child-killing industry . . . and our most Dread Sovereign Lord God requires that whosoever shed man's blood, by man shall his blood be shed."

Shannon was one of the many who had joined the protests in Wichita that summer, and she began editing the anonymously written AOG manuals. Using the lessons learned from these writings, she traveled up and down the West Coast, setting fires at abortion clinics in Portland and Ashland, Oregon, and in Sacramento and Redding, California. She was no longer Shelley Shannon, mother and housewife, but "Shaggy West AOG" and on a mission she was committed to fulfill.

In August 1993, she rode a bus from the West Coast to Oklahoma City, where she rented a car and headed north to Kansas, pausing at rest stops before moving on to Wichita. Early on the morning of August 19, she drove to Dr. Tiller's clinic, a loaded gun in her purse. With a friendly manner, she walked into the WHCS office and told the receptionist that she was a patient looking to consult with Tiller, but once inside she wasn't able to find him. She left and went to a park, rethinking her strategy. Returning to the clinic, she fell in with the other anti-abortion demonstrators on the sidewalk and all of them shared stories about the Summer of Mercy. She introduced herself as "Ann from Sacramento," and the other protesters were thrilled to have her support. At seven p.m., Tiller emerged from his office and stepped into his 1989 Chevy Suburban. When Shannon came toward him, he thought she was going to hand him some anti-abortion literature so he flipped her off.

She quickly fired six shots from a .32-caliber handgun, hitting him in each arm, blood and glass flying all over the car's interior. He raced the engine and aimed the Chevy right at her, but stopped when she raised the gun as if to shoot again. Bleeding badly, he staggered into the clinic, where his wounds were treated by his staff, who insisted that he take as much time off as he needed to heal. He was back at work the next day, helping perform an abortion. He'd put on a flak jacket and stuck a sign outside the clinic reading, "WOMEN NEED ABORTIONS AND I'M GOING TO PROVIDE THEM." With grim humor, Dr. Tiller once described the aftermath of being shot:

"The first time I drove my car back into the [clinic] parking lot . . . I thought, 'This won't bother me.' I was wrong. It did bother me . . . For six weeks, I hired a Brink's armored truck to pick me up at 7:00 in the morning and take me home at 5:00 . . . As you know, that was the only time in my life I've been able to leave the clinic on time . . ."

As Shannon drove away from WHCS following the attempted murder, a Tiller employee jotted down her license plate. That evening when she returned the rental car to Oklahoma City, the police took her into custody. In her possession was a 1991 *Life Advocate* magazine featuring an article about Tiller entitled "The Wichita Killer." Shannon was transferred to a jail in Topeka, where one of her visitors was Scott Roeder, who came to see her every chance he could and now thought of himself as a member of the Army of God. In the backyard of Shannon's home in Oregon, Wichita officials literally dug up an AOG manual. Each new edition of the manual had called for escalating acts of violence, with the third edition advocating the murder of abortion providers. It began with a "Declaration" to doctors:

"After praying, fasting, and making continual supplication to God for your pagan, heathen, infidel souls, we then peacefully, passively presented our bodies in front of your death camps, begging you to stop the mass murdering of infants. Yet you hardened your already blackened, jaded hearts. We quietly accepted the resulting imprisonment and suffering of our passive resistance. Yet you mocked God and continued the Holocaust. No longer! All of the options have expired . . .

"Not out of hatred of you, but out of love for the persons you exterminate, we are forced to take arms against you. Our life for yours—a simple equation . . . You shall not be tortured at our hands. Vengeance belongs to God only."

One major player in AOG was Michael Bray, known as the "Chaplain" of the group and the author of *A Time to Kill*, which quoted biblical verse to justify force against abortion doctors. Another AOG member, Neal Horsley, posted the names and personal information of abortion providers on the Internet, along with photos and video of their patients, staff, and other physicians entering and exiting the clinics. A third AOG associate, Eric Robert Rudolph, later pled guilty to the nail-bomb murder of an off-duty police officer, Robert Sanderson, and the injuring of Nurse Emily Lyons at a Birmingham, Alabama, abortion clinic. He was also found guilty of the murder of Alice Hawthorne and the bombing of 111 other people at Atlanta's Centennial Olympic Park. Another AOG member, Donald Spitz, hosted the group's Web site.

Shannon's attack on Dr. Tiller inspired the Clinton administration to investigate anti-abortion organizations for evidence of a conspiracy to shut down clinics by murdering their physicians. Part of the probe centered on Paul Hill, who'd attended the trial of Michael Griffin after Griffin had killed Dr. David Gunn. In the spring of 1994, President Clinton convinced Congress to pass the FACE (Freedom of Access to Clinics) Act, making it a crime to block access to medical facilities and deny women the opportunity to get abortions. When Shelley Shannon went on trial that March, Paul Hill was in the courtroom offering her support. After deliberating for eighty-two minutes, the jury convicted her and she was sentenced to prison for decades.

Anti-abortion activists were undeterred by President Clinton, the federal investigation, or the FACE Act. They issued "Wanted" or "Unwanted" posters of Tiller and other physicians, offering $5,000 for information leading to their arrest and the loss of their medical license. Dr. John Britton had replaced the murdered David Gunn at the Ladies Center in Pensacola, Florida. Just two weeks after Clinton signed the FACE Act, Paul Hill stood outside the center, yelling again and again, "Mommy, Mommy, don't murder me!" The center called the police and they came to the clinic, but didn't arrest Hill. A few days later, Hill repeated his performance and was busted for disorderly conduct, but soon released. He bought a shotgun and began taking target practice.

On July 29, 1994, he came to the clinic just before seven a.m. and planted twenty-two white wooden crosses in the ground nearby, each one meant to signify the death of a child. Standing near the clinic's front door, he tried to distribute anti-abortion pamphlets and talk to women entering the building, until a policeman arrived and ordered him to remove the crosses. Hill complied, but the officer didn't force him to leave the premises. At 7:27, Dr. Britton arrived in a blue Nissan pickup driven by James Barrett. Sitting behind Britton was Barrett's wife, Jane. All three froze as Hill approached with a 12-gauge shotgun and fired at Britton before quickly reloading and firing again at Britton and then Barrett, killing them both, but not at Jane. Hill trotted away and was arrested within a few blocks.

Those running the Ladies Center contacted the FBI and demanded to know if *now* was the time for them to start enforcing the FACE Act—before more physicians were killed. President Clinton called Britton's death domestic terrorism and asked for a full investigation of Paul Hill. Attorney General Janet Reno ordered U.S. marshals to provide security for clinics across the country and the feds created a task force on violence connected to abortion. That autumn, Hill was the first person tried in federal court under the FACE Act, and his legal strategy was the so-called "necessity defense," contending that he'd killed Dr. Britton to protect the unborn because they could not defend themselves, and to stop the greater evil of abortion. He was convicted in October 1994 and received two life sentences in federal prison. In November 1994, he was tried on state murder charges and the jury took just twenty minutes to convict him. During his sentencing hearing, as the judge ordered him to die in the electric chair, a Kansas City antiabortion activist, Regina Dinwiddie, leaped up in the courtroom.

"This man is innocent," she shouted at the judge, "and his blood will be on your hands and the hands of the people of the state of Florida and on the jury!"

Dinwiddie was arrested for her outburst.

In 1984, after a series of abortion clinic bombings, the FBI had considered investigating the acts as part of a domestic terrorism conspiracy, but the idea had stalled out. In late 1994, a federal grand jury in Virginia, working with the Justice Department to investigate linkages behind the anti-abortion killings, issued subpoenas to Michael Bray, Don Spitz, and Anthony Leake, a Kansas City–area activist. When the feds were unable to establish these criminal links, the grand jury disbanded in 1996.

The violent year of 1994 was not yet over. On December 30, an apprentice hairdresser named John C. Salvi III charged into a Planned Parenthood clinic in Brookline, Massachusetts, and opened fire with a .22-caliber rifle, killing a receptionist and wounding two others. He fled the clinic and drove on to Brookline's Preterm Health Services, killing another receptionist and wounding two more. He left Massachusetts and fired two dozen shots into an abortion office in Norfolk,

Virginia, before he was arrested. Following his conviction, Salvi committed suicide in prison. Despite these murders, and the rising bomb threats and clinic arsons during the mid-'90s, the FBI did not find a conspiracy tying any specific groups or individuals to the spreading bloodshed.

On October 23, 1998, the New York abortion doctor Barnett Slepian was murdered in his kitchen by James "Atomic Dog" Kopp, who then bolted the country. He was caught in 2001, convicted in 2003, and sentenced to twenty-five years to life.

A week after Dr. Slepian was killed, Tiller's clinic received a letter threatening to contaminate his employees with anthrax. Similar letters went out to five other clinics in Indiana, Kentucky, and Tennessee, but the FBI said they were all hoaxes. Clayton Waagner, who was convicted of sending more than 550 fake anthrax letters to clinics in 2001, signed many of them "Army of God."

"In August of 1994," Tiller once said, "I was the first on the anti-abortion hit list or assassination list. And Janet Reno and President Clinton assigned federal marshals to me for thirty months. They came to the house, got me, took me to the office, stayed at the clinic . . . But the good news is, we still live in the United States of America. The good news is that in Kansas, we are able to use the wide definition and the full implementation of the *Roe v. Wade* decision."

During the 1980s and early '90s, Dr. Warren Hern had written extensively about the importance of whom America chose for its president—and how violence against abortion providers had risen dramatically with first Ronald Reagan and then George H. W. Bush in the White House for a collective twelve years. In May 1997, after the Senate passed "partial birth abortion ban" legislation, Hern composed an editorial that appeared in *The New York Times*, saying, "As I watched the Senate debate on late-term abortions, I was struck by the surreal quality of the remarks. The oratory from both sides had nothing to do with the anguish faced by my patients and their families, yet the results will profoundly affect their lives. Families sometimes ask me to do things that might be illegal if the bill the Senate passed on Wednesday ever becomes law . . . The foes of abortion will keep sponsoring legislation that keeps doctors guessing about what they are allowed to do . . . President Clinton is right to object to this dangerous measure. And he would do well to be suspicious of all such attempts to limit later-term abortions . . ."

That June, Hern sent a letter to every member of Congress outlining his position. In November 1997, Hern wrote President Clinton himself, thanking him for vetoing this bill for the second time:

"As a physician providing late abortion services to families whose pregnancies have been tragically complicated by abnormalities and serious illness, I applaud your courage and leadership in this struggle . . . I see women and families each week who desperately need qualified medical assistance in terminating advanced pregnancies that are often complicated with medical, surgical and psychiatric problems. The health and privacy of these women and families are directly threatened by this legislation . . ."

In March 1998, the president wrote back:

"I'm grateful to have your insight on this deeply divisive issue. I vetoed H.R. 1833 because Congress would not include a limited exception in the bill for those few but tragic cases in which the procedure is necessary to save the life of a woman or to prevent serious harm to her health; I vetoed H.R. 1122 for the same reason. Like you, I believe the procedure should be available in the small number of compelling cases where its use, in the medical judgment of a woman's physician, is necessary to preserve her life or to avert serious damage to her health. I remain firm in this belief, and I'm glad to know I have your continued support.

"Thanks again for getting in touch with me on this sensitive issue. Best wishes, Sincerely,

"Bill Clinton."

# XI

After his release from prison, Scott Roeder drifted further into obscure religions, some with ideas similar to the Identity Christianity church in Idaho that had recruited the men who'd killed Alan Berg. One tenet of these belief systems was that born-again Christians such as Roeder were the true descendants of the Old Testament Jews. Roeder kept a kosher diet and celebrated the Sabbath, or "Shabbat" in Hebrew, beginning on Friday sundown and ending on Saturday sundown. He used the Hebrew terms for God (Yahweh) and Jesus (Yahshua). As he practiced these rituals, his ex-wife kept a log of his activities and refused to let their son, Nick, see his father unless she was present. In the log, she noted that the boy hadn't spent any time alone with his father since Roeder had left in September 1994 and that Nick wasn't comfortable with his dad, but fearful, insecure, and embarrassed:

"Nick is too shy and passive and well-behaved and will not talk back or speak up for himself. He does not like to visit with his dad and it's usually by my insistence that he sees Scott."

Occasionally, father and son talked on the phone, but that happened only when Nick picked up the receiver before he realized his dad was calling and he couldn't easily hang up on him. Lindsey's main concern was that if Nick were left alone with him, Scott would kidnap the boy, since one of the groups he was involved with had "kidnapped children from a father and kept them and his mother in a compound."

All the time Nick was growing up, Lindsey had an escape plan if Scott ever tried to take him away.

"My sister," she says, "has a relative on the Cherokee nation down in Texas and we were going to hide out there."

Roeder had recently become involved with the "Embassy of Heaven Church," which was located, according to its return address, in "Stayton, Oregon . . . Kingdom of Heaven." Church members got to pick their names, and the pastor's was Paul Revere. When Lindsey and Scott were still married and he'd received materials in the mail from Revere, she'd hidden them or thrown them away (she'd heard Roeder talk about the violently anti-Semitic novel *The Turner Diaries*, and wondered if he had a copy of it stashed somewhere). During their divorce proceedings, the Embassy of Heaven offered to handle Roeder's finances and sent a request to Lindsey's house asking for the title to their car. She was appalled.

On July 9, 1999, the Embassy of Heaven intervened on Roeder's behalf with a letter to the legal authorities in Johnson County, where Lindsey and Scott were divorced. Pastor Revere described Roeder as a missionary assigned to Kansas and told the Olathe District Court that the church was managing Scott's financial affairs. Revere wanted copies of Roeder's original agreement to pay child support and contended that the court hadn't provided evidence such an agreement existed:

"Scott P. Roeder tells us that he desires to faithfully support his wife and child, but she divorced him and sought the care and protection of strangers. He is willing to again support his family, but only if they will return to his covering.

> Separated unto the Gospel,
> Embassy of Heaven Church
> Paul Revere, Pastor."

Closer to home, Roeder began meeting in suburban Kansas City residences on Saturdays for potluck and Bible study. At the gatherings, worshippers talked about their own Hebrew roots and the "secret societies" that they believed were trying to control the U.S. government. The attendees called themselves "Messianic Jews" and were convinced that Jesus was the Messiah. For a while, Roeder joined a local synagogue, Or HaOlam, led by Rabbi Shmuel Wolkenfeld, but was asked to leave for being too argumentative.

As Roeder moved into and out of these groups and considered paying child support, he kept writing letters to his son, filled with his growing disillusionment with American society. In one, he encouraged the boy not to participate in Halloween with his friends because it was a "high holiday for the devil." In another, he said that because the Bible didn't mention honoring the birth of Jesus, Nicholas shouldn't take part in Christmas. A thirteen-page letter to Nick vividly described his father's 1991 conversion to evangelical Christianity: for some time Yahshua (Jesus) had been working in his life to teach him that he was a sinner in need of a savior, until one day in August Roeder kneeled down in the front room of their home and asked Yahshua to forgive his sins and to help him live his life for the savior. Roeder's prayers were answered, he told Nick, and this wasn't just a religious turning point, but also a political one, and a turning point for the entire family.

When creating the United States, the Founding Fathers had been determined to separate religion and politics, both in institutions and for individuals. Religion was for the private realm, while politics was played out in public. Mixing them, they reasoned, generated too much confusion and too much opportunity for abuse or intolerance. They were now bound together inside Roeder, and the fundamentalist Christian teachings and anti-government rhetoric he'd been absorbing for years came tumbling out to his son.

"Ever since giving my life to Yahshua," he wrote, "and asking Him to be my Savior, His Holy Spirit has been guiding and leading me into certain things that I had not realized before. One of the things the Holy Spirit was showing me concerned the deception there has been over the subject of income taxes . . ."

America had gradually turned away from a government that upheld "godly principles" of truth and justice and embraced an "ungodly system" of socialism and communism, which denied the existence of Yahweh and Yahshua. The United States now "allowed the murder of unborn babies in their mothers' wombs"—just the opposite of what the Bible promoted. He ranted against a political and legal structure that protected abortion doctors, but punished those who picketed in front of abortion clinics. The country had strayed from its biblical foundations and the time was coming when this had to change.

"Whenever a Christian," he wrote, "is shown by the Holy Spirit what is true and rightous [*sic*], that Christian must decide to stand for what is right, <u>no matter what the cost</u>! . . . That Christian must also realize there could be a price to pay for standing for what is right . . ."

It was as if he were telling his son that he was considering new options for stopping abortion, before he told anyone else.

# XII

By the mid-1990s, a revolution was coming to American culture. Cable TV, the Internet, and political talk radio were just starting to break through and become an amplifier for the emotional forces building in the society. New technology was about to collide with the feelings of anger and fear that had been growing for decades on the fringes, but were seeping into the mainstream. Something new, something vast, disruptive, and undefined, was about to be unleashed on the airwaves and online, packaged and presented to a mass audience as entertainment. Those who were already enraged or frightened would be encouraged to feel more so now. Those who were paranoid would be pushed further in that direction. Whatever, or whoever, was unstable was going to be nurtured in its instability. What mattered in the new media wasn't so much political philosophy but how deeply one felt about a government, a group, a crime, sexuality, or, as here, about abortion. A bull market had arrived for accusation, blame, even hatred, and it was driven far less by traditional ideology than by pure emotion.

The 1990s saw a series of spectacular mass shootings at churches, schools, and other public venues. They all had one thing in common: none of these acts was committed for any personal advantage or gain, such as money. Workers at offices, worshippers inside sanctuaries, or teenagers at their schools felt so threatened and challenged by those around them, or by those who held a different viewpoint, that they took up arms in an institutional setting, killing as many people as they could.

My wife, Joyce, and I raised a young son throughout the 1990s, and the eruptions of violence within schools, leading to 263 deaths, were especially difficult for us to watch. Before 1995, such deaths were very rare, but that began to change on November 15, 1995, in Giles County, Tennessee, when seventeen-year-old Jamie Rouse, dressed all in black, went to school and shot two teachers in the head, killing one. While trying to murder the school's football coach, Rouse left another student dead. On February 2, 1996, in Moses Lake, Washington, fourteen-year-old Barry Loukaitis walked into a math class wearing a long Western coat that concealed a high-powered rifle, two pistols, and ammunition. While taking the entire class hostage, Loukaitis killed two classmates and a teacher. That same day, a sixteen-year-old in Atlanta, Georgia, shot and killed a teacher.

In late April 1999, Joyce and I drove out to Columbine High School in southwestern Denver, ten miles from our home, and stood outside a chain-link fence, installed to keep us and others away from the crime scene. We watched as hundreds upon hundreds of teenagers and adults knelt down in the spring mud and burst into tears, grabbing on to one another for support or clutching at the fence and swaying in anguish. A couple days earlier, two Columbine students, Eric Harris and Dylan Klebold, had walked into the suburban school and opened fire with shotguns and semiautomatic weapons, wounding twenty-three students and killing twelve teenagers, one teacher, and themselves. Nobody at Columbine this evening said anything or made eye contact, the shame of what had happened here too deep to be put into words. Our kids had done this, the silence was saying, the boys we thought we knew.

Before Columbine, the country had seen numerous school shootings—in Mississippi, Arkansas, and Oregon—but this one was especially horrifying. Harris and Klebold had built ninety-five bombs and planted most of them around the school. Some of the explosives were supposed to detonate inside the school cafeteria at 11:20 a.m., during the height of lunch hour, killing hundreds of kids as they ate. When the survivors ran outside to escape the mayhem, Harris and Klebold would gun them down. They intended to kill at least five hundred people, dwarfing the Oklahoma City bombing, but when the explosives failed to go off, the young men entered the school and began shooting. The purpose of the bloodbath, revealed on a home video discovered after the killers' deaths, paralleled that of the neo-Nazis' before they'd killed Alan Berg. Harris and Klebold wanted to "kick-start a revolution" against their enemies: "niggers, spics, Jews, gays, fucking whites . . . humanity." They were motivated by extreme hatred, and Adolf Hitler was one of their heroes. Their day of infamy at Columbine—April 20, 1999—was the 110th anniversary of the Fuhrer's birth.

Those who'd killed Berg were tucked away in the Idaho woods and held obviously fanatical beliefs. They were young, angry, uneducated, and unsuccessful working-class white men, without good prospects in front of them. Harris and Klebold (who drove a BMW) had every privilege one could want: money, family support, friends, and opportunities to attend good colleges. But they also had bottomless reservoirs of hurt and anger. Their act of terrorism had evolved inside Eric Harris's well-furnished suburban bedroom, and they were not alone in their feelings. In the weeks following the massacre, the National Safety Center reported that three thousand other high school students across the country concocted bomb threats or other schemes meant to result in death.

"I'm sorry I have so much rage," Klebold said on the videotape.

"I really am sorry about this," Harris said, addressing his mother, "but war's war."

Both expressed their hatred toward different groups and individuals at Columbine, because of things like hair and clothing.

"You've given us shit for years," Klebold said of his classmates. "You're fucking going to pay for all the shit. We don't give a shit because we're going to die doing it."

"We need to die, too," Harris echoed.

Getting ready to leave Columbine that evening, my wife and I noticed a tall dirt mound to the south of the school, maybe a hundred feet in elevation. A large wooden cross rose above it in the fading sunlight, put there in the past few days, stark against the sky. Long lines of people were wending their way upward toward the cross, as if drawn by an invisible hand. A wet, cold wind blew over them, pounding their hair and clothes, but they lowered their heads and marched on through the dirt and mud, determined to reach the top. When they arrived, they reached out and grabbed the cross, holding on to it and gazing down onto Columbine, now surrounded by thousands of bouquets of flowers and handwritten messages to the dead. The scene was stunningly biblical, evoking the hill at Calvary outside of Jerusalem, where Jesus had been crucified. This wasn't a pilgrimage to an ancient holy site, but a shrine to human violence and hysteria, to our incomprehension of ourselves, and to our growing private and public rage.

On every side of us people were crying. For a few moments all the blame and hatred seemed to evaporate, and we were not strangers to one another anymore, or enemies, and had all been hurt and diminished by these deaths. There was no "us" or "them," no left or right, at Columbine. Turning away from the park and moving slowly past the waves of incoming mourners, we wrapped our coats around us and leaned into the bitter wind, which hinted at worse things to come.

Six months after Columbine, President Clinton was now so disturbed by what was happening across America that he spoke publicly about a recent rash of murders: twelve office deaths in Atlanta; eleven hate crime shootings over the Fourth of July weekend against Asians, Jews, and African-Americans in Indiana and Illinois; a church massacre that killed seven in Fort Worth; the shooting of Jewish children at a Southern California daycare center; and the neo-Nazi murder of a minority postal employee. These were no longer aberrant events, but almost predictable eruptions of violence. What distinguished the president's comments was not that he offered any solutions or hope, but that he understood that something fundamental had changed inside the culture.

"All you think about is the new millennium," he said at a Los Angeles fund-raiser in October 1999. "Isn't it ironic that the thing that's holding us back most . . . is our inability to form a community around our common humanity because of our vulnerability to mankind's most ancient fear—the fear of the other?

"I see people in this so-called modern world, where we're celebrating all of your modern ideas and your modern achievements and what is the biggest problem? We are dragged down by the most primitive of hatreds. It's bizarre."

And it was just beginning.

# INTO THE
# MAINSTREAM

# XIII

On January 31, 1996, the media mogul Rupert Murdoch announced that he'd be launching the Fox News Channel, a twenty-four-hour news service airing on both cable and satellite.

"The appetite for news—particularly news that explains to people how it affects them—is expanding enormously," Murdoch said at the time.

Fox News premiered on October 7, 1996, and after a few fits and starts was soon reaching about 10 million American homes. As the network developed, it was usually described as a "conservative" alternative to the rest of the media—an imprecise term. Some Fox commentators held the traditionally conservative belief of opposing big, intrusive governance, but they also supported spending vast amounts of money on domestic surveillance. Others at Fox were all for individual freedoms, but not ones that extended to gays or women's reproductive rights. What Murdoch was selling was something bigger and vaguer than a strict political point of view. Seeing a void in the media marketplace, he was there with a compelling strategy, reaching out to a large, discontented, and mostly neglected TV audience (on talk radio, Rush Limbaugh had been working the same demographic for years, on the way to becoming the most successful radio personality in American history). At Fox, the feelings of viewers mattered more than their party affiliation.

Those feelings represented the unspecified anxiety, the anger and fear, the underlying discomfort, of our time. It was everywhere, it was easy to aim it at the imperfect and cumbersome institutions that formed the basis of our society, and it had not yet been fully exploited as a TV business opportunity. Putting aside what Fox's strategy might mean in terms of public policy or journalism, it was a great vehicle for generating attention and dollars.

I paid little attention to Fox or to its most popular host, Bill O'Reilly, until the fall of 1999. The previous June I'd published a book, *Presumed Guilty*, about the six-year-old beauty queen JonBenet Ramsey, murdered in Boulder in December 1996. For the past three years, I'd been driving the thirty miles from Denver to Boulder and interacting with many of the principals in the case. One was the veteran Boulder district attorney Alex Hunter, who was open-minded, a good listener, and deeply curious about the girl's death (hard qualities to find in such an experienced DA in the middle of a major homicide investigation). He was willing to speak with a journalist, and many other outsiders, to see if he could learn something new about this confounding criminal mystery. It was the only homicide in American and perhaps world history in which a ransom note and a body had been found in the same location. The child had incriminating DNA samples in her underwear and beneath her fingernails, all belonging to a single unknown male.

Faced with such complexity, Hunter quickly brought in the nation's top forensic scientists, starting with Dr. Henry Lee, the director of the Connecticut State Forensic Laboratory, and assembled a first-rate legal team around him. In October 1999, after presenting the evidence to a grand jury for more than a year—unheard of in a murder case— Hunter decided not to indict the Ramsey parents for the crime of killing their daughter.

It was then that I turned on the TV and saw Bill O'Reilly launch into a personal attack on Hunter and Boulder itself (in his view the town was run by far-left secular progressives). Because O'Reilly was angry and personally hurt that the criminal justice system had let him down in the Ramsey matter, the evidence in the case had become irrelevant. Audiences responded to his outrage; he was a rising star in the new media and *The O'Reilly Factor* was on its way to reaching 102 million American homes and more than 3.3 million viewers each weeknight.

O'Reilly wasn't merely assaulting Hunter, which many other commentators from both sides of the political spectrum had done. Long before the evidence in the case was known, the generally liberal Geraldo Rivera had held a mock trial of the Ramseys on his program—and found the parents guilty. The issue was deeper than politics and had more to do with the absolute need to be right, at the expense of everything else. Both O'Reilly and Rivera were attacking the legal system itself and the very thin veneer of social agreements that Americans live by. Expressing their feelings was more important than due process, constitutional rights, courtroom evidence, or forensic analysis. For his efforts, NBC offered Geraldo a reported $30 million contract. He and O'Reilly were succeeding on a grand scale precisely because they didn't care about any of these bigger issues and were encouraging viewers to demean, if not hate, the people who did.

No journalist, or even journalism itself, could compete with the spectacle unfolding on Fox and elsewhere. The new wave of megastar commentators were not reporters, nor were they accountable—their only job was to generate listeners and ad sales. They were entertainers, people like Michael Savage and Mark Levin, Laura Ingraham and Anne Coulter, and they were excellent at what they did, representing a new form of mass popular entertainment. They amused audiences by demonizing individuals, but more important, by demonizing legal rules and systems of government—the handful of words on paper that bound together the American social and political experiment. The contempt for those rules and systems, once isolated on the fringes, was becoming a very hot commodity. Another upcoming Fox commentator, Glenn Beck, addressed the larger problem succinctly in his best-selling book *Glenn Beck's Common Sense*. Americans, he wrote, "know that SOMETHING JUST DOESN'T FEEL RIGHT, but they don't know how to describe it or, more importantly, how to stop it." And they were rarely encouraged by the media to examine the roots of these feelings or how to manage them better. Venting was the new game, the only thing that mattered in this new emotional reality.

In the fall of 1999, the issue was not whether O'Reilly was right or wrong about the Ramsey case, although time showed him to be wrong. (During the summer of 2008, two samples of "touch DNA" from Jon-Benet's underwear were found to be consistent with the other genetic material at the crime scene. As a result, the new Boulder DA, Mary Lacy, finally cleared the Ramsey parents—Patsy had died in 2006—of murdering their daughter and the case remained wide open.) O'Reilly had long since gone on to attack other processes and people, as his fame—and fortune—continued to spread. Some nights he reached 3.5 million viewers and his message never wavered. The surface of things, he implied from his bully pulpit on the nation's airwaves, was the truth of things. There are no facts that aren't immediately obvious.

If thirty years of reporting had taught me anything, it was that the surface of things was exactly that—just the surface. Journalism was and always had been covered with scars and warts. Like the legal profession, it was often not as pure or as noble as reporters and attorneys wanted it to be, but it remained an important piece of what insulated a society from the most dangerous forms of manipulation and control.

Watching O'Reilly, I felt that the professional world I'd come of age in was near its death. In the Ramsey case, he'd dismissed the legal system. Now he was ready to take on the world of science and Dr. Tiller. What the fringe abortion opponents had failed to do to the physician, the mainstream was about to attempt—with voices that had become not just respectable, but paragons of success.

# XIV

By middle age, George Tiller was a far different man from the one who'd been raised a conservative Republican, in a state that hadn't sent a Democrat to the U.S. Senate since 1932. Nothing in his professional life had turned out quite the way he'd envisioned it, and he'd had to adapt constantly to the upheaval around him. Ensnared inside a battle he could never have imagined, he could only hope for a new era and a nation less divided.

"We have given war, pestilence, hate, greed, judgment, ego, self-sufficiency a good try, and have failed," he once said. "We need a new paradigm that consists of kindness, courtesy, justice, love, and respect in all our relationships."

He tried to implement his own new paradigm, speaking to his staff about reconciliation and healing, and inviting Reverend George Gardner into his clinic to provide counseling to his employees. How could they cope with the constant stress of working at WHCS and rise above the verbal attacks and ongoing abuse at the front gate? How could they learn not to hate the people screaming at them each day, but to forgive and even love them? The employees needed all the help they could get.

Abortion foes parked a "Truth Truck" at WHCS, its side panels depicting large color photographs of dismembered fetuses. On the gates leading into the parking lot, demonstrators hung a large banner reading,

"Please Do Not Kill Your Baby." Scores of small white crosses stood in the grass along the sidewalk, showing the average number of abortions protesters believed were performed at WHCS each month. When patients left the clinic after an appointment, they were followed to their homes or hotels and anti-abortion literature and pictures were slipped under their doors. Tiller's enemies took long-range, telephoto-lens images of some of these patients and posted their faces online. People searched through the trash behind the houses of his staff, looking for any scrap of information to use against him. When pregnant women arrived at WHCS, demonstrators approached them with baby blankets and told them to walk next door, where they'd set up their own office. Choices Medical Clinic had opened in 1999, after six years of fighting city zoning rulings. Its sign faced into Tiller's parking lot and offered a "Free 4-D Sonogram" to women who could come in and discuss their options without an appointment.

While these tactics did little to change the actual number of abortions being performed in Kansas or the United States, the number of abortion providers was steadily falling. In 1992, Kansas had had 15; by 2005, it was down to 7. Nationwide, the decline was from 2,400 to fewer than 1,800. Several factors were causing this, including tightened regulations making abortions more costly; public protest and social pressure; and the medical industry trend to consolidate into bigger, more specialized practices. Not long ago, Wichita had had four abortion clinics. Only Tiller's was now left, with Operation Rescue having bought the next-to-last local office to shut it down, and turning it into its headquarters. The great majority of young doctors weren't learning to perform abortions, because this field wasn't just controversial, but dangerous.

In 2001, Operation Rescue celebrated the ten-year anniversary of the Summer of Mercy with another wave of dissent in Wichita. While not nearly as disruptive as the first event, putting Tiller out of business remained one of its major goals. In 2002, the organization, now led by Troy Newman, moved its headquarters from Southern California to Wichita, in order to target Tiller at closer range (the same year, Scott

Roeder first stalked the doctor at Reformation Lutheran Church). Demonstrators began their longest vigil ever at WHCS, coming there for the next 1,846 days. With the clinic under siege, Tiller gave pep talks to his staff, constantly repeated "Attitude is everything," and tried to boost office morale by handing out a dozen roses to his employees and a T-shirt depicting Rosie the Riveter.

"We can do it Team Tiller," it read.

Dr. Tiller had no intention of giving up his practice or caving to the pressures surrounding him. The struggle between the anti-abortion forces and WHCS had become permanent fixtures in the local landscape.

"One night I was working very late," says the Wichita author Robert Beattie, "and I needed to go to Kinko's at three a.m. I got in my car and drove past Tiller's clinic. There were several protesters out there walking around. At three a.m.—in pitch darkness! If you were ever lonely in Wichita in the middle of the night, you could go over there and find some company."

The protesters brought their graphic Truth Trucks to Tiller's church and parked them in front of Reformation Lutheran during Sunday services, loudly demonstrating out front or playing musical instruments. They demanded that church officials excommunicate the doctor and his family, while yelling at members of the congregation entering the sanctuary that a murderer worshipped with them. They came inside the church and interrupted communion with anti-Tiller chatter, grabbed the microphone from the pastor, pushed the organist away from the keyboard, and found the addresses of the congregants and mailed them postcards showing aborted fetuses. Roeder himself had visited the church and been questioned by a police officer patrolling the scene. A few people left Reformation Lutheran because of these incidents, but church leadership stood by the family. Tiller was in a Bible study group there and his wife, Jeanne, sang in the choir (his three daughters and one son were now grown and two of the young women were studying to become physicians). The church staff had talked with Tiller about bolstering security with a camera at the front entrance, but he said that wasn't necessary. Despite all the protest and disruptions, surely no one would further violate the sanctity of Reformation Lutheran.

Abortion foes spread rumors about him and his patients throughout Wichita. An especially inflammatory one was that years ago he'd helped Nola Foulston, the DA of the Eighteenth Judicial District, adopt a baby. In 1989, Foulston had been diagnosed with multiple sclerosis, and the scuttlebutt was that Tiller had helped her become a mother as part of his ongoing political agenda; down the road she'd surely return a favor or two for him during his impending legal battles. When asked about this rumor by *The New York Times*, Foulston's office would neither confirm nor deny it.

The anti-Tiller crowd accused the doctor of getting rich from performing abortions and of having a "decadent, lavish lifestyle." WHCS was indeed a lucrative business and the physician lived in an 8,300-square-foot home. He charged $6,000 for a late-term abortion and did 250–300 per year, with a profit margin of around 35 percent, for an estimated income upward of half a million dollars. But he spent hundreds of thousands of dollars on armored vehicles, lawyers, bullet-proof glass, video monitors, security systems, and an armed staff. He often paid his employees above the norm so they'd stay with him, making sure to hand out bonuses after a particularly bad stretch at the office. He urged them not to give up the fight and said that if a stake had to be driven through the heart of the anti-abortion movement, he wanted to have his "hand on the hammer." Whether he admitted it or not, the environment at work took a toll.

"When I first met Dr. Tiller," says Julie Burkhart, who helped establish his political action committee in 2002, "I was intimidated by him. He said, 'I need to know that you'll do whatever it takes to raise money or whatever else we need done here. This might mean taking out the trash one night, if that's what necessary.' He wanted to know right then that I was totally committed to this work. It wasn't easy for him to trust people. I'm sure that came from being bombed and shot at and having his name dragged through the mud for so long. But as the years moved on, and he saw that I *was* committed, he had a level of affection and trust in me that really bubbled to the surface.

"He never liked talking about all the things going on right outside the clinic because that was a real energy sucker and took time away from the medical work going on inside the walls of his office. He believed there was a solution to every problem and our job was just to focus on that and make health care better for women."

Out in Boulder, Dr. Warren Hern wasn't so optimistic, or reticent, when it came to the protesters who also camped out at his clinic and distributed flyers around town about him. One began, "A baby killer lives in your neighborhood . . ."

In March 2001, the United States Court of Appeals for the Ninth Circuit in California overturned a judgment against abortion opponents who'd targeted several doctors, including Hern, for assassination. Two years earlier, following the 1998 murder of Dr. Barnett Slepian, Hern and three other physicians had decided to take action *before* another doctor was killed. They sued those making the threats under a federal racketeering law and another law against inciting violence against abortion providers. For a month, the four doctors sat in a Portland courtroom next to their potential assassins. The physicians took the stand and described to the jurors how they'd been stalked and placed on the defendants' "Wanted" posters and hit lists, which were then posted on the Internet. It was an opportunity for Hern to talk about the lethal process of "target identification"—a doctor's face showed up on a poster, over and over again, and then he got killed. This process was continuing, Hern argued, and had to be stopped. After listening to the testimony, the federal jury decided for the doctors, but the judgment was later overturned on appeal.

Commenting in *The New York Times* following the second court ruling, Dr. Hern called the appellate decision "crushing." He'd recently been sitting by a window in his office, speaking with a reporter, when he noticed that the Venetian blinds were slightly open. Without interrupting their discussion, he reached over and closed the blinds, as he always did at work or home now when near an open window.

"Whoever shot Dr. Slepian," Dr. Hern wrote, "accomplished his purpose—to strike terror into my heart. It was an act of political terrorism, as have been the assassinations and attempted assassinations of 10 other abortions doctors . . ."

Hern described the view from his home of the renowned Flatirons Mountains rising above Boulder, but he no longer had the luxury of looking out at the reddish, vertical slabs of rock:

"My name, along with those of other doctors, is on an Internet abortion hate list—called the 'Nuremberg Files'—now found to be acceptable free speech by the appellate court's decision. Dr. Slepian's name has had a line drawn through it. Who's next?"

# XV

In addition to the ongoing death threats, the efforts to close Tiller's clinic were moving into mainstream politics. Since *Roe v. Wade*, Kansas had placed only minor restrictions on late-term abortion, but that was changing. Tiller's Web site claimed that he'd done more of these operations "than anyone else currently practicing in the Western Hemisphere." In 1998, the Kansas legislature began requiring that abortion doctors submit medical information to the state's Department of Health and Environmental Statistics. Between 1998 and 2008, Tiller would perform about 4,800 late-term abortions, at least twenty-two weeks into gestation. Roughly 2,000 of these involved fetuses unable to survive outside the womb, because of genetic defects or fatal illnesses, but the other 2,800 abortions involved viable fetuses, although some had severe abnormalities.

In 1998, the Kansas legislature outlawed abortions on viable fetuses after the twenty-second week of pregnancy, except under certain conditions: *"(a) No person shall perform or induce an abortion when the fetus is viable unless such person is a physician and has a documented referral from another physician not legally or financially affiliated with the physician performing or inducing the abortion and both physicians determine that: (1) The abortion is necessary to preserve the life of the pregnant woman; or (2) a continuation of the pregnancy will cause a substantial and irreversible impairment of a major bodily function of the pregnant woman."*

In the original spirit of *Roe v. Wade*, the new law allowed the primary doctor leeway in making his own decisions about particular cases "according to his best professional judgment." Still, this was a victory for anti-abortion forces.

To comply with the statute, Tiller engaged the attorney Rachel Pirner, who'd helped him with his adoption cases. She contacted the Kansas State Board of Healing Arts (KSBHA), which holds the power to license or unlicense doctors, and asked the executive director, Larry Buening, for a clarification. Did the phrase *"a documented referral from another physician not legally or financially affiliated with the physician performing or inducing the abortion"* mean a Kansas physician? Or could it be someone from out of state? The questions were critical. Getting any Kansas doctor involved with abortion after the death threats Tiller had received over the years, not to mention the bombing of his clinic and the gunfire he'd taken in both arms, was a huge challenge.

On April 27, 1999, the KSBHA issued a subpoena for ninety days' worth of Tiller's patient records to see if he was in compliance with the new statute. If not, he could lose his medical license. As Pirner considered a federal lawsuit to stop enforcement of this law, she asked the KSBHA to stay or postpone its decision. According to Tiller's handwritten notes from June 21, 1999, Larry Buening called Tiller that day and literally told him not to make a federal case out of the matter. He could use a Kansas doctor named Kristin Neuhaus as his referring physician. She ran a small abortion clinic in Lawrence and could drive to Wichita once a week to consult with his patients. As long as Tiller and Neuhaus did not have a financial arrangement, this would satisfy the interpretation of the new law. Their conversation, Buening pointedly told Tiller, was strictly off the record. If asked about it in the future, Buening would deny ever having had it. Neuhaus became Tiller's second physician and his legal battles appeared to be over. Then Phill Kline arrived.

Kline grew up in Shawnee, a suburb of Kansas City, Kansas, and when he was five his father abandoned the family, leaving the boy to be raised by a single mother. At Kansas University, Kline headed the college Republicans and became a broadcaster for the Kansas City radio station WHB, honing his language skills before going on to KU law school. Even his strongest adversaries admitted that he was a polished and powerful orator. After entering private practice in Kansas City as a corporate lawyer, he moved back into radio, hosting the *The Phill and Mary Show* and *Face Off with Phill Kline.* He and his wife, Deborah, were members of the Central Church of the Nazarene and he served as finance director of the Johnson County (Kansas) Republican Committee. A fierce believer in lowering or eliminating taxes, he was even more fiercely against abortion. In 1992, he was elected to the Kansas House of Representatives and he then ran for the U.S. House of Representatives, but lost.

In 2002, when he campaigned to become attorney general of Kansas, stopping abortion was one of his major campaign themes, which meant stopping George Tiller. This time Kline won, and he began hiring those who felt as he did. One employee was Bryan Brown, arrested multiple times for protesting in Wichita during the Summer of Mercy. In picking him to head the AG's consumer affairs division, Kline compared Brown to Martin Luther King. Another hire was Steve Maxwell, as assistant prosecutor. After entering office in January 2003, Kline and Maxwell decided to launch what would become a very lengthy and expensive investigation into late-term abortions at Comprehensive Planned Parenthood of Kansas and Mid-Missouri (CHPP) and at WHCS, but they needed a plausible reason for doing so. Kline judged that underage sex abuse was underreported in Kansas. If in the process of looking into this, his staff discovered that abortion providers were violating a law or technicality by not reporting sexually abused girls who were getting abortions, he could build a case against the doctors.

In Kansas, the official term for this type of inquiry is an "Inquisition," and Kline's office soon developed an "Overall Plan."

One problem quickly arose. According to an internal AG memo,

"There potentially exists a legal obstacle to building a Judicial Inquisition due to the absence of a definitive complainant or allegation that a medical provider unknowingly failed to report a specific incident of sexual abuse."

In other words, no one had intentionally done anything wrong. But that, according to the attorney general, the head legal official in Kansas, was not a problem that couldn't be surmounted. The AG's office would approach the Kansas Department of Social and Rehabilitation Services (SRS) for statistics on the sexual abuse reports for girls under sixteen—but not inform SRS about what they were really after.

"If asked to explain the nature of the inquiry," the memo read, "SRS will be told that the Attorney General desires to determine if there is a serious latent sexual abuse problem in Kansas."

After speaking with SRS's Betsy Thompson, Kline's chief investigator, Tom Williams, reported back to his boss that "we have initiated step one of the overall plan."

"I advised her that I was attempting to assess the sexual abuse problem in Kansas . . ." Williams wrote to Kline in an e-mail. "I stayed away from the underlying issue we are interested in . . . I kept the conversation in very general terms . . . There was nothing said to suggest that SRS will resist providing the requested information."

Williams then gave Kline a warning: if they sought only the SRS records of girls nine through fifteen this might "alert them to the focus of the inquiry and may result in legal action to resist disclosure. I recommend that we continue as planned and ask to review all the reports."

In time, the Kansas Board of Discipline of Attorneys would file an ethics complaint against Assistant Prosecutor Steve Maxwell and Chief Deputy Attorney General Eric Rucker for their roles in Kline's Overall Plan (and then go on to file seven ethics complaints against Kline himself). The board accused Maxwell of using his personal views on abortion to mold the investigation for the AG and to deceive a judge. According to the complaint, Maxwell told Judge Richard Anderson of Shawnee County District Court that the clinics weren't reporting instances of child abuse and backed this up with child abuse statistics that he knew were "obviously flawed." Yet the Inquisition continued.

The AG sought search warrants for both clinics in order to gain access to private medical records, but all of this was taking a considerable amount of time. By August 2004, he'd developed an "Operations Plan" for executing the warrants, which sounded like the agenda of Operation Rescue. Kline's investigators were to obtain "complete identities including addresses and telephone numbers of all physicians, nurses, medical personnel and administrative employees who work at the clinics." They were to record "the license numbers and vehicle descriptions of all vehicles parked in and around the clinics."

In order to get all this data, according to Tiller's lawyers, Kline's office was to use its Operation Rescue contacts, who had been gathering such information for years. When executing these search warrants, multiple state and local agents would, in SWAT-team fashion, "assume a discreet proximity" to the clinics. All the officers would "be armed," but with their sidearms concealed. They'd execute the warrants with "handcuffs, flashlights and OC [pepper] spray immediately available upon their person."

The plan stalled out because the Kansas courts would not allow it— ruling that the state's attorney general would be overstepping his boundaries. Kline came up with another plan, going after the patient files of sixty women and girls who'd had late-term abortions at WHCS and thirty similar files at CHPP. Judge Richard Anderson issued subpoenas for the files and the AG obtained other subpoenas for Wichita's La Quinta Inn, near Tiller's clinic, where many out-of-town women stayed when they came in for evaluation at WHCS or an abortion. Operation Rescue and other anti-abortion groups did surveillance on every part of Tiller's life and business; protesters had long demonstrated at La Quinta against WHCS patients at the motel and slipped anti-abortion literature under the doors of their rooms. La Quinta was now ordered to provide Kline's investigators with all registration records for those who'd checked into the motel and received a "medical discount for lodging." With his

Inquisition under way, Kline began urging attorneys general in Texas, Indiana, Florida, and Michigan to go after abortion records in their own states. Even though Kline had gained access to these highly sensitive files, the Kansas Supreme Court had lain down very tight rules for handling the materials, to protect the women's privacy.

David Farnsworth, a retired college professor who lived in Wichita, was on a panel that made recommendations to Governor Kathleen Sebelius for new candidates to the state's Supreme Court. Seven justices sat on the court, and whenever a seat came open, the panel sent names to the governor for consideration.

"In all of the work we did screening candidates," says Farnsworth, "we never asked a single question about a lawyer or judge's position on abortion. Dr. Tiller's name never came up in any of our discussions. The reason for this was simple. Abortion was a matter of settled law in both the U.S. Supreme Court and the Kansas Supreme Court and this was just not an issue."

For Phill Kline, it was the most important issue in America, and he was about to test the Kansas High Court in ways it had never been tested before.

# XVI

As he rose in prominence in the anti-abortion movement, Kline joined forces with Bill O'Reilly and Fox News (the TV talk show host also had a national radio show). In 2005, with Kline's Inquisition under way in Kansas, O'Reilly began referring on the air to "Tiller the baby killer," a mantra that had started years before in Wichita and gradually spread across the country. O'Reilly had found another ally in Mark Gietzen, who ran the Wichita-based anti-abortion group Kansans for Life. Like Scott Roeder, who'd made it his mission to save unborn children, Gietzen had issues with rearing his own young child. In July 2003, the head of Kansans for Life was divorced from his wife, Donna, and according to Sedgwick County court documents he was alleged to "have struck or slapped the parties' minor son on or about the face causing visible injuries." Donna now asked for full custody of the nine-year-old boy, and if Gietzen showed up at her home without approval, she had to call 911 and the child would be placed under police protection. In November of that year, the couples' custody arrangement before the July incident was reinstated.

Gietzen, who'd begun feeding tips to O'Reilly's staff about Dr. Tiller, claimed to have six hundred volunteers scattered around the Midwest. As soon as he gave the word, they'd drive hundreds of miles to protest at WHCS, or look for dirt on Tiller, or try to persuade pregnant women entering the clinic not to get abortions. Between 2004 and 2009, Gietzen told *The New York Times*, his volunteers had made 395 "saves" on the sidewalks outside WHCS, which amounted to about 4 percent of those going into the clinic.

While Gietzen and Kline hooked up with Fox, O'Reilly ratcheted up his attacks on Tiller. One program began, "In the state of Kansas, there is a doctor, George Tiller, who will execute babies for five thousand dollars if the mother is depressed."

The physician had "blood on his hands."

"Tiller destroys fetuses for just about any reason . . ."

Then O'Reilly started reaching for historical comparisons: "He's guilty of Nazi stuff.

"This is the kind of stuff that happened in Mao's China, Hitler's Germany, Stalin's Soviet Union."

During a radio program in 2006, he said, "If I could get my hands on Tiller . . . Can't be vigilantes. Can't do that. It's just a figure of speech."

On television, O'Reilly and his guest hosts brought up the doctor on at least twenty-nine episodes between 2005 and 2009, again and again repeating the phrase "Tiller the Baby Killer."

As he sat in New York and broadcast a drumbeat of heated sound bites, something happened inside the walls at WHCS that revealed the actual risks, the heartbreaking realities, the medical challenges, and the human complexities surrounding abortion. Operation Rescue would seize on it as another opportunity to close the clinic.

Christin Gilbert was born in 1985 and spent most of her life in Keller, Texas. She had Down syndrome, but was active in the Special Olympics and won a gold medal in the softball throw in 2003. The following year, Christin was raped by an unknown male and became pregnant. A grand jury was convened in Tarrant County, but no one was ever charged with the crime. On January 10, 2005, Christin was twenty-eight weeks pregnant when her family, after much debate and anguish, finally decided to bring her to Wichita for a third-trimester abortion.

At the clinic, she was evaluated by Dr. Kristin Neuhaus, who gave her approval for the operation as the required second physician on the case. Dr. LeRoy Carhart, the retired Air Force surgeon who traveled to WHCS every third week to assist Dr. Tiller, would perform the abortion. As a medical student in the years before *Roe v. Wade*, Carhart had seen women whose botched abortions had led to untreatable pelvic infections, protruding intestines, perforated uteruses, and many deaths. In 1987, a nurse had asked him to spend a day at a clinic where she worked; he left the facility committed to receiving abortion training, which he did in Philadelphia. Then he returned to Omaha and eventually made abortion care a full-time practice.

Dr. Carhart began Christin's operation with the standard procedure of injecting the fetus with digoxin. He induced labor after the heart had stopped and sent the young woman back to her motel room at La Quinta Inn, also standard procedure. The following morning, she was riding to the clinic in her family's van when she expelled the dead fetus. At WHCS, doctors discovered a tear in Christin's uterus, which was sutured, and she was diagnosed with dehydration, given intravenous fluids, and driven back to the motel. That evening, she began vomiting, cramping, and passing out. After midnight, her family phoned Tiller's employee Cathy Reavis, who was on call at the motel. Reavis put Christin in a warm bath and then to bed. In the morning, she fainted and her family couldn't revive her. They rushed her to WHCS about 8:00 a.m., where her heartbeat stopped.

At 8:48, the clinic called 911 and emergency responders arrived nine minutes later. Entering WHCS, the paramedics saw Dr. Carhart lying on top of Christin, trying to force liquids from her stomach. A responder ordered Carhart to step away from the patient and the ambulance crew spent the next quarter hour trying to revive her. At 9:14, she was transported to Wesley Medical Center's Emergency Room (throughout this crisis, anti-abortion protesters were at WHCS snapping pictures of the action and of Tiller's arrival at Wesley). The ER team worked to save Christin but could not, and she died from systemic organ failure.

Neither Christin's family nor WHCS wanted to call attention to the tragedy, so it didn't immediately become public. Operation Rescue wasn't certain what had taken place after Christin had been transported to the ER, and several days after her death, Troy Newman was at Wesley looking for answers when someone in law enforcement told him that the young woman had not survived.

Anti-abortionists immediately blamed her death on WHCS and on the procedure the clinic had used to induce Christin's abortion. Within days, Newman and his Operation Rescue colleagues were at the Topeka office of Governor Kathleen Sebelius, speaking with Vicki Buening, the state's director of constituent services. After Newman had shared his views, Buening gave him the standard answer that if patients were unsatisfied with their care at WHCS, they could file a complaint with the Kansas State Board of Healing Arts (KSBHA). As those in Operation Rescue were well aware, Vicki Buening was the wife of Larry Buening, executive director of the KSBHA. Several years earlier, he'd recommended to Tiller that Kristin Neuhaus become his second consulting physician on abortions.

Operation Rescue's senior policy adviser, Cheryl Sullenger, a veteran abortion protester, was present. In 1988, she'd pled guilty to conspiring to bomb an abortion clinic in California, serving nearly two years in prison. She now pointed out to Vicki Buening that a patient could file a complaint only if she were alive.

"Certainly, that is true," Buening said.

"If they are dead," Sullenger said, "they can't file a complaint, can they?"

"I don't have an answer to that question."

On January 25, Operation Rescue issued a press release stating that Christin had died from her abortion. Sullenger filed a complaint against Tiller with the KSBHA and received a letter from Shelly Wakeman, KSBHA's disciplinary counsel, advising her that an investigation had been opened.

The people most affected by Christin's death, her grieving family, were nowhere to be found in this legal and political battle. They didn't publicly blame anyone for the loss of their daughter and sister.

When Christin died, a bill had just been introduced in the Kansas House of Representatives, HB 2503, designed to place more regulations on doctors performing abortions. It was strongly opposed by Governor Sebelius and by Tiller's political action committee, ProKanDo, which had conducted fund-raising on the governor's behalf. As Phill Kline had campaigned for the attorney general's job in 2002 as an archconservative Republican, Sebelius had won the governor's office as a liberal Democrat. From Cincinnati and raised a Roman Catholic, she was the daughter of the former Ohio governor John Gilligan and became part of the first father-daughter governor duo in U.S. history. Sebelius was strongly pro-choice, yet her office claimed that abortions had declined 8.5 percent during her tenure as governor, and the numbers backed her up. According to the Kansas Department of Health and Environment statistics, induced abortions in the state fell by 1,568, or 12.6 percent, from 2001 to 2007. Her administration attributed this to health care programs Sebelius had initiated, including "adoption incentives, extended health services for pregnant women . . . sex education and . . . a variety of support services for families." As governor, she'd vetoed anti-abortion legislation in 2003 and 2005, and would repeat this pattern in 2006 and 2008.

On February 2, 2005, Sebelius sent a letter to Larry Buening asking him to look into Christin's death. Six weeks later, Operation Rescue held a press conference at the capitol rotunda in Topeka, where a former Tiller patient spoke about her inability to bear children since having her abortion and Cheryl Sullenger talked about the demise of Christin Gilbert. On March 25, Buening sent a letter to Governor Sebelius indicating that Christin had received care that "met the standard of accepted medical practices . . ." Later that day, the Kansas Senate passed HB 2503 by a two-thirds majority, but Sebelius vetoed the measure and an attempt to override her veto failed.

Seven months passed before Christin's autopsy report was released, concluding that she'd "died as a result of complications of a therapeutic abortion." The day before Thanksgiving 2005, the KSBHA issued its final report on the case, absolving Tiller and his staff of any wrongdoing, but his opponents were hardly satisfied. They'd been studying an 1887 Kansas law that allowed citizens to impanel grand juries and issue criminal indictments. Operation Rescue and Kansans for Life launched such a petition in Wichita and Sedgwick County, calling for a grand jury to investigate Tiller's role in the death. They collected signatures—7,700 in all—and on April 19, 2006, the petitions were certified, and a month later the grand jury went to work. That July, Nola Foulston, the Sedgwick County DA, announced that the grand jury had been dismissed without issuing an indictment. It wasn't the last time she'd take action to prevent Dr. Tiller from being prosecuted.

The DA's dismissal further angered Operation Rescue. Grand jury proceedings were supposed to be secret, but Troy Newman claimed to have had an anonymous source inside this one. The jurors, according to the source, were given the runaround by KSBHA witnesses and told that what had happened at WHCS was "standard protocol."

Cheryl Sullenger claimed that the board's behavior was putting "all Kansans" at risk.

In April 2006, at the height of the conflict over Christin Gilbert's death, a protester kneeled down in the gutter running alongside Tiller's clinic and began to pray. As a WHCS nurse steered her car into the driveway, the demonstrator refused to move. She honked her horn for so long that a clinic guard intervened and told the praying man that he'd be reported to the police. The following morning, Mark Gietzen was in the same gutter when Tiller drove up in his armored SUV. In a report Gietzen filed with the authorities, he said, "Tiller floored the accelerator, and aimed his Jeep directly at us!"

Gietzen claimed that the car hit and bruised him, so he demanded a $4,000 settlement from the physician. When that failed, he asked Nola Foulston to charge the doctor with attempted murder, which also went nowhere. Gietzen kept protesting by kneeling in the gutter, and when Tiller passed by him in his car, he held up an editorial cartoon depicting Gietzen as a madman. The fringes and the mainstream had joined forces over abortion.

Phill Kline, Bill O'Reilly, Operation Rescue, and Kansans for Life had all clearly identified their target, as Scott Roeder continued to drift.

# XVII

Sitting behind bars in the late 1990s, he'd prayed over whether to pay child support to his son, Nicholas, after he was freed. While turning to God and his political cohorts for advice, Roeder sent a letter to his ex-wife in January 1998, stating that he intended to pay back child support, but didn't want this held over his head when he got out. Once again, he expressed concern about how his beliefs and actions were affecting the boy. Was Nick feeling better now that Roeder's conviction had been overturned because evidence had been illegally seized from his car? Did the youngster miss him?

If Nick still didn't want to come visit him, the inmate wrote plaintively, "I'll understand, but I hope you'll help him to see that it wasn't my fault, being sent to prison."

He all but begged Lindsey to let him know if Nick's attitude toward him had softened.

After leaving prison, Roeder went from one low-paying job to another, from one address in Topeka or suburban Kansas City to the next, and from one set of extremists—people adamantly opposed to abortion or paying taxes, or those convinced they were the descendants of the biblical Jews—to another. No longer tied down by the responsibilities of a family, he dropped into and out of whatever organization he'd latched on to at the moment. The Kansas City area had a small band of anti-abortion activists whom Roeder had become aware of. Anthony Leake had helped edit *Mix My Blood with the Blood of the Unborn*, the book Paul Hill had written in prison leading up to his 2003 execution for murdering Dr. John Britton. In 1995, Leake had been subpoenaed by a federal grand jury in Virginia investigating violence against abortion clinics and doctors.

A local activist, Regina Dinwiddie, had signed an Army of God "justifiable homicide" petition following the murders of Drs. David Gunn and John Britton. In Kansas City in 1995, a federal judge had ordered Dinwiddie to stop using a bullhorn within five hundred feet of any abortion clinic. She met Roeder the next year when they picketed together outside the Kansas City office of Planned Parenthood. Roeder had walked into that clinic and asked to see Dr. Robert Crist, and after coming back outside he hugged Dinwiddie and told her that he loved what she was doing. She was one of his heroes, like Shelley Shannon. Another Leake associate, Eugene Frye, led a victorious civil rights lawsuit against police officers trying to break up a 2001 anti-abortion demonstration in Kansas City, Missouri.

Roeder was moving further toward the edges, forging an identity in the far-right underground. In January 1999, he wrote to Lindsey that he'd been offered a job in Kansas City and was relocating there February 1. He wouldn't say where he was working or the type of employment he'd found because of his "politically incorrect views" on taxation. If the state wanted to find him and punish him for those views, he didn't want to give them any help. He'd spoken with a woman at the Johnson County Courthouse about their divorce arrangement and promised Lindsey that there "will be no interruptions of my child support payments . . . I'm looking forward to being able to visit Nicholas more often."

But neither his ex-wife nor Nick wanted to see him, so he wrote her a snappish letter, refusing to talk to her anymore and declaring that the only page he'd respond to from her was a 444-4444 emergency call. If she violated this rule, he'd hang up on her.

Then his mood changed again, this time to remorse. He wrote Lindsey and apologized for bringing a girlfriend to their home years ago and kissing the woman in front of her and his young child.

During another mood swing, he decided not to support his son financially, after all.

In July 1999, he mailed Nick a letter saying he hoped the boy wasn't angry at him for not making child support payments. Roeder wasn't doing this because he didn't love his son, he explained, but because he'd studied the issue in depth and realized he shouldn't pay anything until Lindsey agreed to take him back. He badly missed his child:

"Would you still like to visit with me? If you would, please page me at . . . I'll call you back as soon as possible."

But Nick didn't call.

By 2001, Roeder was asking for unsupervised visits with his fifteen-year-old son, but Lindsey didn't want to give him that privilege, fearful that he'd run off with Nick to another state. She needed money for a special Boy Scout camp and for dental work on the teenager, and asked her ex to help her financially with both things. When he refused, she found it profoundly ironic that his goal in life was to save the million or so unborn children aborted in America each year, but he wouldn't support the one child he'd fathered. Her sense of betrayal went deeper than dollars and cents.

Like countless other teenagers, Nick had begun experimenting with marijuana and alcohol. The first time he drank, he consumed so much that he got alcohol poisoning and passed out, and his friends had to call 911. When Lindsey tried to reach Scott during this episode, she couldn't because he was asleep; he had sleep apnea, and he slept more soundly than most people. After she learned that drinking was occurring at the home of one of Nick's young buddies, with the approval of the parents inside the house, she confronted the couple and told them exactly what she thought of their behavior. They were indifferent to anything she had to say. Maybe, she told herself, they'd listen to a man instead of a woman, a large man who could look intimidating, a man who'd been accused by the state of Kansas of being a potential bomber and domestic terrorist, even if his conviction on those charges was later overturned.

At the time, Scott was living in the Kansas City area with a friend, in what they called a "farmhouse." Chickens crowed and skittered around in the yard, the structure was heated by a wood stove, and the kitchen was filled with water jugs holding the liquid that Roeder drank because of his belief that unpurified tap water was dangerous, if not lethal. The place was filthy, with grunge and grime on every surface, and the only thing that brought Lindsey out to the farmhouse was her great concern about her son and the people he was now hanging around. Even if Roeder wouldn't support Nick financially, would he stand up for him and try to get him out of a situation that could be physically threatening? Lindsey asked her ex to go to the parents who were allowing teenagers to drink booze at their home and tell them this was placing the kids at risk.

It was a just a phase Nick was going through, Scott told her, kind of like when he'd done drugs back in Topeka as a teenager. A lot of kids went through things like that and it would pass . . . She kept pushing him to speak to the parents and he eventually did talk with one of Nick's friends about the matter, but not the man and wife, and Lindsey could never quite forgive him.

"I really, really struggled with this one," she says.


In the summer of 2001, Roeder announced that he was moving to Illinois and marrying a woman named Sue Archer. He invited Nick to accompany him to the wedding, but Lindsey wouldn't let her son go. Scott and his bride-to-be held similar religious beliefs and had talked about having a full Jewish wedding, with a rabbi, kosher food, and the couple standing under a chupah, or four-poled canopy. The groom would smash a glass with his foot, symbolizing that the marriage would last as long as the glass remained broken—forever—but some of the plans got cancelled and they were joined together instead in front of a few friends. Sue became pregnant with Scott's child, and in June 2002 she gave birth to a girl named Olivia.

"Sue called me that summer after Olivia arrived," Lindsey says, "and I was shocked to hear that Scott had had a little girl with her. Things weren't going well for them. She already had five children and lived on a farm where there were a lot of chores to do. She was just learning how much Scott liked to sleep. She began asking me how to get sole custody of Olivia and keep her away from Scott. I told her, 'Good luck with that,' but our talk was cordial. It was like we had our own little support group because another woman now felt about Scott the same way I did. I worried that if Nick had gone to their wedding ceremony in Illinois, Scott was planning on keeping him there."

After Sue asked Lindsey how to keep Roeder away from her family, Lindsey told her about his arrest for having bomb-making materials and how this had helped her win sole custody of Nick. Sue said that Scott had given one of her young sons a gun, and Lindsey suggested she call the bureau of Alcohol, Tobacco, and Firearms to report the incident. The two women communicated off and on about how to protect their children from Roeder, who wanted to see his daughter as much as his son.

In 2003, Roeder sued for visitation rights with Olivia, and in a Pennsylvania court, Archer and her new husband, Mark, argued against this. Two years later, the court ruling stated that Roeder had much earlier been diagnosed with schizophrenia "for which he takes no medication, which may pose a clear and present danger to the female minor child." The Archers mentioned Roeder's political affiliations, stating that "past conduct and association with anti-government organizations is ongoing and poses a risk to her daughter." They "feared that [Roeder] would kidnap and hide their daughter since he threatened to do so with his son." The court awarded Roeder supervised visitation rights with Olivia and he could be with her for an hour at social services, with a social worker and her mother or stepfather present, but Roeder wasn't allowed to take pictures of the girl or tell her who he was. In the next few years, he saw his daughter several times in Pennsylvania, but the legal battle between himself and the Archers was not finished.

# XVIII

With the protesters in Wichita continuing their 1,846-day vigil at Tiller's clinic, Phill Kline's Inquisition ground forward, month by month and year by year. In May 2006, Judge Richard Anderson ruled that the AG could have access to women's medical records from WHCS and Planned Parenthood of Kansas and Mid-Missouri, but absolutely no copies of these files could be made without his approval. Kline's efforts to get at these records and prosecute Tiller had generated widespread opposition, but at no place more strongly than in Governor Sebelius's office in the state capitol building. Through her vetoes, she'd kept the legislature from tightening Kansas abortion laws, but the Democratic Party needed a broader strategy if it wanted to stop the AG's assault. It needed to get rid of Phill Kline.

The governor worked in downtown Topeka on Tenth Avenue. Just to the north was the attorney general's office, and a few yards north of that was the headquarters of Kansans for Life, whose front window was filled with pictures of healthy babies and a photo exhibit of the developmental stages of a fetus. Inside the office were many more images of babies and handouts featuring articles and statistics designed to underscore the evils of abortion. In very polite tones, those who worked at KFL patiently explained to visitors why Tiller's clinic should be closed. Kline and KFL were as committed to shutting down WHCS as the governor was to keeping it open. Right across the street from the state capitol and the AG's office was the Judicial Center, home to the Kansas Supreme Court and its seven justices. Most of the major players were within a block of one another for the next round of political warfare, whose implications would reach far beyond Kansas.

Inside the national Democratic power structure, Governor Sebelius was a rising star and everything the party was looking for: an accomplished and gifted politician, fresh and strong, articulate and attractive, but not too liberal and without the baggage of a Hillary Clinton. Sebelius held office in a conservative red state, but because of her influence and many supporters Kansas was turning toward blue. She was surrounded by speculation that one day she'd be in a presidential cabinet or become the vice-presidential candidate in 2008. Grooming her successor in Topeka had become important and she needed her own overall plan. That plan involved removing Phill Kline as attorney general and replacing him with a Democrat who could become the next governor of Kansas. Sebelius had her eye on one man, and most agreed he was the right person for the job. There were just two problems.

I'd met Paul Morrison, the district attorney for Johnson County (in the Kansas City, Kansas, suburbs), while writing a book about the first known serial killer in the history of the Internet. Before his arrest in June 2000, John E. Robinson had been running financial scams and luring women to Olathe, Kansas, for several years, then murdering them. His case was high-profile and Morrison decided to prosecute it himself. In the spring of 2001, we met in his office in the Johnson County Courthouse in Olathe. Morrison was a natural-born prosecutor who was learning to become a good politician, folksy and shrewd, with a good sense of humor and a common touch in the courtroom. Bald-headed and blue-eyed, he wasn't exactly handsome but he was smart and forceful and tuned in to the local population. Addressing a jury, he didn't add a "g" to his gerunds (talkin' or thinkin'), which complemented his down-home demeanor. He came across well on television, when laying out for the people of greater Kansas City how successful his office was at rounding up the most dangerous people in the area and putting them away for good.

He'd gotten convictions against the serial killer Richard Grissom, Jr., and Dr. Debra Green, who'd burned down her mansion and killed two of her three children. He was going to convict John Robinson, and when I visited Morrison, he was riding about as high as a prosecutor can—admired by his constituents and adored by his staff. Born in Dodge City, Kansas, home of the legendary lawmen Bat Masterson and Wyatt Earp, Morrison conjured up those who'd once brought cattle rustlers and Old West killers to justice. On his desk he kept a coffee mug featuring Earp's face.

The first problem was that Morrison was not a Democrat, but a lifelong Republican. He was married with three children, and the DA made a point of telling me that he and his wife were instructors at the Good Shepherd Catholic Church in Shawnee, Kansas. He and his wife, Joyce, a tallish brunette, taught young couples about what to expect after their wedding.

"It's all about marriage," Morrison said, "and it's not really very religious. It's about living together and getting along. People who have been married a long time tell you what to expect—and you're not going to get this from your parents."

Morrison kept his religion out of his job. He was pro-choice but not, he once told me, "all that pro-choice." In his work as a big-city prosecutor, he focused on major crimes, like felony theft and murder. By 2006, he'd been running the Johnson County DA's office for nearly two decades and had never paid any legal attention to the activities at CHPP, the Planned Parenthood office of Kansas and Mid-Missouri, whose records Kline was now pursuing. In Morrison's view, the U.S. Supreme Court had long ago ruled that abortion was legal in America, so he focused on people who were breaking the law.

Could he be persuaded by Kansas Democrats to switch parties? With a little arm-twisting that was accomplished and he was groomed to run against Kline in 2006. The second problem was something Governor Sebelius and her party knew nothing about—because the surface of Morrison's life was anything but the whole truth. And that truth would eventually spill over onto Wichita and George Tiller in devastating ways. The bizarre was about to become business as usual.

# XIX

Linda Carter first surfaced in Kansas politics in 1987 as the executive director of the Chamber of Commerce in the town of Marysville and the head of the Marysville Travel and Tourism Bureau. Her husband, John Carter, was the Marysville city administrator, and the couple had three children. Within two years, Linda had resigned both positions because, according to the *Marysville Advocate*, of "controversies and criticisms." In her resignation letter, she wrote that her jobs had been "terribly incompatible" with her husband's.

"People," she added, somewhat vaguely, "expect you to be so perfect."

After a few years in McCook, Nebraska, the Carters resettled in Johnson County and John found work as city administrator of the town of Roeland Park. In 1996, Linda became a part-time secretary for the Johnson County DA, at $8.19 an hour. She had a nose for office politics and a thing for her boss, Paul Morrison, confessing to several other women in the courthouse that the DA was the sexiest man she'd ever met. By late 1997, Carter had been promoted to part-time victims' advocate in the property crime unit. Two years later, Morrison hired her full-time as a victim-witness coordinator, and they began working more closely together. She had big blond hair, a Southern drawl, large expressive eyes, and a face suggesting both determination and experience. If she'd been a few pounds overweight when entering the DA's office, she was shedding them now and wearing tighter clothes.

Halfway through 2000, the director of administration left the office and Carter wanted the empty post. She'd gotten to know her boss's wife, Joyce, and called up Mrs. Morrison, hoping she'd put in a good word for Linda with her husband. Joyce was happy to because everyone liked Carter and felt that she'd blossom in this new position. On January 21, 2001, the DA gave her the job and bumped her salary up to $49,004. Morrison had thirty-three lawyers under him and countless cases to keep track of—he needed to hand off some authority and decision-making to a trusted subordinate, and Linda was always there to handle the extra duties. Putting in long hours without complaining, she was soon running seven staff supervisors and the DA's fiscal coordinator.

With her power consolidated, Linda formed a women's group inside the office, the Rose Club, where she began expressing parts of herself hidden throughout the past half decade. She liked taking the ladies out for dinner and collecting gossip about other employees, including members of the Rose Club. Over drinks, Carter invariably turned the conversation toward sex. She was insatiable, wanting to know what the women liked and didn't like, whom they found attractive in the workplace, and if they had fantasies about that person. Most of hers centered on the DA—"the sexiest man alive." Rose Club members were disturbed by Carter's erotic chatter, but what could they do? She was their supervisor now, and challenging her could place their jobs in jeopardy. Better to order more drinks, keep laughing at her outlandish stories, throw in a few tidbits of gossip yourself, and hope for the best.

As the director of administration, Carter got as much pleasure bossing around the female employees as she did talking with them about sex. When reports of her heavy-handed behavior filtered back to Morrison, he dismissed them. Linda was an excellent worker who got things done, both for the office and the DA himself. It was important to keep her happy so the system would continue running smoothly, yet Carter was becoming increasingly prickly. When she suspected one member of the Rose Club was having an affair with a lawyer in the office, she confronted the woman, who quit and wrote a sharp critique of her supervisor. Carter disbanded the group and cultivated a new set of female workers, the Doll Club. The name came from a local theater production of *Valley of the Dolls*, based on the racy 1960s Jacqueline Susann novel.

Instead of business outfits, Carter began coming to the DA's office dressed in leopard-print miniskirts and matching shoes. She once commanded the Doll Club to gather in her fifth-floor office, where she locked the door, dropped her skirt, and showed off a new pink thong. She liked to think of herself as the real "Wonder Woman," as opposed to the fictional Wonder Woman made famous on television by that other Lynda Carter. Linda showed up at the DA's office one day wearing a shiny blue dress, a red neck-scarf, knee-length golden boots, a golden bustier, and a red cape—Wonder Woman in the flesh.

For years, she and Morrison had been trading glances and smiles in the office and courthouse hallways. Finally, in June 2005, they traveled together to New York City for an event at the Vera Institute of Justice, a think tank conducting a study of racial profiling. In their hotel lobby, Morrison approached her and confessed that he wanted a romantic relationship. She didn't discourage him. By September, they were sneaking into an empty space at the courthouse and having oral sex. They made love in the same office where a few years earlier Morrison had told me that he and his wife Joyce offered counseling to young church couples about the challenges of a long marriage.

In October 2005, Morrison announced he was leaving the Republican Party to run for Kansas attorney general against Phill Kline. Nowhere was the news more welcome than in Wichita. Back in 2002, when Kline had first sought the AG's office, Dr. Tiller decided that he needed his own political action committee. He contacted Julie Burkhart, a local pro-choice activist during the Summer of Mercy, now working as an administrator and counselor at a nearby abortion clinic.

"With Kline running for office," Tiller told Burkhart, when offering her the job of overseeing his PAC, "there's a lot to lose."

She took the position, and Tiller spent $153,000 to help defeat Kline, sponsoring a last-minute radio ad blitz questioning the candidate's qualifications and potential violations of his law license. The effort failed.

"Dr. Tiller didn't realize soon enough," says Burkhart, "that if Kline was elected, he'd be nothing but a pain in the neck. When we finally got involved in the race, it was too little, too late. It was a wake-up call for Kansas Democrats who thought they could run and easily win against real right wingers."

In November 2002, Kline had defeated a relatively weak candidate, Chris Biggs, and then launched his Inquisition. Governor Sebelius had watched with dismay as the AG had gone after women's private medical records in order to shut down WHCS. Four years later, Sebelius put her hopes behind Morrison, and Tiller donated more money to the cause. Abortion would be the key issue in a nasty race, with Morrison's team referring to Inquisitor Kline as "Snoop Dog."

After joining the Democratic Party, Morrison began talking up Linda Carter at the governor's mansion. In July 2006, Sebelius selected Carter to be on the state's new Interagency Council on Abuse, Neglect and Exploitation. After she attended council meetings in Topeka, Morrison drove over from Olathe and the couple rendezvoused at a local hotel. During one tryst in the DA's office in the middle of the campaign, Morrison gazed out the courthouse window and wondered aloud if Kline had a spy watching them through a telescope.

They met in other hotels in Wichita, Overland Park, and Salina, Kansas, and in cities in at least three other states. Carter handled the details, making the reservations and paying cash for the rooms. The more they saw each other, the more heatedly they discussed their options. Should they leave their spouses and file for divorce? Who should go first? Shouldn't they wait till the campaign was over? The pair had fallen into a volatile dance. When Morrison was at his most fervent, Carter had a tendency to cool off, which only made him more fervent—a tough spot for a man accustomed to commanding all the lawyers in his office and representing law and order to the outside world. And at work, Carter flirted with other men, blowing kisses at attorneys who walked into the DA's office and talking with the Doll Club about bedding them. It was difficult enough to manage hundreds of criminal cases when things were going smoothly, but now the office was filled with anxiety and tension. The Morrison-Carter relationship was anything but stable when he decided to take it to the next level.

He bought her an engagement ring, appraised at more than $16,000, and gave it to her during a visit to the Carter family home in Western Grove, Arkansas. But he didn't propose, because the timing wasn't right. How would it look to conservative Kansas voters, not to mention Morrison's avowed enemies in the Kline camp, if he bolted from his wife and children on the eve of the biggest election of his career? They needed to be patient a while longer, and to keep their secrets intact.

"When Paul was running for attorney general," says one of his top campaign aides, "I was around him every day for days on end. We traveled together all over the state. I had no clue what was going on."

# XX

With only weeks left before the 2006 mid-term elections, Kline and many other GOP candidates around the country were lagging in the polls (Democrats were about to win a majority of seats in Congress). The war in Iraq that President George W. Bush had started in March 2003 with the claim that Saddam Hussein had weapons of mass destruction was increasingly unpopular—especially after no such weapons were found. Just as disturbingly, reports had leaked out about the U.S. Army's abuse of prisoners of war in Iraq, Afghanistan, and Guantánamo Bay, Cuba. Lawrence Wilkerson, the former chief of staff to Secretary of State Colin Powell, would tell Congress that more than a hundred detainees had died in U.S. custody in Iraq and Afghanistan, at least twenty-seven of those deaths declared homicides by the military. The victims had allegedly been drowned, suffocated, shot, or kicked to death. The graphic photos coming out of the Abu Ghraib prison west of Baghdad—images of American soldiers humiliating and torturing Iraqi prisoners—made the reports unnervingly real. U.S. military personnel appeared to be in violation of international law.

My father, and many like him, had never voted for a Democrat in his life, but by mid-2006, approaching eighty-three, he was changing his mind. It pained him greatly that as he'd become an old man and my son was nearing an age when he could be called into military service,

American soldiers were engaging in torture in so-called "black sites" around the world. They'd disregarded the very rules concerning POWs that had protected him from the Nazis, and kept him alive. He was an unstoppable letter writer and began composing heartfelt messages to politicians, both locally and nationally, including President Bush. He urged Bush to go visit VA hospitals across America, and to talk with the men who'd been wounded in combat and find out how long their injuries and trauma lasted, once wars were declared over. He never heard back from anyone in Washington, and died two months before the 2006 election that provided a mandate against the Republican Party he'd supported so unwaveringly all his life.

While Republicans struggled nationally, Kansans watched the growing combativeness of the attorney general's race, with abortion as the main issue. On February 3, 2006, the state Supreme Court had finally ruled on Kline's request to gain access to the WHCS and CHPP records. The AG would be allowed to see these medical files, but they'd be heavily redacted, with the patient names removed. Kline and his subordinates were ordered not to release these materials to anyone. The files "could hardly be more sensitive," the court said, so everyone must "resist the impulse" to make them public.

Kline didn't resist. He took recommendations on finding medical experts sympathetic to his cause from anti-abortion groups such as Kansans for Life and Women Inflaming the Nation. Then he went out and tried to hire these experts to view the records. At first, he brought in the Kansas doctor Ronald Erken, who informed members of Kline's staff that they had no case against Tiller. Then he went after Paul McHugh of Johns Hopkins University in Baltimore, a professor of psychiatry. Dr. McHugh looked at twenty-eight medical files and discussed them in a forty-four-minute videotaped interview put together by anti-abortion activists. The tape found its way to Fox News, Bill O'Reilly, and onto the Internet. Dr. McHugh contended that the medical reports held diagnoses such as anxiety, depression, and adjustment disorder—conditions that were not "substantial and irreversible," and therefore did not warrant abortion to protect the health of the mother.

"I can only tell you," he stated in the interview, "that from these records, anybody could have gotten an abortion if they wanted one."

The interview failed to mention the facts in many case files, including one that evoked the late Christin Gilbert. This patient was a ten-year-old girl, twenty-eight weeks pregnant, but unlike Christin, she'd been raped by an adult relative.

By late October 2006, Kline was trailing Morrison in the polls and desperate to catch up. On the evening of November 3, four days before the election, Fox featured an "exclusive segment" on *The O'Reilly Factor*. Kline appeared on the show and O'Reilly created the clear impression that he'd had access to the redacted medical records. To an audience of millions, he declared that he had an "inside source" with documentation indicating that Dr. Tiller had performed late-term abortions to alleviate "temporary depression" in pregnant women.

Jared Maag was the deputy solicitor general for the Kansas attorney general's office. Under oath, he later said, "The words that he [O'Reilly] was using suggested that he had a record in front of him because of the statements that Dr. Tiller would perform an abortion because of depression . . . When you listen to his statement in full, the assumption that I came to was that it came from the office of the attorney general."

O'Reilly's performance outraged Morrison, his supporters, and Dr. Tiller. The latter demanded that Kline be held in contempt for sharing the files with outsiders, while his lawyers asked the court to deposit "the records with a special prosecutor or master appointed to investigate any leak of information from, or the mishandling of, the records."

Morrison blasted Kline's Inquisition and said that his opponent, if reelected, would go after other people's confidential medical records. Kline reminded voters that in 1990 Morrison had faced allegations of drunkenly propositioning a DA employee in a bar. The woman, Kelly Summerlin, was a victim-witness coordinator, the same job later held by Linda Carter. Two federal lawsuits based on Summerlin's claims against the DA were dismissed in the early nineties, but in the campaign's final weeks, Kline trotted out the old charges, jolting Morrison's wife into action. In a TV interview, Joyce said that Kline had "lost his moral compass" by delivering this "malicious attack on the integrity of our marriage."

Morrison had more pressing concerns. During a stump speech in Wichita, he'd been rushed by an anti-abortion protester who'd taken a swing at him, before security jumped in and separated the men. The near injury shook the DA and his campaign staff, who now had a first-hand taste of what Tiller and his employees had endured throughout the past three decades.

On election night, November 7, Kline traveled to Wichita to conduct his final press conference in front of WHCS—Tiller and abortion were the centerpiece of his campaign to the very end. Morrison and his team were far away in the northeast corner of the state, huddling together in a Lawrence restaurant, the Free State Brewery, and waiting for the votes to be counted. The toasts were about to begin, as Kansans had had enough of Phill Kline.

Morrison won an easy victory, by 17 percentage points, to the great relief of many. After four years of an Inquisition costing uncalculated amounts of time, energy, and money to all sides, WHCS and CHPP had not been found to be in violation of any laws. At the Democrats' victory party that night in Lawrence, the winners could only hope that the election signaled the start of a new political environment in Kansas and especially in Wichita. Their opponents, of course, felt otherwise.

"Right after Paul won," says one of his staffers, "the anti-abortion groups put up awful things on their blogs. Like, 'Morrison slithers into office on the backs of dead babies.' It was truly disgusting."

Despite the blogs, there was much cause for optimism. Morrison's supporters were certain that he'd drop the Inquisition and Tiller's legal battles might at last be behind him. The grand strategy to get rid of Kline and take the attorney general's office and Kansas in a new direction had worked.

Or had it?

Kline didn't have to vacate the AG's office until noon on January

8, 2007, and he intended to use every remaining minute to accomplish his unfulfilled goals. On December 20, he charged Tiller with thirty misdemeanors, many involving abortions the physician had allegedly performed on minors. Within hours of the unsealing of these charges in Wichita, a Sedgwick County judge tossed them out—after DA Nola Foulston had made this request and said that her office hadn't been properly consulted by Kline about the matter. On December 28, Kline appointed a special prosecutor, the Wichita lawyer Don McKinney, to continue investigating Tiller. It was the most defiant and inflammatory (some said outrageous) thing Kline had done since taking office four years earlier, as McKinney made Kline look like a moderate.

During the Summer of Mercy, Don "the Dingo" McKinney had demonstrated with Operation Rescue at Tiller's clinic and was an associate and admirer of the late Paul "the Jackal" deParrie. The Jackal had been McKinney's Wichita house guest in 2001, at the ten-year anniversary of the massive abortion protests. He was an Army of God supporter who'd publicly endorsed the killing of abortion providers in general and of Shelley Shannon's 1993 attempted murder of Tiller. Papers filed with the Court of Appeals in Oregon in August 1997 read:

"Respondent [deParrie] is a leader of Advocates for Life Ministries, a group that opposes abortion, and is also the editor of Life Advocate magazine. At various times, Life Advocate magazine has editorialized that the use of 'godly force' is 'morally justified' in defense of 'innocent life.' In addition, on two occasions, respondent signed declarations or manifestos of support for anti-abortionist activists who killed abortion providers. In 1993, respondent and 28 other activists signed the following statement concerning Michael Griffin, who shot and killed Dr. David Gunn in Pensacola, Florida: 'We, the undersigned, declare the justice of taking all godly action necessary to defend innocent human life including the use of force. We proclaim that whatever force is legitimate to defend the life of a born child is legitimate to defend the life of an unborn child. We assert that if Michael Griffin did in fact kill David Gunn, his use of lethal force was justifiable provided it was carried out for the purpose of defending the lives of unborn children. Therefore, he ought to be acquitted of the charges against him.'

"The primary sponsor of that declaration was a group called 'Defensive Action,' whose director, Paul Hill, also signed the statement. In July 1994, Hill shot and killed Dr. John Britton and James Barrett, Britton's escort, and wounded Barrett's wife at another clinic in Pensacola. Respondent and 30 others subsequently signed a declaration that reiterated the earlier declaration and stated that Hill's 'actions are morally justified if they were necessary for the purpose of defending innocent human life.'

"In 1994, respondent described Shelley Shannon, who had attempted to kill Dr. George Tiller, a Kansas abortion provider, as 'a hero.' In January 1995, respondent publicly stated that John Salvi was 'morally justified' in killing two receptionists at a Boston abortion clinic."

Following deParrie's death in 2006, McKinney praised the man online, calling him a true Christian warrior. Like Christ himself, deParrie was a genuine leader who went first into battle and inspired everyone by his example—the very best that pro-life has to offer.

"We are each," he wrote, "going to have to step up our own efforts to fill the gap in the wall left by Paul's passing."

Signed, "Donald 'The Dingo' McKinney."

On December 29, 2006, the day after Kline appointed McKinney as Tiller's special prosecutor, talk2.action.org, a Web site that monitored anti-abortion activists, posted the following message:

"Frame it as he will, the Attorney General of Kansas has vested an overt associate of Operation Rescue, and of at least one member of the Army of God, with the full law enforcement power of the state."

As Kline planned further actions before leaving office, Troy Newman of Operation Rescue was considering another citizens' petition drive against Tiller. If he could gather seven thousand more Kansas signatures, he could get a new grand jury to investigate WHCS and possibly subpoena two thousand of its medical records. He wanted the files of every woman who'd gone to the clinic, when at least twenty-two weeks pregnant, throughout the past five years.

While Morrison prepared to depart the DA's office in Olathe and start his new job sixty miles away in Topeka, he was about to be blindsided. And not for the last time.

# XXI

On December 11, five weeks after Kline lost the election, Johnson County officials come together to select a DA to replace Morrison. Because Morrison had been voted into this position as a Republican, the GOP got to choose his successor and they picked Kline, sending waves of disbelief and indignation across Kansas, while shocking Morrison and Linda Carter. There was nothing Morrison could do to stop this, but he demanded that because Kline had never worked as a DA, he should get paid less than his predecessor. With Kline and Morrison flip-flopping jobs, Carter would now go to work for her lover's archrival. Down in Wichita, Tiller immediately suspected the worst.

Five days before Morrison would become the new Kansas AG and Kline become Johnson County DA, Tiller and his lawyers asked Judge Richard Anderson to make certain that the redacted medical files were kept in a secure location during the transition. Kline would be taking over an office 177 miles from Wichita, in suburban Kansas City, where he had no jurisdiction over Sedgwick County or WHCS medical files, but Tiller was still nervous, and with good reason. Despite the urgency of the situation, Judge Anderson did not rule on the matter immediately, giving Kline all the leeway he needed, as a court-ordered investigation later revealed.

On Friday, January 5, his last full workday as AG, boxes of medical records were moved from his Topeka office and transferred into the car of Steve Maxwell, the assistant prosecutor who worked under Kline. They were driven to Maxwell's residence, where he and Kline's chief investigator, Tom Williams, sorted through the boxes. According to the investigation report, some records were then transferred again, into the trunk of Williams's state-owned vehicle, but the critical WHCS and CHPP files stayed with Maxwell over the weekend.

At eight o'clock on Monday morning, January 8, four hours before the job switch, Williams and another investigator, Jared Reed, left five boxes of medical records at Judge Anderson's chambers in the Shawnee County Courthouse, including the WHCS and CHPP files. That morning Kline had told Eric Rucker, chief deputy attorney general for Kansas, to make certain that these records would be available to him as the Johnson County DA. Rucker then told Williams to get them back from Shawnee County. The order surprised Williams, who didn't understand why the files should be taken into Johnson County's jurisdiction, so he asked for a written confirmation of Kline's request. At 3:43 p.m., nearly four hours *after* Morrison had been sworn in as the new attorney general, Rucker e-mailed Williams. He said to "copy all medical files" and that Kline had directed them to be "delivered to the District Attorney for the 10th Judicial District," in Johnson County. Williams and Reed copied the records at a Kinko's and put them in Reed's car. Reed took them to his apartment and stored the women's private medical files in a Rubbermaid container, where they sat for more than a month.

Before leaving the AG's office on January 8, Kline had left three boxes of Inquisition materials for Morrison, but they held no copies of the WHCS and CHPP records.

"When we moved into the office that first day," says a Morrison staffer, "we looked around and couldn't find any of these files. We were absolutely stunned and couldn't believe that Kline had actually taken all the records from Tiller's clinic and Planned Parenthood."

Morrison's staff wasn't the only ones who were stunned. Over in Olathe, the new attorney general was present during the transition at the DA's office, where he learned that the medical files hadn't been left behind in Topeka. He got into a verbal scuffle with Maxwell, whom Kline had just hired to work for him as an assistant prosecutor.

The following day, Judge Anderson sent Morrison a letter asking if Kline's just-named special prosecutor for Dr. Tiller, Don McKinney, had any of these files in his possession. It was a moot point; one of Morrison's first acts as AG was to fire "The Dingo." He also ended Kline's Inquisition, and a new era seemed to be coming to the Kansas attorney general's office and its relationship with George Tiller.

Three months passed before the matter of the copied medical files made its way through the court system and came before Judge Anderson. Not until April 9 did he learn that Kline had taken the WHCS and CHPP records with him to Johnson County. Judge Anderson was mightily disturbed and would eventually testify about the records, Fox News, and Kline's appearance on the November 3, 2006, *O'Reilly Factor*.

The talk show host, Judge Anderson said, had asked Kline "softball questions," while O'Reilly himself was "claiming that he had inside information about this or that . . . I viewed Bill O'Reilly as, frankly, quite a windbag . . . I was very upset with Kline, because he had put himself in a position where O'Reilly could claim he had stuff. And whether it was driven purely by the pressure of that political campaign or not . . . I didn't think he should have put himself in that position as the attorney general because it looked bad."

Judge Anderson ordered Kline to return all the records to the AG's office or face contempt charges. Kline turned the files over to the judge, telling him that no copies of the materials were left in his possession. Only later did he admit that his staff had "created summaries of at least three WHCS patient records" and would use the summaries in their work in Johnson County.

According to Kline's own criminal investigator, Jared Reed, both Kline and Chief Deputy Attorney General Rucker were "willing do to whatever is necessary to get charges filed or to get abortion stopped. Whatever is necessary up to and including going above the law."

As this played out in the Kansas court system, O'Reilly continued to hound Tiller on the air. In one video clip, Fox's Jesse Waters followed around Governor Kathleen Sebelius and unsuccessfully tried to ask her about Tiller. In another clip, Fox's Porter Barry confronted the physician himself on the streets of Wichita.

"They call you 'Tiller the baby killer,' " Porter said. "Is that appropriate?"

Tiller took out a phone and dialed 911, telling a police dispatcher that he was being accosted by a TV producer.

"No matter what you think about the abortion issue," O'Reilly said on his program in the spring of 2007, "you should be very disturbed by what continues to happen in Kansas. This man, Dr. George Tiller, known as 'Tiller the Baby Killer,' is performing late-term abortions without defining the specific medical reasons why. Let's be more blunt: Tiller is executing fetuses in his Wichita clinic for five thousand dollars. And records show he'll do it for vague medical reasons. That is, he'll kill the fetus, viable outside the womb, if the mother wants it dead. No danger to the mother's life, no catastrophic damage if the woman delivers.

"Now, some Kansas politicians want to stop the madness. But incredibly, Governor Kathleen Sebelius is protecting Tiller, citing privacy. The governor vetoed a bill a few weeks ago that would have forced Tiller to provide a specific medical reason for destroying a viable fetus. Now, America is a great country, but this kind of barbaric display in Kansas diminishes our entire nation.

"Tiller has killed thousands, thousands of late-term fetuses without explanation. And Governor Sebelius is allowing him to continue the slaughter. How the governor sleeps at night is beyond me."

On May 14, 2007, CHPP filed a motion asking Judge Anderson to hold Kline in contempt and for him "to surrender all copies of all patient records he had obtained through the Inquisition." The judge denied the motion. On June 6, CHPP filed a "writ of mandamus" seeking for the court to compel Kline to return the medical records to the AG's office. The legal wrangling over the women's records would generate nearly 2,600 pages of testimony and other documentation, which in time would make their way to the Kansas Supreme Court.

While the case against Kline edged forward, Morrison ran the AG's office, parking his car each morning near the back door of the Kansans for Life headquarters. Those associated with the anti-abortion group constantly put up signs near his vehicle saying "Charge Tiller" or other messages that chided Morrison for being both Catholic *and* pro-choice, in their minds an irreconcilable position. Morrison ignored the taunts because he had so many other things to think about, starting with Linda Carter, who now worked for Phill Kline.

# XXII

The last time the couple had had sex in the Johnson County Court-house, according to a sworn statement from Carter, was on Sunday, January 7, 2007, the day before Morrison became AG. With the campaign behind them and Morrison settling into his new job, Carter announced that she was ready to divorce her husband and backed this up by driving down to Western Grove, Arkansas, and bringing back some furniture. She put it in an apartment she'd just rented in Lawrence, about halfway between Kansas City and Topeka, where the lovers could meet in secret. During one stretch that winter, they spent four nights in a row at their new home. They'd begun discussing a tentative wedding date of April 5, though the attorney general hadn't even left his wife.

On Valentine's Day, Morrison told Carter that he'd changed his mind and decided to stay with Joyce. That set off an eruption, until he changed his mind again. In March, he moved some personal items into the Lawrence apartment and began going there more often. Things were smooth for a while, but then the two began arguing about a highly divisive subject they just couldn't agree on: Dr. George Tiller. Morrison had never prosecuted an abortion doctor or shown any intention of doing so. Right after becoming AG, he'd dismissed the thirty last-minute charges Kline had filed against Tiller in late December 2006.

"It was clear, after looking at the case," Morrison said when announcing this decision, "Kline's investigation of Dr. Tiller was not about enforcing the law. It was about pushing a political agenda."

When visiting Carter's Lawrence apartment, Morrison was intensely interested in finding out from Linda if Kline was investigating the Planned Parenthood clinic in Kansas City and, if so, what tactics he was using. As the director of administration for the Johnson County DA, Carter had inside information about the Olathe office, but she wasn't very forthcoming with her lover. Abortion was a serious point of contention between them. Morrison had made clear to her that he thought Kline's Inquisition had been unethical, if not illegal, and that he'd manufactured evidence against Tiller. Carter was strongly opposed to late-term abortion, especially after Kline had taken her into his confidence and shown her some of the WHCS medical files. She felt that Morrison, with his statewide powers of prosecution as AG, should take action against the Wichita physician.

"Are you going to do the right thing and charge Tiller?" she demanded of Morrison during one of their fights in her apartment.

With two decades of great success as a high-profile prosecutor, he bristled at anyone telling him how to do his job, and he tried to deflect the question by encouraging Carter to look for work in another field and get away from Kline. She wasn't easily put off. The conflict over abortion, which had affected many American families during the past several decades, had angrily come to life between the lovers.

Had Morrison, she pressed, taken campaign contributions from Tiller when he was running for AG?

He lied and said no.

When she continued interrogating him, he erupted and stomped out of her apartment.

She dumped all of his possessions into a pile by the door so he could pick them up when he came back and get out of her life for good. She also decided to sell her engagement ring, but first hid it in her apartment. When her husband, John, stumbled onto the ring and an appraisal document holding Morrison's name, he sold the $16,000 piece of jewelry for $4,750, depositing the money in a joint account with his wife.

Ten days after Morrison stormed out, he called Carter and said that he'd left his wife and taken an apartment in Topeka, where they could now be together. And he was ready to go to St. Louis and have his vasectomy reversed, so he and Linda could have children. He gave her the key to his new apartment and she saw him there in April and May. By now, Joyce Morrison had learned of the affair and she called Carter, demanding that Linda stop seeing her husband.

What neither Carter nor Morrison knew was that Kline had also been tipped off. In March 2007, two months after he became Johnson County DA, a staff supervisor wrote Kline detailing Carter's inappropriate behavior at work. It mentioned her "flirtatious manner with defense attorneys, law enforcement officers and other individuals." One man she'd flirted with was Tom Williams, the former chief AG investigator who now had a similar job in the DA's office. The supervisor's allegations were passed along to the Johnson County Board of Commissioners and to the DA's new chief deputy, Eric Rucker, who'd also worked for Kline back in Topeka.

On March 19, Kline received another letter, this one anonymous, outlining Morrison's affair with Carter. On two occasions, it stated, employees had heard Morrison and Carter having sex in the DA's office. Kline gave the letter to Steve Maxwell, who'd tangled with Morrison on the day Kline had moved into his new job. The DA, who was still involved in his own legal battles at the Kansas Supreme Court, decided to sit on the explosive information. Several months went by as his contempt case moved forward and he pushed on with his plans as DA, doing what Morrison had never done in nineteen years of running the Johnson County office. Using the women's medical records he'd gathered as attorney general, Kline filed 107 criminal charges against Planned Parenthood of Kansas and Mid-Missouri (CHPP) for its abortion practices. For all practical purposes, the Inquisition was back on.

As Kline went after CHPP, the attorney general made a move that baffled and angered his supporters. It may have been because he was under the influence of his lover. Whatever the reason, he asked a lawyer in his employ, Veronica Dersch, to look at the WHCS files Kline

had earlier gotten his hands on. Did they, he charged Dersch with finding out, show that Dr. Tiller had had a financial relationship with Dr.
Kristin Neuhaus, who'd given him so many of the second medical opinions needed to perform late-term abortions? Had Tiller violated the
legal statute that read, "*No person shall perform or induce an abortion when
the fetus is viable unless such person is a physician and has a documented referral
from another physician* not legally or financially affiliated *with the physician
performing or inducing the abortion* . . ."?

Both CHPP and WHCS were again under investigation.

On June 22, 2007, the Kansas Supreme Court ordered Kline to explain to its seven justices why he shouldn't be held in contempt for violating a judge's orders and distributing the medical records to outsiders,
including perhaps Fox News. Five days *after* the court issued this directive, Kline had a subordinate make a copy of CHPP patient records and
give them to yet a fourth medical expert. Then Morrison jumped into
the case, writing a legal memorandum stating that "CHPP patient records and other materials had been taken without authorization from
the Attorney General's office when Kline's term was over; that patient
records had been mishandled; and that copies of the records had been
disseminated improperly."

On June 28, with his relationship with Carter as volatile as ever,
Morrison filed nineteen misdemeanor charges against Tiller. By late July,
he and Carter were again discussing their marital options and Morrison kept pushing her to reveal the activities taking place inside the
DA's office. What was Kline doing with the medical files still in his
possession? How much money had the DA's staff spent hiring expert
witnesses to prosecute CHPP? When Kline became DA, he'd fired
seven lawyers and an investigator who'd worked for Morrison. The
"Olathe Eight" had then banded together and sued the new district attorney in a wrongful-termination lawsuit. Morrison insisted that
Carter keep him informed about the suit and wanted her to write letters of support to staff members who'd joined the case against Kline.

Carter balked, feeling divided between her loyalties to her old boss and her new one, who was paying her $90,001 a year. When she refused to write the letters, her relationship with Morrison again went to the brink.

On September 18, he called her and said the moment had arrived to prove his love for her once and for all. He drove the couple to a Kansas City parlor, where a tattoo artist inked a heart into his pelvis, and inside the heart were two initials: "L.C." She was supposed to get a similar tattoo with "P.M." engraved in her flesh, but backed out and ten days later told him she wanted Morrison out of her life forever. The quarrel escalated, over the tattoo but also why she wasn't keeping him informed about Kline's investigation into Planned Parenthood.

She feared that if she left the DA's office to hunt for a new job in Arkansas, Morrison would sabotage her efforts. In late October, he tried to reconcile with her by saying that if she'd have him as a husband, he'd make peace with Kline and get an emergency divorce from his wife.

She told him never to call back.

# XXIII

The Kansas Judicial Center on Tenth Avenue in Topeka, right across from the state capitol and attorney general's office, was as quiet and sober as the affair between Carter and Morrison was heated and tempestuous. Its exterior was made of cottonwood limestone and its lobby was cavernous—sixty feet high and featuring Vermont marble and South Dakota granite, with the minerals symbolizing the permanence of the law in the face of constant cultural, social, and political change. In the middle of this large open space rose an off-white, graceful-looking sculpture of a half-kneeling woman holding aloft a prairie falcon. The bird was native to Kansas and the sculptor, Bernard Frazier, intended it to represent swift and dynamic justice. While politicians came and went and justice was rarely swift or dynamic, the seven Supreme Court justices working inside the Judicial Center were the last bulwark against chaos and lawlessness, even when it involved the state's highest legal officials.

In the fall of 2007, District Judge David King conducted a fact-finding mission into Kline's behavior with the medical files and turned his findings over to the justices, letting the court decide whether or not to find the former AG in contempt. In his sworn testimony, Kline told Judge King that he had "no knowledge of any 'inquisition' records and/or documents transferred by me in my position as Attorney General to myself in my position as District Attorney." In his opinion, he was *both* the AG of Kansas and the DA of Johnson County for one hour on January 8, 2007, but "performed no acts in that capacity." Judge King told the Supreme Court that Kline had not handled patient records in a manner that "stood up to the highest scrutiny. Such scrutiny surely should have been expected." The High Court didn't hold Kline in contempt, but showed far less restraint toward him than Judge King had.

"The record before us," they wrote in their final report, "discloses numerous instances in which Kline and/or his subordinates seriously interfered with the performance of his successors as Attorney General and seriously interfered with this court's effort to determine the facts underlying this action and the legal merits of the parties' positions. Kline was demonstrably ignorant, evasive and incomplete in his sworn written responses to Judge King . . . Kline's responses . . . showed consistent disregard for Kline's role as a leader in state law enforcement; and they delayed and disrupted this court's inquiry . . . He was thorough only when digressing from the point."

The justices chastened Kline for violating women's "constitutional privacy rights" and said that he'd "hustled to deflect responsibility and any attendant blame. We are deeply disappointed by Kline's casual treatment of the WHCS patient records . . . Kline exhibits little, if any respect, for the authority of this court and for his responsibility to it and to the rule of law it husbands. His attitude and behavior are inexcusable, particularly for someone who purports to be a professional prosecutor . . . He is interested in the pursuit of justice only as he chooses to define it."

On October 23, 2007, Linda Carter, exasperated with Morrison and convinced their relationship was finished, went to Kline and Steve Maxwell and told them about her affair with the AG (she didn't know that they already knew about it). Within days, Morrison learned about this and began calling her frantically. On October 31, he phoned her twenty-two times between 11:58 a.m. and 12:47 p.m. According to Carter, he threatened to tell her prospective employer in Arkansas that Linda was "a monster, fucking sociopath, liar, bitch, and a bad manager." Maxwell and a DA employee, Shawna Chambless, a former Rose Club member, listened in on four of these calls. They reported back to Kline, who now launched a sexual-harassment investigation into Morrison. The first step was Tom Williams sitting down with Carter and taking her sworn statement.

"On November 1, 2007," Williams's record of the interview began, "Linda Carter was contacted at a discreet location [Shawna Chambless's apartment] in Johnson County, Kansas, for the purpose of providing an interview concerning a federal Equal Employment Opportunity Commission Complaint that Carter had filed against the Johnson County District Attorney's office and former Johnson County District Attorney Paul Morrison."

For her revelations, Carter would be given full immunity from any prosecution. On November 2, her complaint was faxed to the EEOC, and her interview with Williams made its way to *The Topeka Capital-Journal* newspaper. On November 14, Carter delivered an affidavit supporting Kline's sexual-harassment case and in it she said that Morrison had made "derogatory references" to the new DA. When referring to Kline's incoming staff in Olathe in early 2007, Morrison had told her to "give the fuckers what they want."

Morrison, Carter concluded, "led me to believe that whether I agreed with his position on the investigation and prosecution of the Tiller clinic would affect the status of our personal relationship."

On November 21, Kline e-mailed his staff a message entitled, "Wishing Linda Carter success in her future endeavors."

"I am sorry to announce," he wrote, "that Linda Carter has submitted her resignation as Director of Administration effective November 30. Linda is pursuing other opportunities and we wish every success . . ."

Carter took off for her family home in Western Grove, Arkansas, anxious to get out of Kansas before the fallout started. On December 8, the *Capital-Journal* broke the story, which was widely read across the state, including by the shell-shocked staff in Morrison's Topeka office.

"We had absolutely no idea this was coming," an aide to the attorney general later said. "Everybody who worked for Paul loved him and thought he had a great future as a prosecutor and a public servant. So much for him becoming the governor of Kansas."

On December 14, Morrison held a press conference by himself. Neither his wife nor other family members were present as he resigned and was replaced by the new attorney general, Steve Six.

"I've made mistakes in my personal life," Morrison said to the media, "but I've always obeyed our laws and done the right things as a professional. My actions caused pain and sadness to many people I love. I have been working for some time to get right with God, get right with my family, and get right with friends and address my personal problems—and I will continue to do so."

He went back home to Olathe to look for a job, where more fallout awaited him.

Kline disagreed that the ex-DA and ex–attorney general had "always obeyed our laws" and opened a criminal probe into Morrison for telephone harassment for his twenty-two late October calls to Carter—and for possible blackmail. Morrison dropped his contrite tone and called the investigation the "politics of sewage." Kline chose two people outside the DA's office to handle the matter, in an effort to demonstrate that he had no bias toward Morrison. Yet one man, Tom Keck, had been an assistant DA under Kline until recently and the other, Robert Arnold, had contributed money to his last political campaign. Nine months later, on December 17, 2008, the pair cleared Morrison of any criminal wrongdoing. While trying to repair his broken marriage and salvage his career, he went into private practice as a defense attorney, his office just across the street from the Johnson County Courthouse, where he'd once ruled over the entire scene.

In November 2008, Kline was defeated in the election for Johnson County DA and the Kansas Supreme Court admonished him, once again, to give up *all* copies of the WHCS and CHPP medical records before leaving office. Clearly no longer trusting him, the court gave Kline a hard deadline for completing this task: December 12, 2008, at exactly 5:00 p.m. The court thought about ordering him to reimburse the thousands of dollars in "personnel expenses" his behavior had cost the legal system, but chose not to. Johnson County taxpayers would have had to pay some of these expenses and "they didn't elect him in the first place and have now shown him the door," said the court. During the Inquisition, Kline had racked up around $200,000 in other legal fees, now personal debt. He needed a job and soon found one as a visiting professor of law at Liberty University, the fundamentalist Baptist college Reverend Jerry Falwell had started in 1971 in Lynchburg, Virginia.

Early in 2009, *The Wichita Eagle* reported that when departing the DA's office in Olathe for the last time and leaving Kansas behind, Kline attempted to mail the Tiller clinic medical records to himself in Virginia, but they were returned because of a faulty address.

If he wasn't finished with Tiller, neither were Troy Newman and the members of his Operation Rescue. In 2008, they succeeded in getting a second grand jury to investigate the doctor and hoped to subpoena thousands of WHCS medical records for the jurors' examination. Many former Tiller patients, aided by the Center for Reproductive Rights in New York City, came forward and offered their support to WHCS in an effort to protect these files. CRR succeeded in keeping the great majority of patient records from reaching the grand jury and no names or other identifying information were revealed. Jurors had access to the files of 150 randomly selected patients who'd had late-term abortions, and after studying these records they, like the earlier grand jury, refused to indict Dr. Tiller. It was another defeat for Newman and the anti-abortionists, who continued showing up at WHCS with their "Truth Trucks," featuring aborted fetuses and their new message, "Abortion is an ObamaNation."

Tiller faced one more legal battle, and if he won it, the seemingly endless Inquisition launched by Phill Kline in 2003 would at last be at an end. Under the new attorney general, Steve Six, the nineteen-count misdemeanor case against the physician for allegedly having an illegal financial relationship with Kristin Neuhaus was moving forward. Across the state and around the nation, abortion foes held out the hope that finally, after so many years of frustration, Tiller would be taken to court and convicted of these charges. He could lose his medical license and abortion practice.

One man watching these developments closely had higher hopes than almost anybody else.

# THE RULE OF LAW

# XXIV

In 2004, Scott Roeder had invited his son, Nick, to go with him to Worldview Weekend, a Christian gathering in Branson, Missouri. Nick was eighteen and could now make his own decisions about being with his father. This group was far more in the mainstream than many of the religious activities Roeder had been involved with throughout the past decade, and his ex-wife felt that he might be leaving the fringes behind. He and Nick went to Branson and had a good time.

"I thought he was moving away from the dark side," Lindsey says, "but it didn't last long. He went back to interacting with the same people he'd been around before, and we didn't see as much of him. He'd call Nick, but Nick would usually try to avoid him, so he wouldn't have to listen to his dad talk about conspiracies."

Roeder found people with his same beliefs online. The Internet linked him to many far-right organizations and let him vent with those who felt as he did about abortion, stem cell research, and Dr. Tiller. He posted his opinions on various Web sites under the name "Servant-ofMessiah."

On May 19, 2007, he brought up an Operation Rescue event held a few days earlier in Wichita, praying for the end of Tiller's "death camp" and calling for all unborn babies to "once again come under the protection of law." He hoped to organize as many people as possible to attend a service at the physician's church to ask questions of the pastor and other leaders.

"Doesn't seem like it would hurt anything," he wrote, "but bring more attention to Tiller."

Three months later, Roeder posted on a site sponsored by Operation Rescue called "chargetiller.com." He compared what was happening in Kansas to "lawlessness" mentioned in the Bible.

"Tiller," he wrote, "is the concentration camp 'Mengele' of our day and needs to be stopped before he and those who protect him bring judgment upon our nation."

On this site, another post read, *"TILLER MUST DIE* PUBLICLY, OBSERVED BY THE WORLD TO SEE, OPENLY, THAT PEOPLE WHO ARE INVOLVED WITH THIS PRACTICE MUST BE AWARE TO TURN ON THERE WICKED WAYS."

By mid-2007, like so many others with his political and religious leanings, Roeder felt alarmed and even more motivated to speak out because of Barack Obama's campaign for the presidency of the United States. There was a chance he might even win. During the past eight years, Roeder and his cohorts had had someone in the White House with whom they'd shared certain core beliefs: the anti-abortion, born-again Christian George W. Bush, who'd opposed stem cell research for use in scientific labs. His administration had been lax in enforcing the FACE Act, which made it a crime to block access to medical facilities and to deny women the opportunity to get abortions. Obama was a pro-choice, liberal Democrat and, in Roeder's view, "a man without any character." Whatever respect he might have had for the candidate went away during the campaign, when Obama avoided directly answering a question about when life begins, saying that that kind of knowledge was above his pay grade.

"What kind of a response is that?" Roeder asked people.

Adding to his discomfort was that his ex-wife and son were big Obama supporters. One time they put an "Obama" magnet on his car, just to annoy him.

"Scott had very negative feelings about Obama," says Lindsey. "He believed that if he got to be president, Obama would strongly back abortion rights and just be horrible and ruin the country. Scott's feelings were really racial."

All the more reason that the legal case to bring down Dr. Tiller had to succeed.

# XXV

As the 2008 election approached, the charges against Tiller made their way through the Kansas court system. In the 1990s, he'd paid a team of lawyers to help him comply with the statute requiring a second physician to sign off on the necessity of a late-term abortion. During the Inquisition, he'd employed more attorneys to represent him against the new allegations. Now, in the fall of 2008, he'd engaged still more to combat the latest charges. At a November hearing, held right after Barack Obama's election, Tiller's side argued to have the case dismissed. His lead lawyer, Wichita's Dan Monnat, relished the role of defending the doctor and took this opportunity to express himself about what had been happening lately at the highest levels of Kansas law enforcement.

"Your Honor," he told Judge Clark Owens, in his sixth-floor courtroom in the Eighteenth Judicial District, "when former Attorney General Paul Morrison filed these charges, he all but apologized for them, calling them technical violations, and the evidence in this case . . . will establish that these technical violations are really the product of politics and personal problems of at least two former attorney generals . . . This prosecution is the product of outrageous government conduct in violation of both the [state and federal] constitutions . . . with total disregard for the privacy rights of women . . .

"The Kansas Supreme Court, speaking of the behavior of Phill Kline, found . . . the unauthorized scattering of the private medical files of women to a national conservative talk show host, to an Internet DVD, and to the car trunks, kitchens, and apartments of the abettors of former Attorney General Phill Kline . . . Special prosecutors have been appointed to investigate Attorney General Morrison's illicit relationship with Linda Carter, a Kline employee for some of the time, and her role in influencing his decision to charge Dr. Tiller. Is that outrageous? Is it outrageous that Dr. Tiller, an innocent man, and the rights of innocent women and the people's system of justice are just the pawns of those politicians?"

Monnat was determined not just to defend Tiller, but to put his inquisitors on trial. When he called Kline as a witness at the November hearing, the former attorney general was nonresponsive to the questions. Then Monnat called Kline's chief investigator, Tom Williams, whom Carter had flirted with in the DA's office. Monnat pointed out that when Williams was supposedly trying to learn about child sex abuse going unreported in Kansas, he'd focused on abortion providers.

"That's where the record sort of led," Williams said.

"Well, hospital records and birth records are a pretty obvious record to think of in the first place, aren't they?"

"Well, maybe."

"And what about dentists, optometrists, psychologists, nurses, teachers, school employees, marriage therapists, family therapists, alcohol and drug abuse counselors, licensed child care providers, social workers, firefighters, EMS personnel, juvenile intake assessment workers, and law enforcement officers?"

"That's a long list."

"Any of them wrong?"

"No, not that I'm aware of . . ."

Despite Monnat's efforts to have the case dismissed, Judge Owens disagreed and scheduled Tiller's trial for late March 2009. On the twenty-third of that month, the parties assembled at the Sedgwick County Courthouse in downtown Wichita for opening arguments. As anti-abortion demonstrators gathered on the streets outside and Operation Rescue members came into the courtroom to protest Tiller in silence during the proceedings, six jurors had to decide if the doctor had had an unlawful financial or legal relationship with Dr. Kristin Neuhaus.

One of those inside the courtroom watching the trial was Scott Roeder. For a decade he'd been hearing from moderate anti-abortionists that the legal system could bring Tiller down and throughout that time he'd hoped and prayed they were right. Now was its chance.

Roeder had been spending more time in Wichita lately, driving down from Kansas City and checking in to one of the cheap motels on East Kellogg Street, just up the road from Tiller's clinic. He didn't have much money, but spent what he had on this pilgrimage to the heart of the war over abortion. He rode by Tiller's church and parked in front of it, staring at the stately red brick structure in the northeast part of Wichita, the money side of town. He stood with his allies on the sidewalk outside the clinic in the late winter cold, continuing the "sidewalk counseling" that he'd been doing for years, talking to women going inside and trying to change their minds, holding his worn Bible and reading certain passages again and again, closing his eyes and beseeching God with all the intensity he could muster for Tiller to come to his senses and give up his medical practice. In years past, he'd visited WHCS, but usually held himself apart from the other demonstrators, carrying a cross and a bundle of red roses, a symbol of the anti-abortion movement. Because of the flowers, the protesters had nicknamed him "the prom queen."

He no longer had the roses or stood away from the others at the clinic, but joined with them and their prayers. He believed that if he prayed hard enough, if he found just the right words and feelings, if he was sincere enough in his beliefs, Tiller would change his mind and stop performing abortions forever. Wichita would no longer be the abortion capital of the world and an evil would have been removed from Roeder's home state. That's what so many abortion foes had wanted during the last three decades, but now they had something much more to hope for, everything building toward this climactic moment.

They'd been frantically texting and twittering one another, calling and e-mailing about this pivotal moment in their history. They'd been trading information about Tiller—his clinic, his residence, his place of worship, and his daily routine—about how he got around town or to and from work. Operation Rescue had an online "Tiller Watch" that posted his home and church address. Demonstrators sent pictures of him on their cell phones, as he traveled from one location to the next, stopping for a bite to eat or to pick up his clothes at the dry cleaner's, each technological advance adding to their surveillance. On February 20, 2009, Operation Rescue's senior policy adviser Cheryl Sullenger twittered her cohorts, "Meanwhile, bloody business as usual at Tiller's shop of horrors."

On March 5, as the legalities were about to begin, she sent out another message, "Inviting all to Tiller trial in Wichita March 16."

# XXVI

When he wasn't in Wichita, Roeder returned home to his new apartment. He now shared a few rooms in Westport, a bar-and-restaurant
district on the Missouri side of Kansas City, with a man he'd known for
years through their common interest in Messianic Christianity. Kamran Tehrani was born in Iran and his father had worked in the shah's
regime, but after the 1979 overthrow of the Iranian government and
the rise of Ayatollah Khomeini, Kamran's family moved to America.
He was raised a Muslim, but became an atheist living in Washington
State and California. In 1988, he had a personal crisis and asked God to
reveal Himself.

"I had a dream and saw Christ's deity," Kamran says, "and this presence nearly killed me. He shrouded his glory so that I could look right
at him, and that started my Christian journey."

Kamran, who'd earned a master's in business administration, came
to Kansas in 1991 and worked as a mortgage broker. In the late 1990s,
he met Roeder through the Prophecy Club, a religious group in Topeka, led by Pastor Stan Johnson. To Kamran, the Prophecy Club was
a "cutting-edge, national ministry." It embraced many of the same anti-
tax, anti-immigration, and anti-gay-rights convictions held by the far
right. In a quiet and polite Midwestern tone, Pastor Johnson could be
heard on the Internet asking the faithful for money and decrying the

state of modern America, while delivering a broad-based attack on those he felt were outside the Christian fold. His delivery was much softer than that of Fred Phelps, who preached savagely against gay people at Topeka's Westboro Baptist Church, but their messages over-lapped.

"The Prophecy Club didn't meet at a church but a motel," Kamran says. "We had discussions about a wide range of subjects, including our Hebrew roots."

He ran into Roeder at the motel and at similar events held by the International House of Prayer (IHOP).

"The Lord," reads the IHOP Web site, "has called us to be a com-munity of believers committed to God, each other and to establishing a 24/7 house of prayer in Kansas City—a perpetual solemn assembly gathering corporately to fast and pray in the spirit of the tabernacle of David."

Small clusters of Prophecy Club or IHOP followers got together at their homes and held Bible study sessions, with an emphasis on carry-ing on Old Testament traditions. For a while, Kamran lived at the Merriam, Kansas, home of the lawyer Michael Clayman, but he moved out and Roeder moved in. In mid-decade at Clayman's, Kamran led a course called the "Four Quadrants," about what had become of the Bible's Lost Tribes of Israel. Kamran's teachings echoed those given to the men in the Order back in the early 1980s, when they were hearing sermons at the Aryan Nations compound in Idaho: these lost tribes had formed the countries of Europe and eventually came to America. At Clayman's, they also studied what Kamran called the "Synagogue of Sa-tan," made up of Freemasons, Catholics, Mormons, Jehovah's Witnesses, and Jews.

"People today," says Kamran, "call themselves Jews, but they're not. They're really the Synagogue of Satan. We're going to be revealing all this in the Last Days."

After both men had left Clayman's and Kamran took an apartment in Westport, Roeder settled in with him. They continued studying these subjects in their new living room, but abortion wasn't really a part of their discussions. Nor was it a large part of Kamran's belief system or interests. The men kept the Sabbath on Saturdays, when students got together and pored over the Bible. Kamran was born Persian, and a Persian proverb says that if you want to get to know someone well, either live or travel with that individual. Sharing an apartment with Roeder, watching his habits and listening to his rants, Kamran got to know the hulking, balding, fifty-one-year-old man with the light-colored, wispy mustache much more intimately.

"He was just very dogmatic in his feelings about the unborn," Kamran says. "He had a real strong passion on this issue. I tried to tell him that my calling is for the born versus the unborn, and that you cannot force women to not abort their children. Not even Operation Rescue can do that. He talked a lot about Operation Rescue and I'd hear him in the apartment speaking with one of their leaders on the phone. It was a woman. They were talking about Tiller and his trial.

"He also talked about Tiller with me and one time he went to Topeka for an anti-abortion demonstration. Scott was very tight with his money, so that really impressed me. It was a long way for him to drive to protest. He told me that Tiller had become a multimillionaire as an abortion doctor and had aborted seventy thousand children. He once asked me my opinion about shooting abortion doctors. I said if you want to go to prison for life that is your decision and nobody can stop anybody from what they choose to do."

What Kamran didn't know was that over the years Roeder, by his own claims, had donated at least a thousand dollars to Operation Rescue—a large amount for someone beyond frugal, who held minimum-wage jobs and was occasionally out of work. He also didn't know that in August 2008, Roeder had driven to Wichita one weekend and attended a Sunday service at Dr. Tiller's Reformation Lutheran Church, concealing a 9-millimeter handgun in a shoulder holster.

"Scott once asked me," Kamran says, "what I thought, biblically, about killing an abortion doctor. I told him that if you act it out, you'll pay for it with prison time. I didn't say, 'No, don't do it,' because in America people have guns and people get shot all the time. They just do what they do."

As someone born and raised in another country, Kamran was often struck by how well armed Americans were, with ninety guns for every hundred citizens. It further impressed him that the United States is believed to be the most heavily armed society on earth, owning 270 million of the world's 875 million known firearms. Between 1980 and 2006, firearm death rates in America averaged 32,300 annually, well over twice that of the next highest country among industrialized nations.

Roeder had thought about running Tiller over with his car, but that might not work. If he was able to get close enough, he could chop off the doctor's hands (his ex-father-in-law kept a sword in a cedar chest in Lindsey's home, left over from World War Two, and Roeder himself had a long, nasty-looking serrated knife under the seat of his car). But even if he removed Tiller's hands, the physician could teach others how to perform abortions. Roeder considered climbing onto a rooftop across the street from the clinic and using a high-powered M50 sniper's rifle as Tiller came to work in the morning, but it would be extremely difficult to get a clean shot at the man inside the armored car or after he'd entered WHCS through a security fence and parked in a locked garage. The Tillers lived in a gated community that was virtually impenetrable, so Roeder couldn't do it at his home. That really left only a single option, and wasn't it the best one of all? Where were people more trusting and open than at a Sunday church service? He'd walked right into Reformation Lutheran carrying a Bible and a hidden handgun and nobody had suspected a thing. Several people had welcomed him that day and all they'd wanted to talk about was bringing him into their fold.

# XXVII

Deputy Attorney General Barry Disney was the prosecutor in the Tiller trial, which opened on March 23, 2009, with bomb-sniffing dogs patrolling the courthouse for explosives. Disney didn't seem to have nearly as much fire for his job as Dan Monnat had for defending the doctor against the nineteen misdemeanor charges. Some spectators in the gallery, including Roeder, noticed this, and he talked about it angrily on the phone with the woman from Operation Rescue. Couldn't the attorney general's office have come up with somebody more forceful? How did the prosecution expect to win if its leader conducted himself like this? Didn't law enforcement in Kansas understand how important it was to convict Tiller? And why did things move so slowly in the courtroom when it was so obvious that Tiller was guilty? Anti-abortion protesters had parked a "Truth Truck" near the courthouse for the trial, so the media and public would see it as they came and went. In their eyes, this was an effective strategy for spreading their message, far more effective than Barry Disney himself.

On the twenty-third, following the prosecutor's limited opening remarks, Monnat stood and delivered a much lengthier statement, reminding the six Wichita jurors what most of them already knew from years of living in the city. Every patient who came to WHCS from across town or around Kansas or from a distant state or foreign country was "heckled and discouraged and approached by the protesters . . . [who] will pursue her to her motel . . . [bringing] more fear and inconvenience to an already bewildered and frightened pregnant woman . . ."

Monnat then laid out the fundamental questions and full substance of the defense's case, a moment that Tiller and his attorney had been building up to throughout the past decade. This was their chance to establish the physician's innocence once and for all, in a court of law, by a jury of the doctor's peers, in his own hometown. As he was about to reveal in the courtroom and in front of the national media in Wichita for the trial, Monnat was more than prepared for this occasion.

Inside his well-appointed office a few blocks south of the courthouse, the attorney kept a row of thick law books in neatly aligned rows behind his desk. Nothing was even a fraction out of place. He was punctual, dressed nattily, had pointed features that seemed to define his highly focused personality, and spoke in measured, clipped tones, as if offering a summation to a jury when he was only meeting with a journalist. With virtually no prompting, he spoke with conviction and passion about the value of the American Constitution and the rule of law in the United States, and you couldn't help thinking that if you ever got into serious trouble with the police, you'd want him at your side. One had to look a little deeper into his life to learn that he was known around town as a pretty fair rock 'n' roll drummer who liked to jam in nightclubs on the weekend.

If his opening statement seemed exhaustive, it was because he was determined to lay the entire Phill Kline Inquisition and pursuit of Dr. Tiller by the state of Kansas to rest for good. According to the prosecution's own brief, Monnat began, the term "legally affiliated simply means . . . a formal business association that would include physicians who are part of the same corporation or who practice together in a partnership or a limited liability company. But the evidence will show that Dr. Tiller and Dr. Neuhaus are not associated as employer and employee, are not associated as business partners, are not associated as joint venturers, are not associated as separate stockholders in the same corporation. They're not even associated as landlord and tenant. More importantly, Dr. Tiller never has had any sort of written, oral or implied contract with Dr. Neuhaus.

"In other words, Dr. Neuhaus can refuse to consult with Dr. Tiller's patients at any time, and Dr. Tiller can stop referring patients to Dr. Neuhaus at any time. Neither is contractually, that is, legally obligated towards one another in any way to accept or give referrals to or from the other. The evidence will also be clear that Dr. Neuhaus and Dr. Tiller are never knowingly and intentionally financially affiliated in any way. Dr. Tiller never pays any money or anything of value to Dr. Neuhaus, whether as salary, stock ownership, investment, profit or expenses. Dr. Neuhaus is always paid directly by the patients themselves and usually in cash, because Dr. Neuhaus doesn't want to have to worry about whether a check is going to bounce . . . Dr. Neuhaus meets separately with each patient and conducts her own independent evaluation of the patient. Dr. Neuhaus keeps her own files on the patients . . ."

If Neuhaus recommended that Tiller not do an abortion on a patient, he accepted her view and didn't seek another opinion. She wasn't paid any differently if an abortion was or was not performed.

"Dr. Tiller and Dr. Neuhaus," Monnat said, "have no shared bank accounts, they have no shared equipment leases or purchases. They have no profit sharing. Dr. Neuhaus maintains her own policy of malpractice insurance and is not covered by Dr. Tiller's. Dr. Neuhaus has a separate Medicare reimbursement number and a separate Canadian health care system number. Dr. Tiller files income taxes completely separate from Dr. Neuhaus's obligation to do so.

"The evidence will show that the evaluations are scheduled and done at Women's Health Care Services, not because Dr. Neuhaus and Dr. Tiller are affiliated but because it is too unsafe, complicated and obnoxious to ask pregnant women who have come to Kansas for an abortion to turn around and then drive two and a half hours to Lawrence for a second evaluation, turn around and drive back, both times having to withstand the ever-present gauntlet of protesters out in front of the clinic who will approach them, heckle them and try to discourage them . . . Actions taken merely by both doctors for the safety and comfort of their patients do show each doctor's affiliation with the patient, but they don't show any affiliation between Dr. Neuhaus and Dr. Tiller."

Dr. Neuhaus, Monnat conceded, occasionally used the WHCS printer, but always paid for the paper and the toner she consumed.

"She used a Tiller car in 2006," he said. "It was a 1997 Toyota Camry that I think belonged to Jeanne Tiller at one point that had been parked on the lot of Women's Health Care Services, so that visiting doctors from time to time could use it to get around . . . Dr. Neuhaus and Dr. Tiller, of course, were worried that somebody might suggest that if she bought the car from Dr. Tiller that would be some kind of financial affiliation. So very conscientiously they had the car appraised by a dealership in Wichita who gave them a $300 figure for what this kind of junker car was worth with its bashed-in side and bashed-in rear end, and that's what Dr. Neuhaus paid to Dr. Tiller, and I submit that will be insufficient to establish the affiliation in 2003 that the prosecution is required to . . .

"The evidence will show Dr. Neuhaus didn't shut down her women's clinic in Lawrence because she is making so much money from these consults. Really, she charged $250 to $300 for each consult in part because she saw it as a humanitarian thing to do for other women who were in desperate circumstances. Dr. Neuhaus is . . . married to Michael Caddell, who is a private investigator in Lawrence, Kansas. Unfortunately, in about August of 2002, as their five-year-old son was starting kindergarten . . . they learned for the first time that their son suffered from severe juvenile onset diabetes and that he needed to have his blood sugar checked five to six times a day and needed to have insulin injections twice a day. Now, what can a mother who also happens to be a medical doctor do for her only child under those circumstances? Dr. Neuhaus does it. She shuts down her women's clinic in Lawrence so that she can be with her son and watch over her son during this critical time.

"The evidence . . . will fail to show beyond a reasonable doubt that Dr. Tiller was knowingly and intentionally legally or financially affiliated with Dr. Neuhaus at any time . . . I will ask each of you to return a fair verdict of not guilty and permit Dr. Tiller to return to continuing to serve the women who so need his medical care. Thank you very much."

The anti-abortion protesters, both inside and outside the courtroom, were further upset when Barry Disney called only one witness, Dr. Kristin Neuhaus, a close ally of Tiller's who underscored this when she came in to testify by hugging the doctor in front of the jury. After her earlier dealings with Phill Kline and the attorney general's office, she was so fearful of the prosecution that she'd sought and obtained immunity from the state before agreeing to testify at the trial. Her hostility to Disney on the witness stand no doubt contributed to his lack of passion for the case.

She told the jurors that she'd received death threats because of her work with Tiller and could never give out her home address to anyone she didn't personally know. If WHCS received a call from somebody asking for her cell or home number, it was usually from abortion foes trying to find out where she lived so they could come to her house and demonstrate. Some female "patients" who'd tried to contact her were impostors just looking to harass her. She sounded permanently afraid.

Once Disney had finished questioning her, Monnat asked her about being subpoenaed by Kline in December of 2006, as he was about to leave office.

"At the beginning of that Inquisition," Monnat said, "it was announced to you that also in the room was Special Agent Jared Reed of the Attorney General's Office, correct?"

"Yes."

"And Special Agent in Charge Tom Williams of the Kansas Attorney General—is that correct?"

"That's right . . ."

"And you were questioned then by Mr. Steven Maxwell. Did you regard him as Phill Kline's number one man?"

"Absolutely."

"And just share with the ladies and gentlemen of the jury what it felt like being interrogated under those circumstances."

"The Inquisition, minus the torture chamber. You know, the Spanish Inquisition. That's what I felt like."

"You told that attorney [Maxwell] sometimes the women were too chemically impaired to make an informed decision on anything at that moment and so you would not refer them to Dr. Tiller for an abortion, correct?"

"That's correct."

"You told that attorney sometimes the women's cognitive processes were too impaired to make a decision and they didn't have a guardian with them, correct?"

"Correct . . ."

One patient had flown all the way from England to Wichita, but Dr. Neuhaus turned her down for an abortion.

How did she feel about being called a "rubber stamp" for Dr. Tiller?

"Well, it's outrageous," she testified. "I always put the patient at the center of every interaction. I would not be able to live with doing other than that . . . I always find that to be my highest and most important duty, to never facilitate harm for anyone. And this is a very, very serious process and a very difficult decision for people . . . And I don't want to make a mistake . . .

"If someone tells me right off the bat that they have reservations, I would never proceed. I . . . make sure that every aspect of their health—their physical, psychological, emotional and spiritual health—are all being addressed."

On redirect examination, Disney wasn't as friendly with his witness—not after Neuhaus said that the trial was a political prosecution of Tiller and it was "open season" on doctors who performed abortions. Disney asked if she'd considered that Tiller could have provided patients with a list of physicians willing to give a second opinion, instead of just repeatedly relying on Neuhaus herself.

"The question is so illogical," she said, "I don't even know where to start."

"Just say yes, ma'am, or no."

"It's an illogical question . . ."

"So you didn't consider it?"

"It's impossible. It's a ridiculous question."

During the trial, Roeder sat a few feet away from George and Jeanne Tiller, watching the couple and listening to the state's case with deepening dismay.

# XXVIII

The prosecution rested and the defense called Dr. Tiller. He talked about his background, along with the 1986 bombing of his clinic and being shot in the arms by Shelley Shannon in 1993. Monnat asked about the protests going on today at WHCS.

"On Wednesday at noon," Tiller said, "we have one or two or three men who come over and drag a kitchen table onto the sidewalk that's outside of our elevated fence—a privacy, security fence. These one or two people stand up on a table with a bullhorn yelling . . . over the fence [and] describing the patients, 'You, getting out of the red car. Don't go in there. Don't kill your baby.' Intensive, unpleasant intimidation."

Why, Monnat asked, don't you just quit?

"Quit is not something that I like to do. Why have we continued? First, the strong support of . . . my wife, the strong support of my daughters, the strong support of my son. I remember one time during one of the protests, we were under a lot of pressure and . . . two of my daughters came into my study . . . and they said to me, 'Daddy, if not now, when? If not you, who?' And that means who is going to stand up for women with unexpected or badly damaged babies? Who was going to be their protector—if you won't—and when was that going to happen?"

Tiller's reference to his daughters and his wife, Jeanne, who was watching the proceedings, was part of a conscious strategy. With her short, stylish frosted hair, her understated but tasteful clothes, and a face that conveyed strength and suffering, compassion and endurance, Jeanne looked like someone who'd walked every step of his treacherous medical journey with her husband throughout the past three-plus decades. If she and her daughters felt that he had the best interests of women at heart, how could others, and especially other women serving on the jury, dispute that?

"Doctor," Monnat said, "as you sit here today, do you feel the extreme pressure that you're always under as a provider in this dangerous situation?"

He nodded and said, "Yes."

On the trial's final day, another defense lawyer, Laura Shaneyfelt, asked the Tiller attorney Rachel Pirner if the Kansas State Board of Healing Arts had ever found any wrongdoing by the physician.

"No," Priner said.

"Were there any follow-up inquiries or any subpoenas issued by the Board of Healing Arts regarding any issue regarding any financial or legal affiliation between Dr. Neuhaus and Dr. Tiller?"

"No."

"Did anyone from the board ever raise any concern to you . . . about any improper or unlawful affiliation with those two doctors?"

"Absolutely not."

Early spring in Kansas can bring a rare blizzard, and one was brewing throughout Friday, March 27, as the lawyers made their closing arguments. By afternoon the storm had begun rolling in from the west, ice and snow covering downtown Wichita, emptying the streets and making everyone in the courthouse eager to get home for the weekend. Once the arguments were finished, the jury went into its deliberations,

contacting the judge less than thirty minutes later to announce they'd
reached a decision. As they walked back into the courtroom and prepared to deliver their verdict, security personnel in the courthouse
was increased and put on high alert. Tiller's enemies, as well as his supporters, had gathered in court to hear the outcome. But by then Roeder
was back in Kansas City.

Members of the Sedgwick County Sheriff's Department formed a
wall between the doctor and his defense team, and the gallery of spectators sitting behind them; rumors had been circulating that if Tiller
was acquitted, somebody planned to throw battery acid in his face.
The moment both sides had been praying for had arrived. The anti-
abortionists had waited nearly thirty-five years for Tiller to be found
guilty of a crime and go on to lose his career. The defense hoped that if
he were found not guilty, he could finally move away from his legal
troubles and focus solely on practicing medicine.

With everyone in place, Judge Owens asked the jury for their verdict, which was followed by several moments of silence.

"Not guilty," came the reply, again and again. Not guilty on count one
and on all eighteen subsequent counts.

Relief seeped out from around the defense table, with smiles and
quiet congratulations and a few tears. Tiller and his lawyers embraced
with hugs and backslaps, certain that the Kline-Morrison saga was at
an end and the doctor could relax this weekend and go back to work
afresh on Monday morning. He might even be able to stop paying some
of these attorneys' fees and focus more resources on his clinic and staff.

The gallery disbanded without incident and rode the elevators down
to the lobby, a few of them bitterly discussing the outcome. The jurors
had finished their courtroom obligations, but for security reasons
they'd have to be led to their cars by armed guards because protesters
were lingering outside. Prior to putting on their coats, and despite their
eagerness to leave before the snow got any deeper, they wanted to perform one more civic duty inside the courthouse—something beyond
the normal boundaries of due process. The jury foreman asked the
judge if they could write a note and have him pass it along to Tiller and

his lawyers. Judge Owens agreed to this and the note was quickly composed and delivered. It pleased Dan Monnat about as much as the verdict had.

"Dr. Tiller," he says, "was confident throughout the process that led up to the trial and throughout the trial itself. He liked to say 'Attitude Is Everything' and his confidence never wavered. He believed in the goodness of the people of Wichita and in their awareness and decency. He felt that if he took the witness stand, he could explain to them the integrity and legality of what he did. In the middle of all these fractured personalities who were involved in Kansas politics, he followed a moral compass and remained confident of his own innocence.

"The six jurors who heard the evidence in this trial showed us a lot about the greatness of our jury system and its continuing viability. That system still does what it was designed to do five hundred years ago, when it was used to protect people against monarchs. It gives defendants the right to counsel, to trial by jury, and the chance to confront your accuser through cross-examination. In this case, it showed that the jury felt that the charges were absolutely without basis.

"A twenty-five-minute verdict in Kansas of not guilty on nineteen counts of performing illegal abortions is very clear evidence of a jury's belief in the rightness of what Dr. Tiller was doing. In the note they gave him after the verdict, they wanted him to know they were happy to do this for him, and they were proud that a safe, secure, and sanitary clinic existed for these operations, as opposed to the back alleys and motel rooms women had once used to get abortions."

Not everyone, of course, felt this way about the verdict. The Rev. Patrick J. Mahoney, director of Washington's Christian Defense Coalition, told *The New York Times* that it was "a setback." Both Phill Kline and Mary Kay Culp, executive director of Kansans for Life, publicly expressed disappointment in how the state had presented its case, but showed restraint. One prominent figure did not and spoke out against the jurors' decision with the loudest voice of all, as he'd been doing for the past several years on the most-watched cable talk show on evening television. On the day of the verdict, Bill O'Reilly said on the air,

"Now, we have bad news to report, that Tiller the baby killer out in Kansas—acquitted. Acquitted today of murdering babies. I wasn't in the courtroom. I didn't sit on the jury. But there's got to be a special place in hell for this guy."

Seven days later, O'Reilly reiterated on Fox, "Tiller got acquitted in Kansas, Tiller the baby killer."

Then a few weeks after that O'Reilly said that Governor Sebelius "recently vetoed a bill that placed restrictions on late-term abortions in Kansas. The bill was introduced because of the notorious Tiller the baby killer case, where Dr. George Tiller destroys fetuses for just about any reason right up until the birth date for five thousand dollars."

The afternoon of the verdict, as the wind picked up and the sky turned grayer and the blizzard descended on Wichita, George and Jeanne Tiller prepared to leave the courthouse and go home. One attorney who'd been practicing law in the city for twenty-five years saw them standing off by themselves, smiling and quietly celebrating their victory. Like so many others in Wichita, he was aware of the Tiller family and their legal ordeals, and this image stayed with him.

"They looked so relieved and happy that day, with the trial behind them," he said months later. "As I watched them in that moment, I tried to imagine what their lives had been like for the past several decades and what they'd lived through as a couple. I thought about the threats and their fears. The truth is that I really couldn't imagine it."

# XXIX

With the case over and Dr. Tiller acquitted, Kamran Tehrani once again heard his roommate talking angrily on the phone in their Westport apartment. Speaking with the woman from Operation Rescue, Roeder was more upset than ever. Why hadn't Disney called more witnesses? Why hadn't he been more aggressive with Neuhaus? If this was the best the state of Kansas could do . . .

"Scott just felt that Tiller's lawyer," says Kamran, "had just shredded the Operation Rescue argument."

For the anti-abortionists, only one more hope existed. Immediately after the verdict, the Kansas State Board of Healing Arts, no longer headed by Larry Buening, announced that it disagreed with the Wichita jurors, so the board itself might take steps to revoke Tiller's license. Some in the anti-abortion movement took solace in this possibility, but Roeder wasn't one of them. He'd been hearing such things for the past two or three years and nothing had changed. How long would it take for this process to unfold, and what if Tiller's legal team crushed the KSBHA as easily as they had the attorney general's office?

For his part, Dan Monnat questioned both the merits and the timing of the KSBHA pronouncement.

"The board's case," he says, "was based on eleven of the nineteen alleged incidents that the Wichita jury had just swiftly and resoundingly acquitted Dr. Tiller of. The timing of this announcement might well be perceived as something done to blunt the thumping the state of Kansas had just taken by the jury."

Roeder was disturbed by more than the recent verdict. Two months earlier, President Obama had moved into the White House and was in the process of overturning the Bush administration policy preventing nearly seven hundred embryonic stem cell lines from being used to study various illnesses and develop cures. The new president had reached out to Kansas and nominated Governor Kathleen Sebelius to be his secretary of health and human services. Obama couldn't, in Roeder's mind, have chosen a worse candidate; early in 2009, she'd vetoed a bill requiring doctors to provide more details to the Kansas Health Department when justifying late-term abortions.

He was hardly alone in his opinion of Sebelius.

"Sebelius," Troy Newman once told Christian Newswire, "is a radical supporter of abortion and is not above misleading the public as to the militant nature of her abortion support."

In March of 2009, Archbishop Raymond F. Burke, prefect for the Apostolic Signatura, the Vatican's highest court, declared that Sebelius should not approach the altar for Communion within the United States because "she obstinately persists in serious sin."

Sean Hannity said of the governor, "I think it speaks to the character of somebody who says they are 'personally opposed to abortion' and yet they accept money from somebody like George Tiller. Absolutely disgraceful."

On his Fox News program, Bill O'Reilly echoed Hannity, saying that Sebelius "is pro-abortion. She wants the babies done for . . . She supported Tiller the baby killer out there."

During Sebelius's confirmation process in Washington, she came under attack from congressional Republicans because Tiller and his staff had attended a 2007 reception at the governor's mansion, and because she'd initially failed to account for donations from the doctor. In response to the Senate Finance Committee, Sebelius revealed that she'd received $12,450 from Tiller between 1994 and 2001, but the

Senate eventually learned that Tiller had given at least $23,000 more to her political action committee between 2000 and 2002.

In the conservative publication *Human Events*, Marjorie Dannenfelser wrote that Sebelius's record revealed that she'd support the abortion industry "even if it means abandoning the needs of women." While calling on pro-life senators to fight the nomination, Dannenfelser said that if such opposition was ever needed, "that day is today." But the governor was confirmed and the only good news for Kansas antiabortionists was that she was no longer running their state.

On May 15, as Roeder absorbed this development, O'Reilly said on Fox that Sebelius was the "most pro-abortion governor in the United States. Based upon Dr. Tiller—the baby killer in her state—and all of that. All right? So there's no doubt."

Roeder had had six weeks for the impact of the verdict to settle into him, and that impact was only expanding.

"I did not know what Scott was thinking about that spring," says Kamran, "but he did talk about buying a gun. One time he said he was going to an auction to get a gun, but I'm not sure if he bought one. He said he needed it for protection. Jesus said to get swords for his followers for their self-defense, and that's how Scott justified it.

"If he'd been doing something really questionable inside our apartment, I'd have asked him to move out. You have to understand. I'm a foreign national in the United States, from Iran, and in my position I cannot be involved in certain things."

Throughout that winter and early spring, Roeder told Kamran that he was going to Topeka fairly often to visit his aging mother, Doris. On his way back to Westport, he liked to stop at a farm near Lawrence and buy goat's milk, a special treat, a rare indulgence, as both he and Kamran enjoyed this "kefir." Roeder saved a few dollars each week from his work as a driver for an airport shuttle service, so he could buy kefir and put aside a few more dollars for a night out with his son. He didn't have that much contact with Lindsey anymore, but called Nick with some regularity, hoping to meet him on the weekends and perhaps share a meal. Nick often had other things to do or made up excuses not to see his father.

Because Kamran and Roeder kept different schedules, they didn't see a lot of each other during the week. Kamran wasn't aware that at odd hours of the night or very early in the morning Roeder had been going to the Central Family Medicine clinic, an abortion office near downtown Kansas City, and conducting his own one-man protests. Or that instead of being in Topeka with his mother, he drove down to Wichita to protest at WHCS, or to meet with anti-abortion demonstrators outside the Sedgwick County Courthouse and to drop in on Tiller's trial. He traveled alone and quietly, keeping much to himself. Like others who knew Roeder from his involvement in religious groups, Kamran saw him as a devoted student of the Bible more than a man of action. Yet he was a large figure and a menacing presence— especially when he was in a manic phase and hadn't slept much— lingering in front of Tiller's church or standing on the sidewalk outside an abortion clinic.

Kamran worked late and might not get home until midnight. He usually went into his room, closed the door, and watched television before drifting off to sleep, uncertain if Roeder was even in the other bedroom or had disappeared for a few days. Months later, Roeder would say that in the weeks following Tiller's trial he'd begun consulting with "numerous people" about what he should do, before "things had come together."

# TARGET
# IDENTIFICATION

# XXX

In the last week of October 2008, I attended a rally for Barack Obama in downtown Denver, his final Colorado appearance before the presidential election. One hundred thousand people turned out to see him on a clear, chilly morning, but the candidate was more than twenty minutes late, giving me time to study the overflow crowd. Most people looked cheerful and optimistic about Obama's chances of election, and relieved that the lengthy campaign was almost at an end. As we stood and waited in the hard-edged autumn sunshine, I thought back to early 2007, when Obama and his wife, Michelle, had appeared on *60 Minutes* and talked about his running for the White House. Michelle was asked about her fear of her husband being assassinated, and her concerns were visible in her body language and facial expressions. She was clearly worried that if he aspired to the highest office on earth, something tragic could happen to him and their family, not to mention the rest of the country. One could only guess at the private conversations the two of them must have had around this subject and the pressures on him not to run.

Obama himself was much cooler on the topic, as if he'd thought about his possible demise and then put it out of his mind. He couldn't do what he hoped to do for himself or America if he were too consumed by violent scenarios, and he hadn't come this far by letting dread limit his dreams. The interview ended, but had haunted me ever since. Watching him campaign throughout 2007 and 2008, I'd had mixed feelings about how he'd dealt with those who attacked him politically and labeled him a "Marxist" or a "racist" or called him other derogatory names. Sometimes, I wanted him to drop his politeness and give criticism back as harshly as he'd received it, but in the back of my mind was Michelle's sense that he had enemies everywhere and might be surrounded by danger. Seeking the presidency in these circumstances was, to say the least, a delicate balance.

When Obama finally showed up that morning in Denver, tens of thousands of us were too far away to see him and the public address system was arranged so that his words collided and reverberated in the October sky, making them unintelligible. That didn't matter. The feeling in the air, one of unity and hope, was more important, as if the country might be able to come together at last after this election and heal old wounds, focus on public issues instead of personality differences, and rally around a new young president. For half an hour on that Sunday morning, it was easy to forget that other Americans were attending rallies expressing their hatred of Obama by shouting, "Kill him! Kill him!" Or that two racist skinheads had just been taken into custody in Tennessee and charged with an alleged plot to murder more than a hundred black Americans—intending to behead some of them—and to assassinate Obama.

Three months later, during the inauguration ceremony in Washington, D.C., the nation's positive feelings toward the president-elect were on full display, as hundreds of thousands of people had traveled across the country and were standing out in the bitter cold to celebrate the swearing-in of the first African-American president. The *New York Times* columnist Gail Collins giddily described the event as "Woodstock without the mud." Regardless of where one stood politically, maybe reconciliation and congressional bipartisanship really could become a reality. The nation was ensnared in two long-running wars and its worst economic implosion in decades. Millions of people had lost their jobs and millions more would soon be out of work, setting off tremors of a total collapse and another Great Depression. For months, financial analysts had been laying out the many intricacies and complexities of the monetary crisis, while searching for solutions.

Bashing the U.S. government had long ago become a lucrative career on the country's airwaves: anyone who relied on public money was dependent, weak, and unable to compete in the marketplace. Now citizens from Wall Street to Main Street, starting with the executives running the housing, auto, and banking industries, turned to the only place they could—the federal government—to help their companies, their families, and themselves. The feds, supported by both Republicans and Democrats, provided them with hundreds of billions of dollars in bailouts, an imperfect solution to a perfect mess. Was this crisis enough to make Americans give up the "us versus them" mentality and work in unison for the greater good? Was it time for the United States, facing dire challenges from every angle, to start pulling itself together instead of apart? One striking answer came four days before the inauguration.

According to a 2001 article in *U.S. News and World Report*, the syndicated radio talk show host Rush Limbaugh had an eight-year radio contract worth $31.25 million a year. On July 2, 2008, Matt Drudge, the creator and editor of the Internet news service the *Drudge Report*, stated online that Limbaugh had signed a new contract extension through 2016, worth over $400 million, breaking all records for any broadcast medium. Six months later, on January 16, 2009, Limbaugh read a letter on his program about a request he'd just received from a national print media outlet. Could he could send them four hundred words on his hope for the Obama presidency?

"I don't need four hundred words," he said on the air. "I need four: I hope he fails . . . What is unfair about my saying I hope liberalism fails? Liberalism is our problem. Liberalism is what's gotten us dangerously close to the precipice here."

(One year after public monies were provided to keep key American industries alive, an independent panel overseeing this process concluded that the program "can be credited with stopping an economic panic").

Hearing Limbaugh call for Obama's failure *before* he became president, with the country in the midst of a financial disaster and countless other challenges, evoked a feeling I had trouble identifying at first. Then it hit me: it was ten years ago and I was back at Columbine High School, watching parents and students kneel down in the mud and cry. We couldn't make eye contact or say anything to one another, because the collective shame at the school was larger and deeper than words. The undeniable truth had finally caught up with us. We'd allowed something to fester and grow, and now we all got to face the consequences and the pain of that indifference or neglect.

But Rush and his media allies were just entertainers, weren't they? What possible effect could all the name-calling have on the general population or the new president during a worldwide crisis? The radio talk show host Michael Savage called the president "a naked Marxist," while Glenn Beck said that America was moving "towards a totalitarian state" and the country now reminded him of the "early days of Adolf Hitler."

In February 2009, as the Obamas were settling into the White House, the Southern Poverty Law Center in Montgomery, Alabama, issued its latest *Intelligence Report*, detailing the current growth of hate groups in the United States, whose numbers had increased by more than 50 percent since 2000 and were expanding once again. The SPLC attributed this rise to fears about nonwhite immigration, but underscored that the election of a black man to the Oval Office was another major factor. The continuing economic meltdown was a third cause, because many blamed this on racial minorities and undocumented Latino immigrants. When the study came out, it initially got little attention, especially compared to the ongoing statements of Limbaugh or Glenn Beck. On March 3, Beck appeared on Fox TV's *Fox and Friends* and said that he wanted to dispel reports that under the Obama presidency the Federal Emergency Management Administration was building secret concentration camps for Americans.

"We are a country that is headed toward socialism, totalitarianism, beyond your wildest imagination," Beck said on the air. "I have to tell you, I am doing a story tonight, that I wanted to debunk these FEMA camps. I'm tired of hearing about them . . . Well we've now for several days been doing research on them—I can't debunk them! And we're going to carry the story tonight . . ."

In December 2008, a month after the presidential election, Amber Cummings, who shot her husband to death in Belfast, Maine, told authorities that James Cummings was "very upset" with Obama's recent win. He'd been in touch with white supremacist groups and had talked about building a "dirty bomb" filled with deadly radioactive materials. When searching Cummings's home, police found components for making that bomb and an application to the neo-Nazi National Socialist Movement, filled out by the dead man. His wife, who served no jail time for the shooting, explained that for years he'd subjected her to mental, physical, and sexual abuse. The day after Obama's inauguration, Keith Luke, a white man in Brockton, Massachusetts, allegedly murdered two black people and planned to kill as many Jews as he could on that same night. Police said he'd been reading white supremacist Web sites, fearful that the Caucasian race was facing genocide.

On March 24, Private First Class Nicholas Daniel Hanke and Kody Brittingham, a former lance corporal now out of the Marine Corps, were charged with making threats against President Obama. In early April, a gunman in Pittsburgh, Richard Poplawski, allegedly killed three police officers. Internet postings by Poplawski showed that he was motivated by racist and anti-Semitic ideology—believing that Zionists were running the world. The postings also revealed anti-government conspiracy theories and the belief that President Obama would pass restrictive gun laws. A New Mexico elementary school teacher, sixty-one-year-old Ellen Wood, was strangled to death as her alleged assailants shouted anti-Semitic slurs at her.

Hate crimes had risen slightly in 2008, with 7,783 incidents and 9,691 victims, including individuals, businesses, and institutions. While statistics were not yet available for early 2009, the violence reported since the election of Barack Obama had generated concern within the

Department of Homeland Security. Three days after the tragedy in Pittsburgh, the DHS issued a report entitled, "Rightwing Extremism: Current Economic and Political Climate Fueling Resurgence in Radicalization and Recruitment." The DHS document reflected many of the conclusions of the Southern Poverty Law Center two months earlier, warning of the dangers of right-wing extremists in the U.S. military and other groups who might "attempt to recruit and radicalize returning [military] veterans . . .

"The consequences of a prolonged economic downturn—including real estate foreclosures, unemployment, and an inability to obtain credit—could create a fertile recruiting environment for rightwing extremists and even result in confrontations between such groups and government authorities similar to those in the past . . .

"Rightwing extremists have capitalized on the election of the first African American president, and are focusing their efforts to recruit new members, mobilize existing supporters, and broaden their scope and appeal through propaganda . . . The current economic and political climate has some similarities to the 1990s when rightwing extremism experienced a resurgence fueled largely by an economic recession, criticism about the outsourcing of jobs, and the perceived threat to U.S. power and sovereignty by other foreign powers."

The DHS document was met with indignation and outrage from GOP politicians and right-wing pundits, who saw it as an attack on conservatives and veterans. The outcry was so strong that Secretary Janet Napolitano felt compelled to apologize to veterans' organizations, but that wasn't enough for some. The Republican Party chairman, Michael Steele, called the report the "height of insult" and the televangelist and former presidential candidate Pat Robertson said that it "shows somebody down in the bowels of that organization is either a convinced left winger or somebody whose sexual orientation is somewhat in question."

Two weeks after the report was released, Joshua Cartwright allegedly shot to death two Okaloosa County, Florida, sheriff's deputies who'd responded to a domestic disturbance call. Authorities said that Cartwright was interested in militia groups, and his wife told police that he was "severely disturbed" by Obama's election.

In the mid-1980s, when Morris Dees was running the Southern Poverty Law Center, he'd been on a hit list put together by the Order in the buildup to killing Alan Berg. Unlike Berg, Dees had survived. In 2009, after the SPLC released its new report, I called Mark Potok, who now headed the organization. With the election of President Obama, he said, the country had entered a cycle that reminded him of the early Clinton administration years, with the inferno at Waco and the prelude to the Oklahoma City bombing.

"In the mid-1990s, the militia movement got bigger and bigger, then peaked in about 1996," Potok said. "Besides Oklahoma City, there were forty or fifty other major domestic terror plots out there that didn't happen. They wanted to blow up a natural gas refinery outside of Fort Worth and kill thirty thousand people. All this caused a real crackdown by law enforcement, who began arresting militia members on weapons violations and giving them seven- or eight-year sentences. That had a real effect and the movement eventually ran out of steam.

"It started to pick back up again after 2000 over the immigration issue. During the next few years, we saw two to three hundred new groups emerge, with people going down to the Mexican border and patrolling it with their own weapons. We don't list these as hate groups, but then the actual hate groups also started talking about immigration, not race. They went whole hog on immigration, saying that it was going to destroy America. In 2000, we had 602 hate groups. By 2008, we had 926.

"We saw seven or eight straight years of hate-group growth driven by immigration, until early 2009. With the falling economy and the rise of Obama, new issues came into play. David Duke [the 'white nationalist' and former Grand Wizard of the Knights of the Ku Klux Klan, former Republican Louisiana state representative, and former presidential candidate] wrote an essay before the election. He said that if Obama won, this would be a visual aid to wake up white America. On November 5, 2008, the day after the presidential election, some white supremacist Web sites crashed from all the activity and concern. Then Obama comes into office and all the racial violence starts. What we have here is a perfect storm for these hate groups to grow. The enemy in the White House has a black face and that brings together a lot of different aspects of the movement. They can all agree on at least one thing—the country's going to hell in a handbasket and the black guy is leading us there.

"It's like the 1990s, except that the media commentators who aid and abet *these* groups, like Lou Dobbs and Glenn Beck and Sean Hannity, are in the mainstream. In the 1990s, radio personalities sympathetic to the militias might reach fifty thousand listeners. Michael Savage now speaks to eight million people a week. There's a lot going on out there. The militias are back in the woods training again, carrying their guns and doing maneuvers. We've just had a whole new security makeover at our office because we're getting a lot more threats."

# XXXI

In early April 2009, the Kansas City FBI office received an anonymous letter warning that a Scott Roeder "would do physical harm" to Dr. George Tiller, or any other abortion provider. The letter's author was Mark Archer, the husband of Sue Archer, with whom Roeder had fathered a child back in 2001. The couple lived in Tunkhannock, Pennsylvania, and was raising the young girl, Olivia. Before writing the letter, Mark had created what he called a "psychological profile" of the suspect based upon Roeder's blog postings, arrest history, and some things he'd said to Sue in Pennsylvania in 2008 when he'd come out to see his daughter. The couple was still involved in a custody battle with Roeder over Olivia, and the purpose of Mark's letter was to get the FBI to place Roeder on a domestic terrorist "no-fly" list so that he couldn't travel to Pennsylvania that spring and visit the seven-year-old girl. According to the FBI, the anonymous letter did not contain a specific or credible threat, so the feds didn't conduct surveillance on Roeder and he made the trip east. Word of the letter was passed along to the clinic in Wichita, but it wasn't unusual enough to draw much attention.

In early May 2009, about a month after Dr. Tiller's acquittal, WHCS was vandalized once again, as it had been numerous times since the 1970s. Somebody snipped the wires to the security cameras and outdoor lights. They cut holes in the roof and plugged the building's downspouts—rain poured in through the openings and caused thousands of dollars of damage to the office. Tiller reported the incident to the FBI and asked the feds to investigate, but no arrests were made. According to a 2008 National Clinic Violence survey conducted by the Feminist Majority Foundation, when federal laws were not applied strenuously in these circumstances, and when death threats were ignored and protesters were allowed to photograph or videotape patients arriving at women's health clinics, the reported rate of violence tripled.

In mid-May, Tiller called Dr. Susan Hill of North Carolina, the president of the National Women's Health Foundation, which operated reproductive health clinics in areas where abortion services were scarce or nonexistent. For many years, Hill and Tiller had provided long-distance support for each other, and he also communicated regularly with Warren Hern in Boulder. The three of them, along with Dr. LeRoy Carhart of Nebraska, made up the remaining old-guard physicians still willing to face the dangers of their profession. Once, when Dr. Hill had been desperate to assist a patient, she'd phoned the "doctor of last resort" in Wichita. A nine-year-old girl from a small Southern town had been raped by her father and was eighteen weeks pregnant. Birthing the baby would severely damage her small body. No area doctor or hospital would help the girl, but Tiller told Hill he'd take the patient for free. After performing the abortion, he kept her in Wichita for three days until she was able to return home safely.

When he called Dr. Hill that May, she told him that she'd recently been threatened by an abortion protester who'd shown up on her doorstep late at night. An image of the man could be found on the Internet, kissing an AK-47. She'd reported this to the feds and local police, but hadn't heard back from them. Tiller asked her to send him pictures of those who'd been harassing her. New waves of demonstrators had been showing up at WHCS, and to him this signaled a general uptick in anti-abortion activity. Hill agreed and wondered aloud why Tiller didn't retire while he still had time to enjoy his good health and family. He gave her the same answer he'd given a few weeks earlier in the courtroom: he wasn't a quitter and couldn't stop serving the women who came to him, because many had nowhere else to go. Drs. Hill and Tiller weren't the only ones thinking about the abortion issue. On Sunday, May 17, President Obama delivered the commencement address at Notre Dame University, with some at the Catholic school protesting his appearance and pro-choice beliefs. On the campus, the president addressed head-on the underlying war that had separated Americans for so long.

"The question, then, is how do we work through these conflicts? Is it possible for us to join hands in common effort? . . . How does each of us remain firm in our principles, and fight for what we consider right, without demonizing those with just as strongly held convictions on the other side? Nowhere do these questions come up more powerfully than on the issue of abortion . . .

"A few days after I won the Democratic nomination, I received an e-mail from a doctor who told me that while he voted for me in the primary, he had a serious concern that might prevent him from voting for me in the general election. He described himself as a Christian who was strongly pro-life, but that's not what was preventing him from voting for me. What bothered the doctor was an entry that my campaign staff had posted on my Web site—an entry that said I would fight 'right-wing ideologues who want to take away a woman's right to choose.' The doctor said that he had assumed I was a reasonable person, but that if I truly believed that every pro-life individual was simply an ideologue who wanted to inflict suffering on women, then I was not very reasonable. He wrote, 'I do not ask at this point that you oppose abortion, only that you speak about this issue in fair-minded words.' Fair-minded words.

"After I read the doctor's letter, I wrote back to him and thanked him. I didn't change my position, but I did tell my staff to change the words on my Web site. And I said a prayer that night that I might extend the same presumption of good faith to others that the doctor had extended to me. Because when we do that . . . that's when we discover at least the possibility of common ground. That's when we begin to say, 'Maybe we won't agree on abortion, but we can still agree that this is a heart-wrenching decision for any woman to make, with both moral and spiritual dimensions.'

"So let's work together to reduce the number of women seeking abortions by reducing unintended pregnancies, and making adoption more available, and providing care and support for women who do carry their child to term. Let's honor the conscience of those who disagree with abortion, and draft a sensible conscience clause, and make sure that all of our health care policies are grounded in clear ethics and sound science, as well as respect for the equality of women.

"Understand—I do not suggest that the debate surrounding abortion can or should go away. No matter how much we may want to fudge it—indeed, while we know that the views of most Americans on the subject are complex and even contradictory—the fact is that at some level, the views of the two camps are irreconcilable. Each side will continue to make its case to the public with passion and conviction. But surely we can do so without reducing those with differing views to caricature. Open hearts. Open minds. Fair-minded words."


In mid-May, as Obama went to Notre Dame, Phill Kline sent out a brochure mentioning Dr. Tiller and asking the former attorney general's supporters to help pay off his $200,000 in personal legal debt. The money would also assist the Life Issues Institute in Cincinnati in launching more aggressive anti-abortion "battles on the national front." While contending that he'd acted in good faith to his duty and oath of office, his opponents "must silence the truth by silencing the messenger; and to date, I am the only one who has been willing to speak the truth."

On May 21, Ann Coulter responded to the president's South Bend speech by unleashing a rant on AnnCoulter.com. Instead of having a constitutional lawyer (like Obama) drone on and on about the "purported constitutional right [to an abortion]," Coulter suggested, why not enact an abortion itself? Why not have the Notre Dame marching band form "a giant skull-piercing fork" and end the life of an infant? Or have the president throw the "ceremonial first fetus," instead of the ball chief executives toss out on opening day of the baseball season? Or maybe Notre Dame could get "famed partial-birth abortion practitioner George Tiller to do the demonstration at next year's graduation." And the Obama administration could give him a hand with the procedure, since Tiller was such a close friend of the Health and Human Services secretary, Kathleen Sebelius.

"This," Coulter concluded, "is a 'constitutional right' like no other."

# XXXII

On Monday, May 18, Roeder drove the roughly forty miles from Kansas City to Lawrence and went into Jayhawk Pawn & Jewelry, where he said that he needed a gun for self-defense. He picked out a semiautomatic PT .22-caliber pistol, worth $229.99, but couldn't take it with him because the store, in conjunction with the Bureau of Alcohol, Tobacco and Firearms, had to follow standard procedure and run a background check on the buyer. In 1996, Roeder had been arrested in Topeka for the criminal use of explosives, but the Kansas Court of Appeals had overturned his conviction, ruling that the police had conducted an illegal search when seizing evidence from his car. In mid-May 2009, the ATF's examination of Roeder uncovered no red flags from his past, but he had to wait a day for this process to be completed. He didn't immediately go back to Lawrence to pick up his new gun, but on May 20 he stopped by the Bullet Hole in Overland Park to buy two boxes of ammunition.

On Saturday, May 23, a tall, balding, middle-aged man was caught on videotape vandalizing the Central Family Medicine office, where abortions were performed, near downtown Kansas City. With the clinic closed for the weekend, he'd glued shut the locks on the doors, a violation of federal law. Following the 1993 murder of the Florida doctor David Gunn, President Clinton had urged Congress to pass the

FACE (Freedom of Access to Clinics) Act, making it a crime to block access to medical facilities. Congress had complied and the Clinton administration had prosecuted thirty-six individuals under this law, which was used on only about half as many suspects during the presidency of George W. Bush. Central Family Medicine had captured a blurred image of the vandal on tape and passed it along to the authorities. Clinic workers could see enough of the man's features to identify him as somebody named "Scott," who'd been coming there for years to meet with others and protest.

Back in 2000, he'd twice glued the locks shut with superglue and the clinic had also gotten his picture back then, but the FBI said it was too fuzzy to make a positive identification. On that occasion, the Central Family Medicine office manager Jeffrey Pederson had jotted down the man's license plate number and given it to the feds, who'd promised to speak with him. For several years the man had left the clinic alone, before showing up in 2006, standing around on the sidewalk and talking with others. By then, the authorities had lost interest in him. After the May 23, 2009, incident, Pederson filed another report with the Kansas City, Kansas, police and again contacted the FBI.

That Saturday afternoon, Roeder drove to Lawrence in his powder blue 1993 Ford Taurus and returned to Jayhawk Pawn & Jewelry to pick up his new gun and some Remington hollow-point cartridges. From Lawrence he took back roads south through farm country because he preferred the scenery and dealing with less traffic—and was committed to avoiding paying the $3.50 toll on the Kansas Turnpike. He headed to Wichita and found a cheap motel, the Starlite, located on the business artery known as both Highway 54 and Kellogg Street, just a few blocks from Tiller's clinic and a few miles from the doctor's church.

The next morning, Roeder attended the 10 a.m. service at Reformation Lutheran, a modern-looking redbrick structure made up of various angles and many windows, positioned to create a sense of open space and to let a maximum amount of sunlight into the sanctuary. Entering the foyer, he carried a worn Bible and a concealed handgun inside his shopworn clothes, the slacks a touch short and the shirt collar frayed. In the foyer, he glanced around at the ushers handing out programs to worshippers. A long table near one wall offered juice and coffee, and several members of the congregation were gathered beside it, chatting among themselves. Not seeing who he was looking for, he walked on through the foyer and into the sanctuary. Toward the rear, he sat down by himself on an aisle and searched the pews, studying the faces, up one row and down the next, confused and disappointed, not quite ready to give up. He stood, returned to the foyer, and went on to the restroom, before going back into the sanctuary.

His contacts in the anti-abortion movement had spent years tracking Tiller and his family and then passing the information along to others. They knew the doctor's weekly schedule and where he attended church, knew the Reformation Lutheran address and when the services were held. Roeder had scouted out the nearby streets and the asphalt parking lot next to the house of worship, which sat in a large undeveloped field in northeast Wichita, surrounded by untouched acres of grass. Because of its isolation, the church had a calm and peaceful aura, almost a rural feeling, especially when the trees and flowers and grass were in full bloom, as they were on this late May morning. The church seemed more than just a few blocks away from the exclusive Wichita Country Club, the clothing boutiques and pricey restaurants along Rock Road.

Adjacent to the church was a property owned by Charles Koch, whose father had founded Wichita's Koch Industries, the oil-refining empire that had become America's second-largest privately held company. Its annual revenues were estimated at $110 billion and, according to *Forbes* magazine, Charles and his brother David had a combined fortune worth $24 billion. The four Koch sons had tangled over ownership of the business, but the family as a whole was known for its archconservative politics. In 1980, David had run for vice president, alongside the Libertarian presidential candidate Ed Clark. Their ticket won 921,299 votes (or 1.06 percent), the most ever for that party.

In 2004, David Koch had started Americans for Prosperity, a Washington, D.C.–based advocacy group promoting the long-time mantra of the GOP's conservative wing: limited government, free markets, and less regulation on business. The organization was headed by Tim Phillips, a former partner in Century Strategies, which became well known after a Senate investigation suggested financial connections among the convicted lobbyist Jack Abramoff, Century Strategies, and Americans for Tax Reform. With the coming of the Obama administration, David Koch and Americans for Prosperity were gearing up to fight the new president and the Democratic agenda, particularly health care reform. Koch had virtually unlimited funds for such activities.

By early 2009, AFP had become the guiding hand behind the "Tea Party" protests about to sweep across the nation. On February 27, AFP launched its opposition to Obama by sponsoring a tea party in the Dallas–Fort Worth area. In May, AFP started Patients United Now, whose purpose was to resist government involvement in the American health care system, including public funding for abortion.

From previous surveillance, Roeder understood that people entering Reformation Lutheran on Sunday mornings didn't use the large double doors at the main entrance but came in through the smaller foyer. He knew that throughout May 2009 Dr. Tiller was scheduled to be one of six ushers handing out programs in the foyer between 9:30 and 10:00 a.m. The service began at ten sharp, but the ushers tended to linger in the foyer before coming into the sanctuary, as a few people usually wandered in late and needed a program. What Roeder didn't know was that on this Sunday, May 24, Tiller was on vacation at Disney World in Orlando, Florida, doing what Susan Hill had suggested he do and getting away from the clinic for a week, spending time with wife and children and grandchildren, taking in the sun, and reading escapist novels.

Upset that he'd driven to Wichita and spent a night in a motel for nothing, Roeder decided to stay for the service and settled into his pew, checking out the congregation. These weren't the kind of real Christians engaged in the in-depth religious study he was accustomed to. These were Sunday Christians who dropped by the sanctuary once a week to sing a few hymns and put a few dollars into the collection plate, but they didn't think much about Yahweh or Yahshua on the other six days. His old Bible, he was certain, had been thumbed far more than theirs. What did these people really stand for, if they weren't willing to stop the evil unfolding just a couple of miles away at Tiller's clinic? Why would they let such a man be a member of their church? Did they have any Christian convictions at all?

When the collection plate came around, he showed them his attitude by placing a handwritten note on top of the money.

"Do you believe in taxes?" it read.

A pair of ushers noticed the foreign object in the plate, and that the bald stranger hadn't mingled with the other worshippers, and that his Sunday morning clothes were shabby and didn't fit on his large frame, but nobody commented much about it. The church, like so many others in Wichita and other locales, was a friendly and welcoming place, despite the anti-abortion protesters who'd gathered outside in years past and come inside to disrupt a communion service or yell at the children attending Sunday school. Maybe the man was down on his luck and had needed the comfort of church today. Folks at Reformation Lutheran wanted to think the best of others and gave him the benefit of their doubts. And because Dr. Tiller had convinced church authorities that they didn't need a security system, Roeder's gun went undetected. When the service was over, he retraced his route to Kansas City, stopping for kefir near Lawrence and reporting to his job at the Quicksilver airport shuttle service.

The following week, Roeder called Eddie Ebecher, an activist in the Kansas City area who went by the name "Wolfgang Anacon." Ebecher had protested with Roeder at anti-abortion rallies, including one at Tiller's clinic, and the men had once lived together. When Roeder phoned him in late May, he seemed out of sorts and edgy, complaining about the movement's inability to stop abortion in Kansas and the rest of America. He mentioned a few of his regrets and casually hinted that he was going to miss certain people. Roeder called his brother, David, who lived in a rural area west of Topeka, a perfect spot for what Scott had in mind. He asked if he could come over and see David that Friday afternoon, the twenty-ninth, but the man was busy so they rescheduled. Roeder then made plans for an evening out with his now-twenty-two-year-old son, Nicholas.

Roeder rigorously observed Shabbat, the Jewish Sabbath, as a day of rest extending from sundown Friday until sundown Saturday, but to-night he was making an exception because he wanted to be with Nick. The young man often dodged his father's calls or failed to respond to his messages, but Scott was insistent about getting together on this par-ticular Friday; he'd offered an extra enticement by inviting Nick to a movie he was eager to see. Throughout the day, Roeder contacted his son several times to make certain they were still on and also called Lindsey, telling her to get home as fast as possible and take over the care of her ninety-year-old father, so Nick could leave the house sooner.

The two of them went to an inexpensive restaurant, watched *Star Trek*, and then lingered over ice cream, Nick noticing that his dad wasn't in any hurry to part tonight. Roeder had always wanted his son to know who he was and why he had such strong political and religious convictions. Nick had his own questions about God, but kept a lot of things to himself, not entirely sure yet what he believed about faith and not ready to speak his mind openly to his father. There was no rush; they had time for those discussions. Nick still thought of his dad as a nonviolent man who wouldn't hurt a bird or a bug. Mostly he let his companion talk and Roeder again shared his thoughts on the issues critical to him, as he'd been doing ever since Nick was a small child. Scott wished his son were different in some ways, and more like him. The young man hurt his feelings on occasion by refusing to take his calls or being ungrateful. He wished he wasn't so influenced by his mother and had more of his own values and showed more appreciation for the things Roeder had done for him over the years, but this wasn't the moment to dwell on that. He'd always wanted to be close to his son, especially now.

As they sat together talking in the falling darkness, Nick didn't observe anything out of the ordinary about his father, not until later on, when he looked back on this Friday evening and scoured every corner of his mind for clues. Something unspoken had passed between the two of them over their ice cream, conveyed with a gesture or a glance or a pause in the conversation—Roeder seemed to be saying good-bye.

# XXXIII

On Saturday morning, May 30, Roeder arose very early and at 5:45 drove back to the Central Family Medicine clinic, but this time he wasn't alone at the office. As he stood in the parking lot and prepared to glue shut the locks, a female employee awaited him inside. When he approached the back door, she ran out and chased after him. Lumbering to his car, he glanced over his shoulder and echoed the words of Bill O'Reilly and many others in the anti-abortion movement, calling the woman a "baby killer." She got a close look at him, his car, and his license plate.

Since the clinic had been vandalized last Saturday, her boss, Jeffrey Pederson, had upgraded the video surveillance equipment and this time it had captured clearer pictures of the man. The woman went into the office and called Pederson at home. He phoned the FBI with the car's make and number: a 1990s powder blue Ford Taurus, Kansas plate 225 BAB. The feds said they'd set up a time to come in and interview his staff about the vandal.

As the sun rose over Kansas City, Roeder drove out of town west and headed for Lawrence, laying out his plans for the rest of the day. At 8:45, he parked next to Jayhawk Pawn & Jewelry and stood in front of the locked door, determined to be first in line when the store opened at nine. A few other men showed up and they all traded small talk and jokes on this beautiful late spring morning, before Roeder stepped into the shop and began looking at boxes of ammunition. He told the manager, Jeff Neal, that he used his gun for target practice, and Neal explained that the five-inch-long PT .22 could take either high-velocity or low-velocity ammo. Low-velocity bullets were quieter and less likely to disturb neighbors, but the firearm couldn't be used in semiautomatic mode without high-velocity ammunition, in case he wanted to shoot multiple rounds without reloading. Roeder bought a box of each.

Leaving Lawrence, he drove across the modest hills of the Kansas countryside, its acres in full bloom by late May, its fertile bottomland filled with stands of cottonwood and rows of grain. Pulling into Topeka, he drove to his old neighborhood, passing up and down the streets of his youth and remembering the people in each of the houses, thinking about the mother of one of his childhood friends, and the father of another. He paused in front of the home of a former Cub Scout leader, recalling the boys in his pack and the good times they'd had together when he was small, before he was sent off to that mental hospital and forced to take drugs. A few people were out on their lawns doing yard work, stirring more memories. He wanted to stay here longer and keep reminiscing, but he was on a schedule.

His brother, David, lived on the western outskirts of Topeka. The two of them didn't spend that much time together anymore, but Scott had to see him today. David knew that his brother had very strong religious views and opinions about abortion, so in recent years the family had tried to bypass those subjects with him. It just led to arguments and strain, and no one ever changed his or her mind. When Scott arrived at David's, he seemed a bit hyperactive or manic. He hadn't gotten a lot of sleep the night before—it was best not to rile him up and to talk about other things.

David and his wife, Karen, had a home on an impressive country spread set back 150 yards from the nearest county road and protected by a gate. David's living conditions were strikingly different from the cramped apartments and hovels his brother had occasionally plopped down in, when he could hardly make ends meet. The brothers were different in many ways, but shared a common interest in firearms. In recent months, Scott had pawned the 9-millimeter handgun he'd taken into Tiller's church the summer before, but David had bought it out of pawn to keep for himself. When Scott arrived, he showed off his new PT .22 and suggested going into the surrounding woods to shoot some rounds. The two men walked out to the tall grass and forest, where Scott fired thirty or forty bullets into the ground and a streambed and a rotting old log, before the .22 jammed.

In separate cars, they drove to the High Plains Gun Shop in Topeka and spoke with employee Rex Campbell. Scott asked about buying some steel bullets, but Campbell said they didn't make them for this particular weapon and the gun had malfunctioned because Roeder was using the wrong ammunition. While recommending a longer Winchester rifle cartridge, he closely examined the PT .22. It was dirty and "dry," badly in need of oil. He gave it a few squirts, pulled the tape off the grip so it fit better in the hand, and made a few other adjustments, tightening up a few parts parts of the firearm. As David stood in the background, Scott meticulously questioned Campbell about the ammunition that was compatible with the .22, while keeping a running total of every penny he was spending. He bought a small can of oil and a couple of boxes of bullets, including some hollow-point Winchesters. In the parking lot of the gun store, he said good-bye to his brother and drove off alone.

Scott had told several people that he was returning to Westport this evening for a five o'clock meeting with his cohorts, but when he left Topeka he didn't head east back toward Kansas City, but south on Highway 75, wending his way over the two-lane roads leading down to Wichita. During the past week, he'd thought about changing his license plate, or obscuring the letters and numbers, but in the end he hadn't bothered doing that. Once or twice this afternoon, he stopped alongside the isolated road and got out and fired a few rounds into a ditch, to make sure that the gun was working smoothly and wouldn't jam again.

Arriving in Wichita, he went to Reformation Lutheran for the 5:30 p.m. Saturday service, pulling into the uncrowded church lot, holding his Bible in one hand and stuffing the PT .22 into his pocket. In the foyer, he looked around for Dr. Tiller, searching the hallways and the bathroom and then the sanctuary, feeling a rush of frustration, doubt. Was Tiller sick or just on a very long vacation? Was he even a member of the congregation anymore?

This evening, the church was holding a special ceremony, conducted in Swahili to celebrate Pentecostal weekend. Pastor Kristin Neitzel, one of two ministers at Reformation Lutheran, was in charge of the service and only about fifty people were in attendance, all of them sitting together in just a few pews. Any stranger was bound to stand out more now than on Sunday mornings, when hundreds showed up. Roeder walked into the sanctuary and scanned the rows for the mop of short brown hair and the bespectacled face he'd seen so many times before on wanted posters, on anti-abortion material, and on the Internet. Kansans for Life had recently published a spring 2009 pamphlet with Tiller's picture on the cover, and the lead story had complained about how he'd been acquitted at his trial with the help of "traveling abortionist" Kristin Neuhaus.

Pastor Neitzel noticed the tall, balding stranger, his presence setting off a dim memory. In the late summer or early fall of 2008, ushers had spotted this same man sitting in their church off by himself, and they'd brought him to the pastor's attention. He didn't seem to fit in and might be trouble or cause the kinds of disruptions Reformation Lutheran had seen inside its sanctuary in years past. Pastor Neitzel had never forgotten about him.

Not finding Tiller among the congregation, Roeder stayed only briefly before standing and walking out through the foyer. Pastor Neitzel went over to the pew where he'd been and sat down. She saw an offering envelope with scribbling on it—something about whether Reformation Lutheran was organized under the 5013C tax code. She left the sanctuary and went out into the foyer, staring through a window at the man, who was crossing the parking lot and getting into a light blue Ford with a front license plate featuring the purple wildcat logo of Kansas State University, up the road a few hours in Manhattan. On the car's rear end was the evangelical fish symbol that in recent decades had become so popular.

Roeder cruised around the east side of Wichita before checking into the Garden Inn and Suites on the Kellogg corridor, just a few blocks from the Starlite Motel, where he'd stayed the week before. He paid in cash, because he didn't believe in credit cards and the computerized trail of numbers they left behind. Using a coupon that dropped the price from $56.14 to $39.29, he also paid the clerk the mandatory $25 overnight deposit for his room. After settling in and trying out the king-size bed, he got back in his car and rode through the streets, thinking about tomorrow and the fastest routes through the city. He ate a cheap dinner and returned to the Garden Inn, waiting for darkness. He put on his pajamas, lay down, and switched on the television, moving through the stations and looking for something to hold his attention, stopping on the History Channel because he liked stories about real people who'd done difficult and important things—things that had altered the direction of history and echoed through generations and made a difference.

For more than thirty years, starting in the mid-1970s, Wichita had been at the heart of America's battle over abortion, but nothing had ever been resolved or really changed. People from across the nation had come here and clashed in the streets and the courtrooms, lying flat on the sidewalks, going off to jail and making speech after speech, fighting one another through the media and then on the Internet. Bombing Tiller's clinic, shooting him in the arms, sending him death threats—none of these had had any effect on the man. He was still going to work all week and doing what he'd always done, in the safety of his walled-in office. Everyone in the movement knew about his armored car and bulletproof vest. Everyone knew that he was the most prominent and busiest abortion doctor in the country, if not the world. In 2008, 10,642 abortions had been performed in Kansas and 5,131 of the pregnant women had come there from out of state, most of them to Wichita.

Nothing had stopped them from making these choices, despite the tireless efforts of Operation Rescue and other anti-abortion groups. Roeder had given these organizations his money, his time and energy, his emotional support and patience and hope. He'd consulted with people enough and sought their opinions, he'd had enough inner debates. He'd talked it over with the woman from Operation Rescue until he didn't want to talk anymore. Ending abortion was a matter of being in accordance with God's law, not man's, and this was what God and those in the movement wanted him to do.

Lying in bed, he was certain that if he completed the mission, the anti-abortion groups would step up and support him the way he'd supported them. They'd regard him as a hero, someone who'd changed the course of history. Then he drifted off and slept so soundly that he overslept. By the time he'd awakened, cleaned up, dressed, and gone to the front desk to collect his $25 deposit, it was nearly 9:30. He wasn't that concerned. The woman behind the desk, Sandy Michael, was standing outside smoking a cigarette, but he told her to finish it before taking care of him.

She was struck by how relaxed and happy-go-lucky the man seemed. A lot of people these days were pushy.

"Take your time," Roeder told her. "I can wait."

It wasn't until he was in his car that he remembered that church started at 10:00, not 10:30, and he barely had time to get over to Reformation Lutheran before the ushers dimmed the lights for the opening of the service.

# XXXIV

For the past half hour, traffic had been steadily turning into the church parking lot, but as ten approached it was winding down. Nearly all the worshippers had entered the foyer, received a program from an usher, and taken a seat on the red pews. At the front of the sanctuary was a lectern from where sermons were delivered, and behind the lectern rose a high brick wall featuring red peace banners and a large golden cross. To one side, the choir loft was elevated above the pews. Jeanne Tiller had come to church early today for choir practice, while her husband had driven another car. On this perfect May morning on the last day of the month, people exchanged nods and hellos, smiles and handshakes. In some ways, they came to church for this feeling as much as anything else, this sense of community and belonging to something larger than themselves, and being able to look forward to an hour of peace and worship before starting a new week.

No one paid much attention to the tall, bald man sitting on the aisle in a rear pew and holding a worn Bible, with a distant air that was neither open nor friendly. He wore a tattered white shirt, dark slacks, and black shoes. On previous Sundays a couple of ushers had unsuccessfully tried to start up conversations with him, but he only wanted to talk about the relationship among churches, taxes, and the federal government. One congregant, Dr. Paul Ryding, a local veterinarian who specialized in caring for horses, thought that the man wasn't there to join in the singing and the prayer. He never put money in the collection plate or signed the guest book. He wore "high-water pants" and he'd once given off a very strong, unpleasant odor. At the same time, he hadn't caused any disruptions inside the church, so why not leave him alone? He might eventually warm up and become a Reformation Lutheran member.

A few minutes earlier, Roeder had parked in the crowded lot—backing into the space, so his rear wheels were up against the curb. He'd entered the foyer and searched for Tiller, who was supposed to be handing out programs but once again wasn't there. Roeder eyed the hallways, before going into the sanctuary and taking a seat. Turning his neck and shifting around, his gaze moved along the rows of pews and up toward the choir loft—Jeanne Tiller was present, but where was her husband? This was the third service in a row Roeder had come to and not found him. Had someone tipped off the physician that Roeder would be in the church this morning?

He stood, exited the sanctuary, and walked to the restroom, carrying his Bible in front of him. For a moment, he thought about bolting before things got started—he didn't want to sit through another hour of Lutheran rituals and a sermon—but decided to return to the pews. As he sat down and glanced over his shoulder, Tiller stuck his head in through a doorway leading into the sanctuary and disappeared back inside the foyer.

Roeder jumped up.

The church was full today because of the Festival of Pentecost, about to be celebrated with a special prelude of international music. A baptism ceremony was scheduled, along with the welcoming of new worshippers into the congregation. Jeanne Tiller and her choir mates were ready to perform the chosen hymns. The trim, short-haired blonde had a good-enough voice to have become a professional singer, but she'd stayed home and spent the past forty-five years raising four children and providing constant support and reassurance for her husband. He'd needed it more with every passing decade—in fact, just a few days earlier, he'd gotten another anonymous letter at the office.

"Somebody should kill you," it read, "so you can't kill anymore."

Reformation Lutheran was one of the very few places in Wichita where Dr. Tiller ever felt safe. In years past, he'd brought a bodyguard with him to the services, but then decided to stop.

At ten o'clock sharp, as the bells rang out from the nearby St. George Orthodox Church, Tiller and the usher Gary Hoepner were finishing up their duties in the foyer and getting ready to join the worshippers inside. Tiller had on a green suit and handsome, hand-tooled cowboy boots, with images of bald eagles stitched into the sides—a symbol of the doctor's patriotism. Hoepner, a white-haired, kindly looking man who did maintenance on the premises, had been a member of the congregation for fifty-two years. Another usher, Ken Hobart, dropped by to ask Tiller about his recent trip to Disney World, the doctor telling him how much fun he'd had in Florida with his grandchildren. A fourth usher, Keith Martin, was milling around the front of the church, near the large double doors at Reformation Lutheran's mostly unused main entrance. In recent months, the church had seen several car robberies during its Sunday morning service; Martin was studying the parking lot, looking for any suspicious movements. Waiting for stragglers to arrive, Tiller and Hoepner stood on opposite sides of a long "hospitality" table in the foyer, holding coffee and doughnuts. The men made small talk about the local breakfast places they enjoyed, while above their heads hung a smaller version of the red peace banner on display in the sanctuary.

Kathy Wegner and her eighteen-year-old daughter, Alison, came into the room and spoke to the men. Kathy was always raising money to help young people at the church, through bake sales, jewelry sales, and other activities. She had another sale planned for today in the foyer, once the service was finished. As Tiller and Hoepner chatted, the Wegners brought in boxes and set up their wares by a far wall. Hoepner briefly dimmed the sanctuary lights, to let everyone know church was starting, then wandered back to the coffee table and spoke with Tiller. Inside the sanctuary, Pastor Lowell Michelson began beating a darbuka drum, providing the rhythm for an African song called

"Celebrate the Journey!" As the sanctuary filled with the gathering sounds of music, Hoepner picked up a jelly roll from the table and took a bite. A side door leading into the sanctuary swung open.

A large bald man marched through it with his head lowered. Hoepner glanced up and remembered seeing him before—just last Sunday. At exactly this time a week ago, he'd come into the foyer carrying an old Bible, before moving down the hallway toward the restroom. His odd manner and weathered clothes had stayed with the usher. His clothing today was no better and he had the same worn Bible in his hand, but instead of going to the bathroom, he kept his head down and came straight toward Dr. Tiller, fumbling in his pocket.

"I was standing close enough to George to touch him," Hoepner later recalled. "The man had brought out a gun, but I wasn't sure if it was real. I saw his hand on the trigger. I saw the barrel go up to Dr. Tiller's head—very close. I heard a loud pop!—like a pop gun. George fell and I thought, Oh, my God! I stood there for a second and the man exited out through the foyer toward the parking lot. As he ran away, I heard him say something. I heard him say, 'Lord, forgive me.'"

Instinctively, Hoepner ran after him, bursting through the foyer door and out onto a patch of grass.

From the corner of her eye, Kathy Wegner had seen a flash and heard the pop. She glanced across the room and saw Tiller lying flat on his back. She saw Hoepner chasing a man through the door.

"Mama," Alison said, pointing at the figure sprawled on the foyer's gray carpet, "that's Dr. Tiller."

At first, Kathy thought he'd fallen down.

"Ali," she said, "you go help him up."

Her second thought, as she saw blood pooling around Tiller's head and realized he wasn't moving, was that she'd better find a telephone.

As Alison walked toward the body, Kathy ran a into a business office just off the foyer and dialed 911.

"Dr. George Tiller was just shot!" she yelled into the receiver, her breath coming hard.

"Dr. Tiller was shot?" the female dispatcher said.

"Yes!" her voice cracked. "I'm at church!"

"Who's the suspect?"

"I don't know!" she cried into the phone.

"Was he black, Hispanic, white?"

"White!"

"What was he wearing?"

"A white shirt and dark slacks!"

What else did she remember?

He was balding, Kathy said, with an "older man hairstyle."

Alison had approached Tiller and was standing over him, only five feet away.

Roeder sprinted toward the rows of cars at the rear of the parking lot, clutching the Bible to his chest and waving the pistol.

"I've got a gun," he shouted over his shoulder at Hoepner, "and I'll shoot you!"

Hoepner quit running and froze on the asphalt, thinking not so much about his own safety—he'd do anything to get his hands on the man who'd come into his church and shot Dr. Tiller—but about his aging wife. He didn't want to leave her a widow. He turned away and moved toward his truck, which he'd left near the foyer this morning so it would be handy for his maintenance chores. Reaching inside the cab, he grabbed his cell phone from under the seat and dialed 911, asking the dispatcher for police assistance and an ambulance.

Keith Martin was drinking coffee near the foyer entrance when he'd heard what must have been a firecracker—until he turned and saw Dr. Tiller lying on the carpet. Glancing out a window, Martin saw a large, bald-headed man angling through some parked cars, going toward the back of the lot. The usher saw Hoepner chasing after him, but then he stopped.

Martin dashed outside, carrying his half-full Styrofoam coffee cup.

"Get his license plate!" Hoepner shouted at Martin from beside his truck. "Get the number!"

Martin followed the man to his car, parked facing outward. The tall, rail-thin usher, a lawyer who'd been a member of the church for decades, came within a few yards of Roeder and stood in front of the pale blue vehicle, looking closely at the stranger. Martin remembered him from his previous church visits—recalling not so much his face or clothes or even his off-putting manner, but his piercing smell, harsh and chemical, which the usher once described as "terrible" and "unusually pungent." Months earlier, when Martin had first seen the man in church, the attorney had instantly been suspicious of him; maybe he was one of those anti-abortion protesters who'd disrupted their services in the past. He could even be the person who'd mailed Martin an ugly letter saying that because of his association with George Tiller, he was unfit to be a Sunday-school teacher and interact with children. But after seeing the man another time or two in the sanctuary, Martin changed his mind and chastised himself because the stranger had never done anything to interrupt the proceedings or harm the church. Martin felt bad about having passed judgment on him too quickly—an un-Christian thing to do.

The two men stared at each other over the hood of the Ford, and these memories and feelings came rushing back; Martin's gut had been right all along. The man hadn't just protested Dr. Tiller's presence at Reformation Lutheran this morning, as many others had. He'd done the worst thing possible, and done it inside their church in the midst of their Sunday service, violating and defiling the space where people came together for one hour a week to celebrate and pray.

"How could you do that?" Martin said.

"He's a murderer," Roeder calmly replied, opening the door of the Ford and sliding into the driver's seat. He started the engine. "Move."

Martin held his ground.

"Move!" Roeder raised the gun and aimed it at him. "Or I'll shoot you."

Martin hesitated, gazing down the barrel, wanting to do whatever was necessary to keep the man here until the police arrived, but not wanting to die.

He stepped aside.

Another elderly worshipper, Thornton Anderson, was late for this morning's service and had just parked his car in the rear of the lot. Stepping out of the vehicle, he heard Hoepner yelling from up near the front of the church, "Get the tag number! Get his license number!"

Anderson saw Keith Martin standing next to a blue Ford with a man behind the wheel. As the car pulled away, Anderson watched the usher throw his coffee cup into the open window and onto the driver.

The Ford passed close enough to Anderson to give him a good look at the Kansas plate: 225 BAB.

Roeder sped out through the lot and onto Thirteenth Street, a main traffic artery leading up to Rock Road or back toward downtown Wichita.

Another middle-aged usher, Charles Scott, had come out of the church and heard Hoepner yelling and seen the Ford take off. Operating on instinct, like the other worshippers, Scott began chasing after the Ford, going the length of a football field, and then farther, all the way to Thirteenth before stopping.

Thornton Anderson came up to Hoepner, who was holding his cell phone to his ear and talking to the 911 operator. Anderson gave him the make, color, and approximate year (early 1990s) of the vehicle, along with the license number, and Hoepner relayed all this to the dispatcher. He stayed on the line while Anderson and Martin went into the church.

In the foyer, Alison Wegner was crying on the phone with the police, hysterical. Martin took the receiver from her and gave the dispatcher an account of what he'd just seen. The hospitality table had been pushed up against a wall to make the room more open. Another worshipper, Bob Livingston, was kneeling down beside the body and holding Tiller's hand. The veterinarian Paul Ryding had heard the commotion and come out from the sanctuary to take a look.

Ryding rolled Tiller onto his left side and bent over him, breathing into the man's mouth and nose, the vet's face and shirt now smeared with blood. Tiller showed no vital signs—no pulse, no heartbeat, no corneal response when Ryding passed his hand in front of his eyes. On his forehead, a flap of skin was loose, and soot and powder covered the wound. He'd been shot once above the right eyebrow, with the gun pressed right up against his flesh, a spent .22 shell casing on the carpet near his body.

Inside the sanctuary, Pastor Lowell Michelson had heard a sharp noise toward the back, thinking someone had dropped a hymnal. As he continued with the service, an usher beckoned him away from the pulpit.

"George has been shot," the man said quietly.

Worshippers were twisting around in the pews, nudging one another and whispering. They, too, had heard an explosive sound—like a balloon popping or a door slamming. Had the percussionist for the choir hit something during the African song?

Pastor Michelson conferred with an assistant who felt that the best way to avoid panic was by proceeding with this morning's program.

In the foyer a woman screamed and the congregation turned in her direction. A few people rose from their pews. The music halted and an usher walked up to the choir box, leaning over to speak to Jeanne Tiller, who sprang out of her chair. Taking her arm, the man escorted her from the sanctuary, as more worshippers stood up.

"Everyone please be seated," an assistant pastor announced from the front of the sanctuary. "Please remain calm. We have had an incident and we are taking care of it. Remain in your seat."

The congregation sat down, but kept glancing back to the foyer.

The usher Keith Hobart was in the sanctuary when he'd heard the sound. He went into the foyer and saw a man lying on his side on the carpet. Hobart thought it was part of a staged protest against abortion, but then he saw the blood on the floor and recognized Dr. Tiller. The usher decided to go back inside to tell his daughter to stay put so she wouldn't see the wounded man. As he was doing so, the foyer doors flew open and Jeanne Tiller rushed in screaming.

"George! George! George!"

In the 1930s and '40s, John Steuart Curry painted *The Tragic Prelude*, featuring abolitionist John Brown, in a mural at the Kansas statehouse. For decades, the anti-abortion movement has compared itself to the anti-slavery movement that led up to the American Civil War. *(Courtesy of KansasMemory .org, Kansas State Historical Society)*

For seven years, Scott Roeder conducted surveillance inside Wichita's Reformation Lutheran Church, where Dr. George Tiller was a member. Anti-abortion demonstrators disrupted services both outside of and within the church itself, but RLC officials chose not to install a security system. *(Courtesy of the district attorney's office for the Eighteenth Judicial District of Kansas)*

The nation's two most prominent abortion doctors—George Tiller, and Warren Hern of Boulder—vacationing together in the Colorado Rockies. Both men had received countless death threats, and following Tiller's murder, Hern called on President Obama to investigate the crime as domestic terrorism. *(Courtesy of the Tiller family and Dr. Warren Hern)*

Twice in the week leading up to Dr. Tiller's murder, Scott Roeder attended services inside this sanctuary at Reformation Lutheran Church. He carried a worn Bible, a concealed handgun, and wrote anti-tax messages on collection envelopes. *(Courtesy of the district attorney's office for the Eighteenth Judicial District of Kansas)*

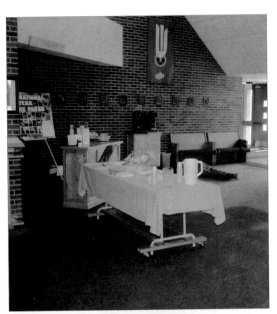

At 10:13 a.m. on May 31, 2009, Dr. George Tiller was pronounced dead in the foyer of Reformation Lutheran Church, ten minutes after he was shot. By late afternoon, commentators nationwide, including President Obama, had released statements on the murder and on abortion. *(Courtesy of the district attorney's office for the Eighteenth Judicial District of Kansas)*

Scott Roeder as a Cub Scout in Topeka, Kansas, in the 1960s. Several years later, he was suspected by a doctor of having schizophrenia and put on medication, which he refused to take. *(Courtesy of Lindsey Roeder)*

Within a few hours of shooting Dr. Tiller, Scott Roeder was arrested near Kansas City. When taken into custody, he was relieved to learn that he'd succeeded in his mission, and that the physician had died from a single gunshot wound. *(Courtesy of the district attorney's office for the Eighteenth Judicial District of Kansas)*

Scott and Lindsey Roeder on their honeymoon in 1986. Their marriage was stable until the early 1990s, when he underwent a born-again religious conversion and joined the anti-abortion movement. *(Courtesy of Lindsey Roeder)*

Scott Roeder and his two-year-old son, Nicholas, at Christmastime in their Kansas City home. Following his arrests in 1996 and 2009, Roeder wrote Nicholas a series of impassioned letters from jail, laying out his political and religious beliefs. *(Courtesy of Lindsey Roeder)*

BOTTOM RIGHT: The anti-abortion Choices Medical Clinic was located next door to Dr. Tiller's office. Protesters at Tiller's clinic encouraged women to go to CMC, where no appointment was necessary, and put their babies up for adoption. *(Courtesy of Stephen Singular)*

Dr. Tiller's abortion clinic in Wichita, Women's Health Care Services, was unmarked, gated, and windowless for the security of those patients and medical professionals who entered. WHCS was the focal point of the 1991 "Summer of Mercy" anti-abortion protests, which led to 2,700 arrests. *(Courtesy of Stephen Singular)*

Right Middle: In March 2008, Dr. George Tiller spoke about reproductive freedom to the National Young Women's Leadership Conference, sponsored by the Feminist Majority Foundation. For decades he was a conservative Republican, but his political views gradually changed because of his involvement in the abortion war. *(Courtesy of the Feminist Majority Foundation)*

Anti-abortion activist Phill Kline was attorney general of Kansas from 2003 through 2006. As AG, he carried out an investigation into Dr. Tiller and his clinic, searching for illegalities that might close down the practice. (*Courtesy of the Kansas attorney general's office*)

Nola Foulston, district attorney for Wichita's Eighteenth Judicial District, has successfully prosecuted many high-profile criminals, including serial killer BTK. In January 2010, she tried Scott Roeder for the first-degree murder of Dr. George Tiller. (*Courtesy of the district attorney's office for the Eighteenth Judicial District of Kansas*)

Linda Carter, dressed here as Wonder Woman, worked in the Olathe, Kansas, district attorney's office run by Paul Morrison. After Morrison became Kansas attorney general, he left office in 2007 when his affair with Carter was revealed. (*Courtesy of the* Pitch Weekly/ *Justin Kendall*)

In 2006, Democrat Paul Morrison defeated Phill Kline to become the Kansas attorney general and ended Kline's Inquisition into Dr. Tiller. Morrison left office in the wake of a sex scandal, which changed the Kansas political landscape. *(Courtesy of the Kansas attorney general's office)*

The founder of Operation Rescue and abortion opponent Randall Terry addressing the media at Scott Roeder's January 2010 trial. Following Tiller's death, Terry called him "a mass murderer" who was "every bit as evil as Nazi war criminals." *(Courtesy of Stephen Singular)*

Every third week, Nebraska's Dr. LeRoy Carhart traveled to Wichita to work in Dr. Tiller's clinic. After Tiller's death, Carhart hired two of the deceased man's employees and became a more prominent target of the anti-abortion movement. *(Courtesy of the Religious Coalition for Reproductive Choice)*

Reverend Dr. Carlton W. Veazey delivering a eulogy for Dr. George Tiller in Washington, D.C. Following the murder, forty-five states held vigils for the slain physician. *(Courtesy of the Religious Coalition for Reproductive Choice)*

# XXXV

The Wichita Police Department had its lightest shift of the week on duty Sunday mornings because automobile accidents and other crimes reached their lowest point during these hours. At 10:02:42 a.m. on this Sunday, the first 911 call from Reformation Lutheran came into the Computer Aided Dispatch (CAD) system for Wichita and Sedgwick County, as the dispatcher took down the information.

Officer Erik Landon was working the east side of town today, the beefy, broad-shouldered patrolman looking for traffic violations or other irregularities. At 10:03:30, he received a call from CAD about a shooting at a church at 7601 East Thirteenth Street. A balding white suspect, about six feet tall and perhaps two hundred pounds, had left the church by himself; he was driving a light blue Ford Taurus and, according to witnesses, moving west on East Thirteenth, toward downtown. He had a small firearm and was obviously considered dangerous. After receiving this bulletin, Officer Landon didn't turn on his red light or speed up dramatically, but drove straight toward the church. At 10:04:10, as Landon was en route, the CAD dispatcher got the license plate number for the Taurus: Kansas 225 BAB. One minute later, or 123 seconds after the first 911 call was made from the church, CAD had identified the car's owner and the shooter's name: fifty-one-year-old Scott Roeder, whose last known address, 5044 Knox Street, was in

Merriam, Kansas, the Kansas City suburb where the suspect had once lived with Michael Clayman and studied the Bible with his fellow Messianic Christians. CAD had already retrieved a photo of Roeder from his most recent driver's license.

At 10:07, Officer Landon reached Reformation Lutheran and went into the foyer, now filled with as many as fifteen people. A crowd was hovering by the far wall, where an older man was leaning down over a body and trying to revive the victim by breathing into his mouth and nose. Landon came closer, observed the situation, and dispatched a brief message to WPD: "Code Blue," meaning near death. He forcefully moved Paul Ryding away from Tiller, telling the veterinarian to go wash the blood off his face. Landon then separated Jeanne Tiller from her husband and she was escorted into another room, as the officer attempted to clear the area around the victim and secure the crime scene. Someone had already picked up the shell casing by Tiller's head, before putting it back onto the carpet.

As Landon tried to manage the chaos inside the foyer, all across the city police cell phones and beepers were ringing. At other Wichita churches where services were just starting, on-call officers received the urgent messages, excused themselves from their families, and hustled to the exits. Most drove to Reformation Lutheran, but some were ordered downtown to WPD headquarters. The metropolitan area saw about thirty murders a year, normally investigated by half a dozen homicide detectives. When a major crime occurred, other officers were called in from the gang unit (the city had about three thousand suspected gang members), and that was happening now.

Officer Valerie Shirkey was also patrolling the east side of town when she got the 10:03 dispatch about the church shooting. Using the police car's siren and red lights, she arrived at Reformation Lutheran at 10:08, dressed in the same casual, summery manner as the other WPD personnel: white pants and a short-sleeved green shirt. Grabbing her camera and two rolls of film, she ran inside and helped Officer Landon take charge of the foyer. Emergency Medical Services were pulling up out front, the Wichita Fire Department had been alerted, and more officers were coming through the church doors and bringing the crime scene under control. Officer Shirkey began snapping pictures of Tiller—of his glasses, which had fallen off and were lying near his head, of the blood pooling around him on the carpet, of the blood splatters off to the sides, and of the brain matter that had been blown onto a nearby trash can.

The police made way for the paramedic Gene Robinson, who leaned over Dr. Tiller and took his pulse, checking for vital signs. At 10:13, he looked up at the others and shook his head.

"Code black," he said.

A murder investigation had officially begun.

Lieutenant Ken Landwehr, commander of WPD's homicide division, had not yet come to the church, but was handing out various assignments to the detectives below him. Sedgwick County District Attorney Nola Foulston, a veteran prosecutor who'd tried many high-profile cases herself, was on her way to Reformation Lutheran and other lawyers from the DA's office were right behind her. So was the local press, as pieces of Wichita were just starting to absorb the shocking news: Dr. George Tiller had been shot and killed inside his church—one more jolt to a metropolitan area that had been divided for decades by the conflict surrounding the physician. When travelers from around America came to this city of something under 400,000 in south central Kansas, they saw a modest skyline rising against the flat Midwestern horizon, and were often struck by the friendliness of the native population, but they couldn't help noticing one other local landmark: those huge billboards proclaiming Wichita "The Abortion Capital of the World."

The ten police officers at the church called an immediate halt to the service and were blocking off the parking lot exits and isolating the witnesses from other members of the congregation and media. A WPD dispatcher had just issued a teletype BOLO—"Be on the Lookout"—alert, sent to law enforcement throughout Kansas, Oklahoma, and

Missouri, and including Roeder's license number and a description of the Taurus. The FBI and ATF were already aware of the killing and had been told that Dr. Warren Hern out in Boulder and Dr. LeRoy Carhart up in Nebraska might both be at risk. The Kansas Highway Patrol and officers from Johnson County, which included the greater Kansas City area, had been told about a 1993 blue Ford being driven by a man with hazel eyes and the rest of Roeder's physical characteristics. Citizens in the Wichita area who liked to tune in police scanners had picked up the news, relaying it among themselves and making calls to others.

Reformation Lutheran had been emptied of worshippers and many were standing outside on a grassy section next to the church, holding on to one another, praying together, and crying. A group of adults had led some small children away from all the police activity, trying to distract them as they told the kids stories and played games and rolled on the lawn, the morning growing warmer in the late May sunshine.

Gary Hoepner was still on the phone with the 911 dispatcher. For the next 21.5 hours, CAD would continue receiving data about the shooting. Throughout that time, Hoepner's grief was just starting to come alive, along with the regret that he hadn't had time or been quick enough or done something to save George Tiller and stop a murder from occurring inside his church.


The powder blue Taurus had in fact not gone west onto East Thirteenth Street toward downtown, as the original CAD dispatches reported to police officers, but east up to Rock Road and then north toward Highway 254. The coffee stains on Roeder's white shirt looked suspect and were itching his chest, but he didn't have time to stop and change. His radar detector was on, to keep track of any cops, and he was determined to avoid the nearby turnpike, by far the fastest way to make the 170-mile trip back to Kansas City. Police might be waiting for him at a toll booth and, besides, the state of Kansas still was not going to get his $3.50 fee. He fiddled with the radio dial, hunting for any news of the shooting.

He took 254 east to El Dorado, home to the highest-security prison in Kansas (BTK, among others, was housed there). Driving the speed limit and conscientiously using all his signals, he departed 254 for Highway 54 and took this two-lane blacktop through the small towns of Eureka and Yates Center, turning north on Highway 75 to Burlington, where he paused to change into the blue denim shirt in his backseat. Sitting behind the wheel, he tossed the stained white shirt over his shoulder, onto some other clothes, ties, papers, and trash. Concealed beneath the car seats were live cartridges and his long serrated knife. Stuffed under the driver's visor was a handout for the recent Reformation Lutheran service conducted in Swahili and on it, he'd written to himself: "Young women. Short dress!" And next to that, "Deliver us from temptation."

In Burlington, he moved along the quiet Sunday afternoon main street, just a few blocks long, until he found an empty parking lot behind a row of buildings and pulled into it. A dirt pile in the lot, maybe four feet high and four feet wide, was being used for a construction project. Wrapping the murder weapon tightly inside a piece of cloth, Roeder buried it as deeply as he could in the dirt. The firearm's magazine was still loaded, with live rounds of ammunition that others might stumble on, including children, but if everything went smoothly, he'd come back for the gun as soon as possible.

Driving sixteen miles north on Highway 75, he stopped at a collection of restaurants and gas stations known as BETO Junction, where he gassed up the Taurus and ate a small pizza, hungry from all the morning's exertions. From BETO Junction, he turned east onto Interstate 35, toward Kansas City, constantly twisting the radio dial and listening for reports out of Wichita. He heard nothing, which was maddening. What had happened in the church after he'd run outside? Was Tiller dead or alive? Had he even shot the right man, and if he had, could the bullet have hit another usher or worshipper? If he'd so much as nicked somebody else, he'd feel awful about it, because that would be a crime and would damage or negate everything he stood for and was trying to achieve. He kept driving and changing the dial, settling in on a talk radio program. He'd made plans to stop by a farm between Topeka and Kansas City to buy kefir and goat cheese, but that would take too much time. There was a paycheck waiting for him at Quicksilver, which he needed to pick up this afternoon.

For months and years, going back to the start of the decade, he'd wondered what it would feel like to make this journey from Wichita up to Kansas City, after fulfilling his ultimate goal. Now he knew. It felt incredibly good and freeing to leave the church behind and to be all alone out on the open road on this clear spring day, a great day for a drive, to roll down the windows and take in the scenery and let the cool air rush over him as he passed through farm country—knowing, or at least hoping, that he'd finally accomplished his mission. The stress and tension building within him in recent weeks, as he'd thought about the plan and put together the details, was easing out of his body. Maybe he'd done something significant and powerful with his life, after all, something historic. All those emotions that had surrounded and tormented him for so long—culminating with the anger and bitter disappointment over Tiller's trial—had at last found a focus and a release. He'd expressed himself.

His only regret was that he hadn't done this sooner.

# XXXVI

Deputy Sheriff Andrew Lento of Johnson County was patrolling a rural area outside of Kansas City at 10:40 on Sunday morning when the BOLO had come in from the WPD. It alerted him to be on the lookout for a 1993 blue Ford Taurus driven by a middle-aged man named Scott Roeder, who'd just shot Dr. George Tiller at Wichita's Reformation Lutheran Church. The suspect was armed and any lone officer would need backup before moving in on him. Lento calculated that if Roeder had left the church around 10:15 and taken the most direct route back to Kansas City, via the turnpike and then I-35, he wouldn't arrive in this vicinity for about three hours. The deputy kept patrolling the back roads until a quarter to one.

In downtown Wichita, Gary Hoepner and Keith Martin, along with several other members of the congregation, had been escorted to the sixth floor of the City Building, just across the street from the courthouse. The WPD brass worked out of this black high-rise, where detectives were preparing to interview the eyewitnesses. The two ushers were separated, put in rooms with one officer each, and questioned about what they'd seen. Hoepner and Martin gave matching detailed accounts of what Roeder had looked like and that he'd been in the church several times before today. Both said that he'd aimed the handgun at them and threatened to shoot. The detectives went over this last point carefully, because Roeder's actions with them could widen the charges to include two counts of aggravated assault. The ushers were shown a photo lineup of half a dozen suspects, including the picture of Roeder from his driver's license, and both identified him as the killer.

While the men were being interviewed, the Kansas City FBI office called Jeffrey Pederson, who managed the Central Family Medicine clinic and whose locks Roeder had glued shut in recent weeks. The feds remembered that a week earlier Pederson had given them a physical description of the vandal and his Kansas license plate number—225 BAB. The tag and description matched the suspect in the Tiller shooting. When Pederson learned that the doctor was dead and the shooter had been identified as Scott Roeder, he literally felt sick.

At 12:45, Deputy Lento arrived at I-35, pulled into the center median, and parked, his car facing the northbound traffic. While taking a call from a local resident about a barking dog complaint, he saw the Taurus approaching in the left-hand lane and traveling the speed limit. Lento got off the phone, and as the Ford went by, he saw the license plate: Kansas 225 BAB. He immediately advised his dispatcher that he'd made a positive ID of the suspect's vehicle, and the information was sent along to Wichita.

At a few minutes after one p.m., Lieutenant Landwehr was in the City Building being briefed about the two eyewitnesses from the church. Detective Brad Elmore walked in and said that a Johnson County police officer had located the Taurus, about twenty miles south of Kansas City. Was it time to move in? Landwehr nodded, ordering his staff to prepare an arrest warrant and telling Elmore to tell the officer to be prepared to stop the Ford and take the driver into custody.

Deputy Lento was readying himself for a "high-risk" traffic stop, by going over procedure and calling for three other officers to assist him as soon as possible. He exited the median, slipped out into traffic behind the Ford, and turned on the yellow hazard lights on the rear of his vehicle, but did nothing more to call attention to himself.

Roeder had slowed down and moved into the right-hand lane, going fifty-five miles an hour. Lento pulled in closer, his car now occupying both lanes of I-35 so that no one could pass either him or Roeder. He held this pattern for the next few miles, until the other officers arrived and were in position at the rear. Lento turned on both his red light and the camera inside his car, installed to record traffic stops or incidents. When the caravan reached the mile 208 Interstate marker, just outside Gardner, Kansas, Roeder slowed down on the shoulder of the highway and stopped, staying inside his vehicle. Lento parked behind him and, using a loudspeaker, addressed the suspect.

"Raise both hands, driver!"

Roeder complied.

"Driver! With your left hand take the keys out of the ignition. Drop the keys on the ground."

He did as ordered.

"Driver! With your left hand, open the door from the outside!"

With the door ajar, Roeder stepped out, wearing a white ball cap and sunglasses. He faced the officers, now bunched up behind him.

"Driver!" Lento said. "Raise your hands—with your back to me!"

Roeder turned his back to the men.

"Raise your shirt with your left hand! Take it out of your pants."

He followed the command.

"Where's the gun?"

He threw his hands in the air, as if to say he was unarmed.

"Lift up your shirt, driver! Step backward."

Roeder began walking in reverse toward Lento, until he was only a few yards away.

"Driver, stop! Get down on your knees."

As he scrambled to the ground and lay flat on his stomach, the cap fell off his head. He put his hands behind his back, in expectation of being cuffed. His blue denim shirt and dark slacks were spread out on the shoulder and he wore a pair of black tennis shoes, spotted with blood.

With guns drawn, all four of the officers approached the figure splayed out in front of them, one policeman aiming a shotgun at the prone figure.

They handcuffed him and frisked him for a weapon but found none, and he was taken to Lento's car. When he was informed that he was under arrest for the murder of George Tiller, the words sunk in and filled him with relief. The doctor was dead. The mission had been accomplished.

As he was being driven to the sheriff's office in Gardner, Wichita police officials, including case supervisor Rick Gregg and Lieutenant Landwehr, boarded helicopters and flew north to the Kansas City area. Another detective drove up from Wichita as fast as he felt he could. While several of the officers attempted to talk with Roeder in Gardner, others impounded his vehicle and began combing it for evidence. They found the knife, the live cartridges, and a note scribbled on an envelope. It read, "Cheryl Op Rescue," with a phone number next to the woman's name. The police wondered if Roeder had a computer in the car, which he didn't, but they eventually found one in his apartment. Their first task was to copy all the files on his hard drive and then search through these copies, leaving the computer itself untouched.

# XXXVII

That Sunday morning Dan Monnat had been in his law office in downtown Wichita, just a few blocks from the Eighteenth Judicial District
Courthouse, where Tiller had been tried and acquitted two months
earlier. Monnat was working on a case when he got a call from Tim
Potter, a crime reporter for *The Wichita Eagle*.

"What have you heard?" the journalist asked him.

"What are you talking about?" the attorney said.

"I'm sorry," Potter replied, "but Dr. Tiller has been shot—again."

Monnat was shocked, but in the next instant he told himself that it
must have been another failed attempt on the physician's life. George
might be wounded, the way he was before, but he'd be back at his clinic
tomorrow or later in the week. Then Monnat learned the grim news:
this time Dr. Tiller was dead.

The lawyer knew that his wife, Grace, was at home working outside
on a ladder, without her cell phone handy. He drove to the house to tell
her in person and both of them returned to his place of business, located inside a secure building not far from WPD headquarters. Monnat was worried about the safety of not just himself and his family, but
of everyone on Tiller's staff and all those who'd been on their defense
team at the March trial. He phoned everybody from that team and said
to come down to his office, now serving as an impromptu operations

site for the press calls pouring in from around the nation. Through people close to Jeanne Tiller, he conveyed to her that his legal staff would handle all media matters and shield the grieving family from the coming onrush of attention—the hundreds of e-mails and phone messages with requests for interviews. Monnat and the other lawyers decided, with Jeanne's approval, that this was no time for passivity or silence, no matter how much they were hurting. They needed to begin speaking out now for Dr. Tiller, so that not just the anti-abortionists and their view of the slain man would be represented on the airwaves.

Monnat stayed at his office until midnight on May 31, talking with National Public Radio and other press. He was back four hours later to go on the air with CBS's *Early Show*, and then MSNBC and CNN. For days that stretched into weeks, he'd be much too busy dealing with the media, funeral issues, the Tiller family, and inquiries about the future of the clinic to reflect on his own personal loss.

"We didn't want to make Dr. Tiller's death a political occasion," he says, "but beginning on the afternoon of May thirty-first we felt that his life should be honored, all of it, not just his work. His life as a husband of forty-five years, a father of four, a grandfather of ten, a navy flight surgeon, a man with a great sense of humor, and an individual committed to his church, his community, and the U.S. Constitution and Bill of Rights. It was our job to let the public know that he wasn't just a human being, but a heroic human being, because we knew that other people were going to be saying a lot of terrible things about him."


That morning Lindsey and Nick Roeder had taken her father to Knox Presbyterian in Overland Park for the Sunday service. At the church, Nick had helped his ninety-year-old granddad get around in his wheelchair, and then he brought him back home, made him lunch, and gave him an insulin shot. Lindsey had to stay longer at Knox because today was kindergarten graduation and she was director of the child care center in the basement. About 1:45 p.m., Nick returned to the church to pick up his mother, and they stopped by McDonald's. A long waiting line held them up, so they didn't get to the house till after 2:15.

At 2:30, someone pounded on the front door, an unusually aggressive knock.

"It must be your dad," Lindsey called out.

Nick's response was reflexive. "Don't answer it."

She opened the door a few inches and a huge man was standing there with a raised fist. He jammed it through the crack and Lindsey wasn't strong enough to shut the door. After identifying himself as a federal agent with the Bureau of Alcohol, Tobacco, and Firearms, he said that he needed to talk to her. Panicking but trying not to show it, she told Nick to take his grandfather to the back of the house. Lindsey stepped outside.

"Is Scott Roeder in there?" the man asked.

She said that for years he hadn't been allowed inside her residence.

"We don't know this for sure, but we think he's murdered someone."

As the words filtered through her, Lindsey didn't seem able to make sense of them. She swayed as if she might faint, but the agent reached out and caught her.

"I don't understand," she said.

"Dr. George Tiller has been murdered."

"I don't understand."

"He's a late-term abortion doctor in Wichita and . . ."

Inside the house, the phone was ringing. She ignored it, steadying herself on her feet and slowly absorbing what she was being told.

"Scott," she said, "was really against abortion."

Who, the agent asked, had left her house forty-five minutes ago in her car?

That was Nick, her son, she explained, realizing that the ATF had been sitting on her street for quite a while this afternoon, watching her residence and everyone who went into and came out of it.

"We need to speak with him," the agent said.

The phone was ringing again, but she made no move to answer it.

If the agent wanted to talk to Nick, he'd have to come outside, because the stranger wasn't going inside her home.

"All right," he said.

She went in and returned shortly with her son, who was telling Lindsey that his grandfather could hear all the activity around their house and was upset by it. Nick turned to the agent and tried to convince him that the only other person left in the house was his ninety-year-old granddad. The phone rang again, so Lindsey unplugged it.

A TV crew from Kansas City, the ABC affiliate, was pulling up in front of the residence. More media trucks were on their way.

His father, Nick told the agent, didn't live in Merriam, Kansas, anymore, but shared an apartment with someone in Westport.

"Can you take me there?" the man said.

They got in an ATF car and drove across the state line into Missouri, to the apartment rented by Roeder and Kamran Tehrani.

Lindsey had gone back inside to try to calm down her father, but more people were knocking on her front door.

Using her cell phone, she called Knox Presbyterian and asked to speak with her pastor, briefly laying out for him what had happened and saying that she wouldn't be coming in tomorrow. Hanging up, she looked out the window and saw a young man approaching her house, thinking it was a TV journalist. When she opened the door, he said he was an FBI agent and needed to talk with her. Before she could respond, a woman jumped out from the side of her house and landed in front of her, frightening Lindsey. It was a reporter, and the agent shooed her away.

When he asked if any other government agencies had contacted her, Lindsey told him that the ATF had been lurking outside her home at least since her son had left to pick her up from church about 1:45. An ATF agent had just left with Nick, headed to Roeder's apartment.

This information clearly agitated the FBI man, who said that he had to talk with her son—at once.

From inside the house, Lindsey's father was watching TV and yelling.

"Scott's been arrested!" he shouted. "Picked up!"

"Scott's been arrested?" she called over her shoulder.

"Yes!"

"He's been arrested," Lindsey told the agent, and the news agitated him even more.

"No way," he said, asking for Nick's cell phone number.

She gave it to him and he dialed, while Lindsey listened to the conversation and looked on in amazement. A U.S. government law enforcement turf war between the ATF and the FBI was unfolding on her front stoop. The ATF agent with Nick wouldn't let the FBI agent communicate with her son or reveal Scott's address in Westport. These people, Lindsey told herself, really don't talk to one another in the middle of a crisis, just like on those TV police shows.

The FBI man walked off and disappeared.

Reporters and TV producers kept coming all afternoon and into the evening, from Kansas City, Topeka, and Wichita. Then they began calling Lindsey from New York and Los Angeles.

"We had press," she says, "out the wazoo."

A journalist asked her to deliver a statement on behalf of her and Nick about the death of Dr. Tiller. As best she could under the circumstances, she put together a few words expressing their sympathy for the physician's family, and it went out across America. Deep into the night, Nick searched Google for information about the crime and his father's role in it. The name Scott Roeder had generated tens of thousands of hits and somebody had already written a song about him, recorded it, and uploaded it to YouTube.

The next morning, after learning that his brother had been arrested for the murder of George Tiller, David Roeder called the local FBI office and told them how Scott had come to his home on Saturday afternoon and taken target practice with a .22 handgun in the woods behind it. He explained that the weapon had jammed and they'd had to take it into a gun shop for repairs and while there his brother had bought more ammunition. David was most interested in telling the feds that his fingerprints might be on the .22, but that he'd had nothing to do with the killing of Dr. Tiller. Later that day, the feds came to his property to retrieve the empty shell casings from the rounds that Scott had left in the ground.

# XXXVIII

Like the shots fired at South Carolina's Fort Sumter in January 1861, opening the War Between the States, the single shot at Reformation Lutheran unleashed the emotions behind the cultural battle the country had been fighting for decades—Americans began either mourning or celebrating Dr. Tiller's death. Some laid the blame on the religious right and conservative commentators such as Bill O'Reilly and Ann Coulter. Others blamed the physician himself. An Operation Rescue Web site, chargetiller.com, was immediately taken down and the Internet was afire with speculation. What did the murder mean for the anti-abortion movement, with its greatest enemy now dead? What would happen to Tiller's clinic? What about his Kansas patients and the five thousand out-of-state women who came to Wichita each year seeking counseling or an abortion? Were his co-workers, friends, and family under threat?

By Sunday afternoon, the news out of Wichita was affecting the highest levels of government. U.S. marshals were mobilized nationwide to offer more protection to abortion clinics, and Attorney General Eric Holder was preparing to order the Department of Justice to launch a federal investigation into the killing. President Obama issued a statement from the White House:

"I was shocked and outraged by the murder of Dr. George Tiller, as he attended church services this morning. However profound our differences over difficult issues, such as abortion, they cannot be resolved by heinous acts of violence."

Warren Hern of Boulder, one of the last doctors left to perform late-term abortions, delivered his own public statement about the murder:

"I think it's the inevitable consequence of more than 35 years of constant anti-abortion terrorism, harassment, and violence."

Because President Obama supported legalized abortion, Hern said, abortion foes "have lost ground. . . . They want the doctors dead, and they invite people to assassinate us. No wonder that this happens. I am next on the list."

On its Web site, Operation Rescue posted: "We are shocked at this morning's disturbing news that Mr. Tiller was gunned down. Operation Rescue has worked for years through peaceful, legal means, and through the proper channels to see him brought to justice. We denounce vigilantism and the cowardly act that took place this morning. We pray for Mr. Tiller's family that they will find comfort and healing that can only be found in Jesus Christ."

Kansans for Life, said its executive director, Mary Kay Culp, "deplores the murder of Dr. George Tiller, and we wish to express our deep and sincere sympathy to his family and friends. Our organization has a board of directors, and a 35-year history of bringing citizens together to achieve thoughtful education and legislation on the life issues here in Kansas. We value life, completely deplore violence, and are shocked and very upset by what happened in Wichita today."

The Kansas chapter of NOW was "deeply saddened at the cowardly act of violence committed against Dr. George Tiller, a champion for women's reproductive freedom—an act that ultimately took his life. Dr. Tiller, although previously surviving many acts of terrorism and violence directed at him and his clinic, did not allow it to stop him from standing up for the rights of all women. Kansas NOW grieves not only the loss of Dr. Tiller, but also the loss that all women needing access to safe abortions have suffered due to this act of violence . . ."

Father Frank Pavone, national director of Priests for Life, said, "I am saddened to hear of the killing of George Tiller this morning. At this point, we do not know the motives of this act, or who is behind it, whether an angry post-abortive man or woman, or a misguided activist, or an enemy within the abortion industry, or a political enemy frustrated with the way Tiller has escaped prosecution. We should not jump to conclusions or rush to judgment. But whatever the motives, we at Priests for Life continue to insist on a culture in which violence is never seen as the solution to any problem. Every life has to be protected, without regard to their age or views or actions."

"Some of us who worked at Wesley Medical Center," said a nurse employed at this Wichita hospital, "felt that Tiller's death was about what goes around comes around. But others couldn't understand why crazies would kill him. I believe in choice and felt that his murder could send us back to the days of coat-hanger abortions."

From Liberty University in Lynchburg, Virginia, Phill Kline said that he was "stunned by this lawless and violent act which must be condemned and should be met with the full force of law. We join in lifting prayer that God's grace and presence rest with Dr. Tiller's family and friends."

"Dr. Tiller's murder," said Nancy Keenan, president of NARAL Pro-Choice America, "will send a chill down the spines of the brave and courageous providers and other professionals who are part of reproductive-health centers that serve women across this country . . . We also call on opponents of a woman's right to choose to condemn this action completely and absolutely. What happened today in Wichita cannot become the beginning of a more aggressive wave of violence targeting abortion providers and the women for whom they provide care . . ."

Operation Rescue's founder, Randall Terry, was unconcerned with being diplomatic.

"George Tiller," he said, "was a mass murderer. We grieve for him that he did not have time to properly prepare his soul to face God. I am more concerned that the Obama administration will use Tiller's killing to intimidate pro-lifers into surrendering our most effective rhetoric and actions. Abortion is still murder. And we still must call abortion by its proper name: murder. Those men and women who slaughter the unborn are murderers according to the Law of God. We must continue to expose them in our communities and peacefully protest them at their offices and homes, and yes, even their churches."

In an extensive videotaped speech running more than six minutes, Terry said that Tiller "had blood all over his hands" and was "every bit as evil as Nazi war criminals." The anti-abortion movement should not stop showing people pictures of dead babies: "our best weapons of rhetoric . . . and our most effective images." In the background as Terry spoke were arrayed Christian symbols, including a cross, several angels, and other religious figurines.

Since 2002, Julie Burkhart had run Tiller's political action committee, ProKanDo, which came to an end on May 31, 2009.

"I was in a meeting that day in Washington, D.C., at the Embassy Row Hilton hotel," she recalls, "and my husband sent me a text message. Then another friend sent me a text, saying Dr. Tiller was dead. There was just this feeling of heaviness that was almost paralyzing, and it's still there.

"When you work every day in this kind of environment—I saw the bulletproof vest in Dr. Tiller's office and rode in his car with the bulletproof windows—you start to think that you're immune to the violence. It's not going to happen to you or someone you work with. I thought he'd eventually retire and spend his time with his grandchildren."

On its Web site's home page, the Army of God depicted flames burning under Tiller's body as it was being carried out of his church on a gurney.

"Large numbers of innocent children scheduled to be murdered by George Tiller," the site read, "are spared by the action of American hero Scott Roeder . . . George Tiller, Babykiller, reaped what he sowed and is now in eternal hell . . . Psalm 55:15, Let death seize upon them, and let them go down quick into hell: for wickedness is in their dwellings, and among them."

"After getting the news," says Julie Burkhart, "I caught the first plane out of D.C. for Wichita. I felt just shock and utter disbelief, and all this anger. It was a life-altering experience for me. All I could think about on the flight was, 'The fuckers got him,' and all the work we'd done together and all the work he'd done before I'd met him had been taken away in an instant. Dr. Tiller always said that until you understand the heart of a woman, abortion doesn't make sense. It's only when you get to know the heart that you can understand. This is not a cerebral or medical issue."

In the spring of 2009 following Tiller's acquittal, Bill O'Reilly had increasingly referred to "Tiller the baby killer." On his first show after the murder, the talk show host declared that "quick-thinking Americans" should condemn his violent death.

"Anarchy and vigilantism will assure the collapse of any society," he said. "Once the rule of law breaks down a country is finished."

Speaking of O'Reilly in *Salon*, Gabriel Winant wrote that no other person bore as much responsibility for the characterization of Tiller "as a savage on the loose, killing babies." Winant cited how Tiller's name had first appeared on the *Factor* in February 2005 and since then O'Reilly and his guest hosts had brought up the doctor on twenty-eight more episodes, including April 27 of this year.

"Almost invariably," Winant wrote, "Tiller is described as 'Tiller the Baby Killer.' "

On June 1, the conservative commentator Michelle Malkin posted online, "Prepare for collective demonization of pro-lifers and Christians—and more gratuitous attempts to tar talk radio, Fox News, and the Tea Party movement as responsible for the heinous crime."

A few weeks after the homicide, Ann Coulter came on *The O'Reilly Factor* and, while indicating that she was personally against the shooting of abortion doctors, said she didn't want to impose her values on others.

"I don't really like to think of it as a murder," she stated. "It was terminating Tiller in the 203rd trimester."

# XXXIX

By late afternoon on May 31, federal agents were at Kamran Tehrani's Westport apartment, interviewing him about his connection to Roeder. He spoke openly to them about his roommate and their mutual ties to Messianic Christianity.

"I was just in shock and awe about the murder," Kamran says. "Scott was passionate over this issue, but it never entered my mind that he'd actually shoot the doctor. As I told the FBI, we've all thought about committing suicide, but how many of us carry it out? After this happened, there was a lot of fear in the people I know. Some didn't want to do Bible study any more, which I think is cowardly. All we had was an innocent Bible study program and there's nothing wrong with that. If people want to stop us from doing this, then shed my blood over that because I will stand on conviction.

"This country is in enemy hands and I make no secret of that with anyone. The truth will ultimately come out. Both Scott and I are strongly anti-Bush, anti-Obama, anti-Satan, and anti- those who want to destroy the country. Tiller is no different from them. I can't regret that he's been executed for what he was doing. But did I know it was coming? No. Am I still Scott's friend? He'll have to walk away from our friendship before I do. I feel very grieved for what has happened with him."

As Kamran talked with the FBI, the police detectives who'd gone up to Gardner, Kansas, tried to question Roeder, but he'd already asked for a lawyer and was withholding comment. That evening, he was placed in a WPD vehicle and driven back to Wichita, making small talk with the officers sitting beside him, while offering up a few comments about his opposition to abortion. He was booked on first-degree murder charges, held on a $5 million bond, transferred to a cell in the Sedgwick County Detention Facility next to the courthouse, and placed in solitary confinement. By the time he was left alone it was after midnight but sleep didn't come, because his cell was cold and he was on suicide watch, with guards constantly walking by and monitoring him. So he couldn't hurt himself, the staff had placed him in a tight-fitting, wraparound garment called a "skirt," designed to limit his movements.

On Sunday afternoon, before Roeder had been booked and locked up, an unidentified friend of his had made a phone call to Ney, Adams & Sylvester, one of Wichita's most prominent criminal-defense offices. Back in 1987, the firm's Richard Ney had gained local notoriety as the key defense attorney for Bill Butterworth, charged with killing Phil Fager and his daughters, sixteen-year-old Kelli and nine-year-old Sherri. A well-respected contractor, Butterworth had been engaged in a construction project at the Fager home when the murders occurred inside this residence. Ney had been able to reach Butterworth before the police interviewed him, and to advise him on a legal strategy. The crime rattled Wichita, in part because it was thirteen years and numerous victims into the unsolved BTK case. Had the region's best-known serial killer, who'd terrorized the city off and on since 1974, struck again?

At Butterworth's trial, he claimed to have gone missing during four crucial days around the murders and couldn't remember what had happened. After undergoing hypnosis, he testified that when he'd found two victims at the house and heard Kelli struggling against an unknown assailant, he'd bolted and fled to Florida. He was acquitted, sending more shock waves through Wichita, since most people had felt Butterworth would be convicted. Ney's reputation as a tough, talented defense attorney had just expanded exponentially. And if Butterworth was innocent, who'd murdered the Fagers?

When BTK, Dennis Rader, confessed to some or all of his homicides in 2005, he didn't bring up the Fager killings, but did admit sending a letter to Phil Fager's widow, just to frighten her. Closing the BTK case in Wichita once and for all, and publicly confirming that Rader had committed "only" ten murders, had been extremely important to DA Nola Foulston, who'd taken great umbrage with media suggestions that there were any unsolved BTK killings in Kansas or elsewhere. It was time to put that nightmare behind the city and local law enforcement. Now, in the spring of 2009, Wichita's legal establishment was about to reveal just how importantly it viewed the death of Dr. Tiller—and the conviction of his alleged assassin.

When the call from Roeder's friend came into Ney, Adams & Sylvester on May 31, Ney was on vacation, but a secretary took down the information. Although it was Sunday, the attorney quickly got the message and phoned the person who'd contacted his office. He didn't know this individual, but later described him as very "concerned and compassionate" toward the accused, and they discussed the possibility of Ney representing Roeder. Ney called his partner, Doug Adams, asking him to go over to the detention facility and set up an initial meeting with Roeder, standard operating procedure inside the criminal justice system.

"When somebody gets arrested," says Ney, "a family member usually calls us and says they need a lawyer and then we go to the jail and talk to the person. It works like this because once you've been locked up you can't just go to the Yellow Pages and look for a lawyer. Someone has to help you do this."

On Monday, June 1, Adams went to the jail to speak with Roeder, but wasn't allowed in. The official reason for this was that because the inmate hadn't personally placed Adams or Ney on a visitors' list, or specifically asked to see the attorneys, they'd been denied access.

When Adams demanded that a judge change this policy, the request was turned down. In effect, this meant that Roeder would now be represented pro bono by public defenders instead of by a high-priced lawyer who'd made his name by winning difficult cases against the DA's office (and there may well have been money available for a pricey Roeder defense team because some of those who most strongly supported the murder of Dr. Tiller had considerable financial assets). Since Adams and Ney couldn't get to the defendant quickly and lay out a possible plan, they also weren't able to instruct him that above all he should talk to no one, starting with the press.

Ney was more than surprised by these developments.

"I was not happy about this," he says. "Almost as soon as we were told that we couldn't see Roeder, reporters were suddenly able to speak with him—but not members in good standing with the bar."

What conclusions did the lawyer draw from all this?

"You can draw whatever conclusions you want to. I have my own conclusions, but I'll keep them to myself. The question in Wichita becomes: Is this how we're supposed to operate in the future or is this just one very special case? If a prosecutor's son or daughter got arrested, do you think they'd be able to get a lawyer of their choice into the jail to see them? The entire criminal bar in Wichita was taken aback by what happened. It's hogwash. The right to counsel is guaranteed under the Sixth Amendment, so this isn't how we're supposed to do business."

For three days after his arrest, Roeder was kept wrapped inside the skirt, which brought on wretched memories of being in a mental hospital as a teenager and didn't make sleeping any easier. Lying awake at night, he thought about the impact of the murder on his family members, especially on his son and aging mother, and hoped they hadn't been affected too adversely. He wondered how those in the anti-abortion movement had received the news and why some of them weren't trying to contact or visit him in jail. Hadn't he done exactly what they'd wanted and prayed for somebody to do throughout the past three decades? Wasn't this why they revered Paul Hill, the man who shot Dr. John Britton, as a hero? When were they going to step forward and support him?

"He's never been a member of KFL and I've never heard of him," Mary Kay Culp, the Kansans for Life executive director, said about Roeder on June 1. "He's not on our mailing list. He's never given us money."

Two other anti-abortion groups, Operation Rescue and the Kansas Coalition for Life, not only immediately condemned the shooting, but tried to disassociate themselves from the suspect. The head of the KCL, Mark Gietzen, who'd repeatedly kneeled in the gutter in front of Tiller's clinic to impede his entrance, said that if Roeder was connected to the pro-life movement, it would set their cause back twenty years.

Troy Newman, director of Operation Rescue, personally denounced the killing and said he was in mourning like everybody else.

"We are pro-life," he told *The New York Times*, "and this act was antithetical to what we believe."

He went even further and said to the *Times* that Tiller had been a "worthy adversary." And that the alleged murderer had "killed more babies than he has saved" because now it would be more difficult than ever to outlaw abortion.

When Newman was informed that somebody named Scott Roeder had posted his thoughts on Operation Rescue's blog, he responded that the man was "not a friend, not a contributor, not a volunteer."

Yet Roeder had told numerous people that he'd contributed at least $1,000 to the organization and had the receipts to prove it. On the day of the murder, an envelope reading "Cheryl Op Rescue," with Cheryl Sullenger's phone number scribbled on it, had been found in the Ford Taurus. Sullenger wasn't just a member of Operation Rescue, but its senior policy adviser. In 1988, she'd pled guilty to conspiring to bomb a California abortion clinic and served nearly two years in prison. After the Kansas City TV station KMBC reported on the discovery of the envelope in Roeder's car, a local alternative newspaper, *The Pitch*, phoned Sullenger to ask about her connection to the alleged killer.

"He hasn't called me recently," she told them.

Then she altered her story and admitted to having had multiple phone conversations with Roeder before Tiller was murdered. Both she and Newman eventually acknowledged that the suspect had contacted Operation Rescue to find out the time and location for Tiller's 2009 trial.

As these comments and developments filtered back into the detention facility, Roeder became angrily disappointed with the people he'd thought were his allies. How could they turn their backs on him now?

Sleep-deprived and upset, confused by the actions of those he'd admired, he began to carp to his jailers. It was still too cold in his cell, he'd been denied phone privileges, the food was inedible, the guards were dealing with him like a common thug, and he needed his sleep apnea machine so he could get more rest. Why were they showing him so little respect? The only positive thing was that Tiller's clinic had been closed since last Monday, while his family and employees mourned and made preparations for the funeral.

Roeder then did what no attorney would have ever advised him to do and took his complaints outside of the jail. On June 4, his fourth full day in custody, he phoned the Associated Press and stated that he wasn't anti-government, as the press had wrongly been reporting, but "anti-corrupt government . . . I haven't been convicted of anything and I am being treated as a criminal . . ."

Increasingly worried about his elderly mother, Doris, in Topeka, he made a collect call to a woman in Kansas City whom he'd once worked with and befriended. In years past, they'd gone out to dinner and had many intense discussions about the Bible. He'd mowed her grass, and she viewed him as a "very kind man," but she was pro-choice and his intensity on this subject disturbed her, so they'd agreed not to talk about abortion. She was stunned to hear that he'd been accused of murdering Dr. Tiller and far more stunned when he called her from jail to ask her for a favor. Could she contact his mother and tell her that he loved her and hoped to be in communication with her soon? The friend fulfilled this request, but Doris replied that she never wanted to hear from or see her son again.

Following his incarceration, Roeder began receiving copies of ex-treme anti-abortion pamphlets, featuring graphic pictures, from the fringes of the movement. When he mailed one of these to this same friend in Kansas City, she said she never wanted to speak with him again, either. Yet those on the far edges of the anti-abortion flank *were* contacting him and thanking him for what he'd done.

While adjusting to his jail routine, he was examined by a psychia-trist to see if he was mentally competent to stand trial. The doctor concluded that he was not legally insane and could be a participant in the courtroom. Because he was basically indigent, Roeder had been appointed two public defenders: Steve Osburn, who'd represented BTK during his confessions, and Mark Rudy. They wanted him to stop talking to the media, but it was too late for that and he wasn't going to listen to their advice anyway.

# XXXX

By dawn of June 1, Lindsey had been contacted by CBS's *Early Morning*, ABC's *Good Morning, America*, and *Inside Edition*. A *New York Times* reporter was camped outside her home and the local press were coming and going on her street. She'd received a call from the *Los Angeles Times* and from a journalist in London, while others were trying to reach her at the church day care center. She said no to most of them, but when she turned down *Good Morning, America*, a producer of the show showed up at her door with a bag of food. CBS countered by sending flowers, while CNN was demanding an exclusive arrangement that she speak only with them. Adjusting to the fact that her ex-husband was in jail for the murder of Dr. Tiller was only one of her challenges.

"Meeting all these media people," she says, "was like having an out-of-body experience."

She and Nick were big fans of cable TV's MSNBC and particularly of Rachel Maddow, the Air America radio talk show host who'd ascended to nightly appearances on the network during the 2008 election cycle. By May 2009, she had her own evening program and was an established star in the progressive wing of American politics. Funny, brilliant, and to the left of most of MSNBC's on-air talent, Maddow was about as far removed from *The O'Reilly Factor* and the abortion views of Scott Roeder as you could get—one reason that Lindsey and her son liked her so much. Right after the murder, Maddow had Tiller's colleague Dr. Susan Hill, of North Carolina, on to talk about violence against abortion providers.

"We're still here," Dr. Hill said, "and we're going to be here."

Maddow invited Lindsey to be on her show, but the appearance didn't take place, yet Lindsey did go on CNN. Nick gave no interviews, and ever since hearing about Dr. Tiller's death and his father's arrest, he'd repeatedly asked himself if he'd observed anything unusual about his dad last Friday during their final evening together, any clues that might have caused him to intervene and prevent this tragedy. The truth was that he hadn't, but that didn't make the killing any easier to understand or accept.

By Wednesday afternoon, June 3, most of the reporters had left Lindsey alone, including the one who'd kept jumping out of the bushes whenever she'd walked outside. She handwrote a sign—"Family Sleeping Please Respect Our Wishes"—and put it by the front stoop, then lay down to rest for the first time since last Saturday night. She hadn't really had any time alone for almost four days, or any time to feel what she'd just been through, and was about to doze off when she heard a soft tapping at the door. It was probably the FBI or the ATF or the WPD. Glancing outside, she saw a middle-aged woman in shorts, who announced that she was a friend of Scott's.

Opening the door, Lindsey was perplexed and a little frightened.

"Tell me who you are," she said.

She was the girlfriend Roeder had brought to the house more than fifteen years earlier, when Nick was five. Lindsey remembered the couple kissing and fondling each other in front of the boy, before Scott took him aside and showed him images of aborted fetuses.

Lindsey slammed the door shut, suddenly filled with memories and fears—the old fear from Nick's childhood that Scott would take the boy away and they'd never come back, the deepest fear that she couldn't protect her son from the man she'd chosen as her husband. Walking back inside the house, she sat down and began to tremble and then to cry, and this time, unlike every other time she'd felt like crying since last Sunday afternoon, she gave in to it. As she sobbed, all the pain she'd pushed aside through all the years came rushing up, the pain of marrying someone who had disappointed and hurt her and failed to stand up for his son; the pain of living with somebody who was unreliable and unstable and verbally abusive, wasting their money and refusing to support their child; the pain of having contacted law enforcement again and again—the FBI and the Kansas City police—and trying to tell them that Scott was dangerous and had to be stopped, but nobody had listened or taken action; the pain of reaching out to Scott's family, but they hadn't wanted to hear about his extremism and hoped it was just a temporary phase.

She cried because she'd wondered for the past two decades what she could have done better as a wife, a mother, and a daughter to help her ex-husband, her son, and her aging father. And because she believed that Scott should have received psychiatric treatment long ago, but he'd refused every opportunity to help himself. And now she couldn't help him and it was clear to everyone just how dangerous he was, and she was afraid that he'd send somebody to her home to harm her or Nick.

She wept for all the times her ex had called her ignorant and demeaned her and she'd endured this, trying to keep the peace, but one day her silence would end and then he'd hear her truth.

# XXXXI

America's press corps was ramping up to come to Wichita for the biggest media event in the city since the February 2005 arrest of BTK. Members of the National Organization for Women (NOW) and other feminist groups, along with anti-abortion protesters from coast to coast, were phoning, e-mailing, and texting one another, offering their opinions or making plans to attend the funeral. South central Kansas would be a battleground once again, even as Dr. Tiller was being buried.

On the night of his death, Wichita held a vigil for him at the heavily guarded Reformation Lutheran, with his wife and family in attendance (in all, forty-five states would hold vigils for the slain man, while in Congress U.S. Representative Louise Slaughter of New York called for a resolution condemning the murder). On Friday, June 5, three hundred people came to an interfaith wake at Wichita's First United Methodist Church, sponsored by Christian, Jewish, and Muslim organizations, but the largest event was the funeral the following morning. Under a sunlit sky fast becoming oppressive, the WPD and U.S. marshals started arriving at 7 a.m. for the ten o'clock service at College Hill United Methodist Church. By eight, the media had assembled along the side streets and neighbors were coming out to watch from their porches, a police chopper circling overhead. At 8:30, fifty American Legion members rolled in on their motorcycles to honor Tiller as a navy veteran and to provide a show of muscle if protesters tried to disrupt the memorial.

Worshippers from Reformation Lutheran stood by the front of the church giving out white carnations, as the Tiller family distributed a handout that read, "Family, friends and colleagues have come together to celebrate the life of a devoted humanitarian and loving father, grandfather and husband, George R. Tiller, M.D. People are here today from across the country to celebrate . . . a man who wholeheartedly dedicated his life to kindness, courtesy, justice, love and respect."

More than a dozen demonstrators showed up from Fred Phelps's Westboro Baptist Church in Topeka. Known mostly for picketing military funerals because of their opposition to U.S. Army policy regarding gays, the protesters were kept a block away from the church by police. They held up a sign reading, "God Sent the Shooter." Phelps's eldest daughter, Shirley Phelps-Roper, led them in singing "Killing children makes God angry" to the tune of John Denver's "Take Me Home, Country Roads." When Reverend John Martin of College Hill United Methodist approached the group and tried to offer them carnations, they screamed in his face. A cop told him to back away, and he did.

Outside the church, one hundred people, including the civil rights lawyer Gloria Allred, formed a long line—a "Martyr Guard"—stretching down the block and designed to protect the Tiller family as they entered the service. The guard wore "National Organization for Women" T-shirts with "Attitude Is Everything" written across the back. Inside the sanctuary, seven hundred people found seats, with a video screen in the overflow room providing funeral coverage to the media and three hundred others, including some former Tiller patients. His casket was draped in a white shroud and to its left was a portrait of the doctor and a towering floral arrangement spelling out, "TRUST WOMEN." Hundreds of mourners also wore "Attitude Is Everything" buttons. The crowd was estimated at a thousand, but no prominent Kansas politician, such as the former governor, Kathleen Sebelius, or the head of a major anti-abortion organization, such as Operation Rescue's Troy Newman, was present.

All four of Tiller's grown children spoke. The oldest, Jennifer, said that her father had told her that "life is like an Impressionist painting. When you are up close to it, it can be confusing and not make any sense . . . Only when you stand back from it can you see the broad, masterful strokes of the artist . . . Maybe my dad wasn't even aware of what he painted because he was so close to it . . . As I look out on you today—all of you, in many colors—I see all the brushstrokes . . . all the dots. I see all the people, the color, the canvas of my dad's life . . . He really did paint an incredible masterpiece, and it's . . . all of you. You are my dad's living masterpiece."

Throughout the service, the word "abortion" was avoided and only Tiller's son, Maury, referred to the shooting: "I struggle with the manner in which he was welcomed into heaven."

The family announced the establishment of the George R. Tiller Memorial Fund for the Advancement of Women's Health, and Larry Borcherding, a Tiller friend since college, delivered the twenty-two-minute eulogy:

"Dear God, get heaven ready because Mr. Enthusiasm is coming. Heaven will never be the same . . ."

The emotional crescendo of the morning came when Jeanne Tiller stood to sing and dedicated her performance to "my best buddy and the love of my life." With her head erect and her back straight, in a voice that didn't waver and over the sounds of weeping, she belted out the Lord's Prayer and received a standing ovation. Even some journalists in attendance had difficulty holding back tears and were talking about the performance months later. As the funeral came to a close, mourners walked out into the burning sunshine and a few pro-choice activists talked to the press.

"First we cry," said Gloria Allred, "and then we fight."

The succinct floral arrangement beside Tiller's casket resonated beyond any of the songs or speeches. The phrase "Trust Women" was deceptively simple and went to the heart of the war over abortion—the two words implying that it wasn't for government, religion, men, or other social institutions to decide what was right for the individual female when confronting one of life's most wrenching moments. Women were ultimately responsible for dealing with the consequences, good and bad, of their choices, and real freedom, real equality, and real responsibility included the right to make a wrong or harmful decision. Some women who'd had abortions weren't haunted by them, but others were and the haunting could live on for decades. I'd spent considerable time at a Denver women's prison visiting an inmate serving a life sentence for killing a young wife and mother, just like herself. She blamed the murder in part on the residue of her teenage abortion. She may have been using this argument to dull some of her guilt and shame over gunning down another woman, but whenever we spoke about this one thing became clear: she'd taken me into an intensely female realm that was outside of my own experience. There were parts of her life as a woman that I could not enter into.

Dr. Tiller could have easily taken a different career path and avoided danger, but he became, as he once put it, "a willing participant" in the abortion war, committing himself to it until death. The flowers by his casket made a fitting final statement about his beliefs: you can't really protect women or men from their choices, so let them have their own lives and trust the process. Given the history of society's efforts to control women's sexuality and reproduction, this remained a revolutionary idea. No wonder it disturbed and frightened some people so deeply.

# XXXXII

One pallbearer in Wichita was Dr. Warren Hern. Four days after the service, the Boulder physician wrote a letter to President Obama, calling on the chief executive to look at Tiller's death in the larger context of investigating and stopping domestic terrorism. Over the years, Hern had received "thousands of death threats" and it was "past time for this continuing anti-abortion terrorism and violence to end . . . We need your help—now."

The following day, Hern expanded on this theme during an address at Denver's Temple Emmanuel, the same synagogue where almost twenty-five years earlier to the day, Alan Berg had been memorialized. The speakers at Tiller's funeral had tried to avoid controversy, but that had never been Hern's style. He didn't narrow his focus on Tiller's assassination, but described the environment that had surrounded and supported it, an environment about to explode across America into more racial and religious violence.

"In the highly specialized world of late-term abortion for women with desperate needs," he said, "George and I were each other's only peers. Within two weeks after starting to do abortions at Colorado's first freestanding, nonprofit abortion clinic in Boulder in 1973, I started getting obscene death threats in the middle of the night. I slept with a rifle by my bed at my house in the mountains, and I expected someone to try to kill me . . .

"After two dozen clinic bombings in 1984, FBI Director William Webster said that the incidents weren't terrorism because 'we don't know who's doing it.' Since those times, the anti-abortion rhetoric has been filled with descriptions of doctors as 'baby killers,' 'mass murderers,' and 'child killers.' The anti-abortion fanatics call themselves 'pro-life' while they are killing doctors and other health workers who help women . . . 'Pro-life' is not a neutral, descriptive term. It is a dagger of psychological warfare that is backed by hate and terror . . . a profound libel and insult to those who help women. Words kill, and the phrase 'pro-life' is an obscene and grotesque sophistry . . .

"Fox News TV host Bill O'Reilly, who calls himself 'pro-life,' made an obsession of obscenely referring to Dr. Tiller as 'George Tiller, the baby killer.' He repeated this epithet dozens of times. He demonized and vilified Dr. Tiller on the public airwaves. This is called 'target identification.' This is electronic fascism . . ."

Because of his outspoken response to Tiller's murder, Hern would soon get a call from an O'Reilly producer in New York, asking him to appear on the show to debate the abortion issue. Hern had been on Fox before, with the talk show host Sean Hannity, who'd angered the physician by referring to him as "Mr." instead of "Dr." Following Tiller's death, Hern was expecting a call from Fox and was prepared for it. He had his own ideas about how to conduct an on-air interview between himself and O'Reilly, and when the call came in, he would give the producer an earful.

Hern said at the synagogue, "We don't have to invade other countries to find terrorists. They are right here, killing abortion doctors . . .

"[Dr. Tiller] represented the value of the individual adult human being as opposed to state control of individual lives. He represented a thought. The man who killed Dr. Tiller tried to kill a thought. The idea that an embryo or fetus is equal to, or more important than, the life of a cantankerous adult doctor is no longer a sick private delusion.

It is a collective psychosis masquerading as religion that has become a political force threatening democratic society . . . The main difference between the American anti-abortion movement and the Taliban is about eight thousand miles . . .

"I am now, once again, under the twenty-four-hour protection of heavily armed U.S. marshals. They risk their lives for me . . . The American anti-abortion movement is opposed to the rule of law, a secular society, the American Constitution, representative government, personal freedom, democracy and thought. The spirit of true freedom, the security of its citizens, the peace of civil society, and the soul of America is at stake here. Dr. Tiller's assassination is the latest blow to that freedom.

"Wake up, America."

On the day of Tiller's funeral, Roeder called the Associated Press from jail and spoke about the crime. His comments quickly became public, and one was provocative enough to change his legal status.

"I know," he told the AP reporter, "there are many other similar events planned around the country as long as abortion remains legal."

Hearing this, Judge Warren Wilbert bumped the inmate's bond from $5 million to $20 million.

But this did not keep "similar events" from happening across America.

Within twenty-four hours of Tiller's death, a father and his nine-year-old daughter were gunned down in southern Arizona. The police arrested Shawna Forde, leader of the anti-illegal-immigration group Minutemen American Defense, as the key suspect in the murder of Brisenia and Raul Flores. The day after Tiller was killed, Private William Andrew Long of the U.S. Army had just completed basic training and was volunteering at the west Little Rock, Arkansas, recruiting office before taking an assignment in South Korea. While smoking a cigarette outside the building, he was shot dead and an eighteen-year-old fellow soldier, Private Quinton I. Ezeagwula, eighteen, was seriously wounded. The alleged gunman, Abdulhakim Muhammad, age twenty-three, told investigators that he wanted to kill as many army personnel as he could "because of what they had done to Muslims in the past."

Echoing Roeder, Muhammad then made a collect call to the Associated Press from the Pulaski County jail.

"I do feel I'm not guilty," he told the AP. "I don't think it was murder, because murder is when a person kills another person without justified reason."

Muhammad's actions were multiplied several months later when Major Nidal Malik Hasan, a military psychiatrist and a Muslim, allegedly opened fire at Fort Hood, Texas, killing thirteen people and wounding thirty others. Hit by return fire, he survived the worst mass shooting ever at an American military base. Hasan was about to be deployed to an Afghanistan war zone and was enraged over how U.S. military personnel treated Muslims and the racial and religious slurs he'd heard at the base. The United States was conducting a "war on Islam" and he wanted "to do good work for God."

On June 10, the day Dr. Hern wrote President Obama asking for help with domestic terrorism directed at abortion doctors, eighty-eight-year-old James von Brunn charged into the crowded U.S. Holocaust Memorial Museum in Washington, D.C., armed with a rifle. The museum draws about 1.7 million visitors a year and sits across from the National Mall and within sight of the Washington Monument. It houses exhibits and records from the Holocaust, and that evening it planned to debut a play about the Nazis' victim Anne Frank and the American civil rights martyr Emmett Till. In 2002, two white supremacists had plotted to build a fertilizer bomb, like the one Timothy McVeigh had used in Oklahoma City, to level this museum.

A few days before Von Brunn came to the museum, President Obama had visited the former concentration camp at Buchenwald, Germany.

"There are those who insist the Holocaust never happened," he'd said at Buchenwald. "This place is the ultimate rebuke to such thoughts, a reminder of our duty to confront those who would tell lies about our history."

James von Brunn had an anti-Semitic Web site and was the author of *Kill the Best Gentiles*. Internet writings attributed to him said that the Holocaust was a hoax and decried a Jewish conspiracy to "destroy the white gene pool . . . At Auschwitz, the 'Holocaust' myth became Reality, and Germany, cultural gem of the West, became a pariah among world nations." Back in 1981, while carrying a revolver, a knife, and a sawed-off shotgun, Von Brunn had entered the room next to where the Federal Reserve Board was meeting. Because of high interest rates and the nation's economic difficulties, he hoped to take board members hostage, but his actions ended in a conviction for attempted kidnapping. In 2004 and '05, he'd lived briefly in Hayden Lake, Idaho, for many years home to the Aryan Nations compound that recruited the men in the Order who killed Alan Berg.

When Von Brunn burst into the Holocaust Memorial Museum on June 10, several thousand people were looking at exhibits. He emptied his rifle, killing an African-American security guard, thirty-nine-year-old Stephen T. Johns, before being shot and hospitalized in critical condition (he died in early January 2010).

"This outrageous act," President Obama said after the assault, "reminds us that we must remain vigilant against anti-Semitism and prejudice in all its forms."

The Secret Service reported that death threats against Obama himself were up 400 percent since he'd taken office, the highest level ever for an American president. Two preachers, Wiley Drake in Buena Park, California, and Steven Anderson of Tempe, Arizona, made no secret of their prayers for Obama's death. On the Internet, the president's enemies were gearing up to sell T-shirts, teddy bears, bumper stickers, framed tiles, and notepads carrying a biblical quotation from Psalms 109:8: "Let his days be few . . . Let his children be fatherless and his wife a widow."

Three days after the shooting by Von Brunn, the longtime Republican activist Rusty DePass added to the racially charged atmosphere spreading across the country by making a reference to First Lady Michelle Obama on Facebook. A gorilla that had escaped from a zoo in Columbia, South Carolina, he said, was "just one of Michelle's ancestors—probably harmless."

# XXXXIII

One day before Von Brunn's attack, the Tiller family surprised many on both sides of the abortion issue by announcing that it was permanently closing WHCS.

"It was," said Julie Burkhart, "the right thing to do. It had to happen."

"We are thankful," said Operation Rescue's Troy Newman, "that Tiller's clinic will not reopen and thankful that Wichita is now abortion-free."

Nancy Northup, president of New York City's Center for Reproductive Rights, stated that the end of WHCS "illustrates the ongoing harassment endured by abortion providers [and] . . . leaves an immediate and immense void in the availability of abortion."

That "void" had now spread to most parts of the United States. According to 2005 statistics from the Guttmacher Institute, a think tank focused on sexual and reproductive health, about 87 percent of American counties had no abortion providers. In Kansas it had been 96 percent before the Tiller homicide.

Following the pronouncement, Roeder called the CNN reporter Ted Rowlands and declared the WHCS closing "a victory for all the unborn children." While not admitting to killing Dr. Tiller, he said that if he was tried and convicted of the crime, "the entire motive was the defense of the unborn."

With Tiller dead, his clinic gone, and a turbulent era in Kansas politics finished, I decided to contact someone I'd been thinking about since the physician's demise. Paul Morrison's law office was in Olathe, where he now worked as a defense attorney, and I was curious about his views on the murder and the shutting down of WHCS. Who could say what would have happened if he'd never met Linda Carter? Or if Dr. Tiller had never gone on trial because of the Inquisition? Since the sex scandal that had led to Morrison's resignation as attorney general in late 2007, he'd tried to keep a low profile and seemed taken aback by my call, making it very clear very fast that he didn't want to discuss any of these matters.

"My opponents," he said in a weary voice, "always painted me as a big pro-choice supporter, but that really isn't true."

When I attempted to pose a question about what had happened to Tiller, the former DA cut me off.

"To tell you the truth," he said, "all I'm trying to do right now is make some money."

Then he hung up.

I dialed another lawyer, Dan Monnat in Wichita, who'd had several weeks to absorb the recent events.

"It's a real shame," he said, "that the history of the world is so much about the loss of our human champions, particularly in the arena of civil rights. That's what this fight is really all about—the right of a woman to choose is a civil right and the slaying of a doctor who allows a woman to make those choices and enjoy that civil right is a political assassination. How do self-serving politicians like Phill Kline and his minions not take some responsibility for the death of someone they unfairly and repeatedly demonized in the press by name-calling and frivolous prosecutions?"

How had the loss of Dr. Tiller affected him personally?

He didn't respond immediately, but sounded as if he were shuffling some papers on his desk, in an attempt to maintain his composure.

"It's our duty as lawyers to help a family in crisis," he said, "but then the emergency subsides and things eventually settle down. The media attention starts to fade away. Time passes and the quiet moments set in when you're alone with your thoughts and it dawns on you that someone's energy and life and vitality are not in your life anymore. You feel that—you feel the absence of it. You realize that you're never going to experience somebody's sense of humor and humanity again. Ever."

He was silent for a few moments, then cleared his throat. "People are free to speak their mind against abortion and to protest against it, but it's illegal to block a woman's access to a clinic or to kill a doctor. These criminal acts are nothing but terrorism. If your goal is to change the abortion law, change it through legal channels."

As Tiller's death continued to resonate and spring became summer in 2009, something building beneath the country's surface for years and intensifying since the Obamas moved into the White House was fully unleashed. Widespread rage erupted against the new president as he tried to go forward with his administration and his plans to reform health care. From coast to coast, people organized protests against him and carried signs comparing him to Adolf Hitler. One racially unsettling poster showed him wearing pancake makeup and a splash of red lipstick, like the Joker in a Batman movie. The "Tea Party" demonstrations against the president and his plan to change health care were just coming into vogue. A nationwide movement of citizens calling themselves "birthers" constantly questioned Obama for not having a proper birth certificate, even though this issue had been resolved to the satisfaction of the American public and U.S. voting laws long before the 2008 election. In Denver, for example, the talk show host Peter Boyles put up on his Web page this headline above an image of American schoolchildren honoring the new chief executive: "BARACK OBAMA KIDS AND HITLER YOUTH SING FOR THEIR LEADER."

Not to be outdone, State Senator Dave Schultheis of Colorado compared the president to the September 11 terrorists.

"Don't for a second," he tweeted, "think Obama wants what is best for U.S. He is flying the U.S. Plane right into the ground at full speed. Let's Roll."

Fox's Glenn Beck, meanwhile, homed in on the issue that had shaped so much of American history and driven the first Civil War.

The president, Beck stated, had "a deep-seated hatred for white people or the white culture. This guy is, I believe, a racist . . . The Manchurian Candidate couldn't destroy us faster than Barack Obama. If you were planning a sleeper to come in and become president of the United States, this is how he would do it."

In the wake of such rhetoric, the same thing began happening to the Obama family that had earlier happened to Alan Berg and George Tiller, once they'd repeatedly been identified as targets of hatred. A man standing on a street corner in Maryland held up a placard reading "Death to Obama" and "Death to Michelle and Her Two Stupid Kids." In New Hampshire, a protester brought a holstered gun to a political gathering, and a North Carolina man pled guilty to threatening Obama, after calling 911 twice from his trailer south of the Virginia border and declaring that he was going to assassinate the president. The Alan Berg story was back with a vengeance, reaching into the top levels of the American government and affecting the new president in ways none of the rest of us could really imagine. What conversations did he and the First Lady now have about the safety of their family? And how did this impact his thinking or acting on public policy issues?

The story I'd personally tried to avoid since the late 1980s no longer seemed avoidable. About an hour after Dr. Tiller was killed, I was contacted by a woman I'd grown up with who told me about the crime before this news had been released to the media. Then I learned that a nurse who'd worked on one of Tiller's last operations at Wesley Medical Center was from my hometown, along with a police officer who'd been assigned to the case minutes after the shooting. My sister's first-grade teacher was Scott Roeder's grandmother and the Kansas militia had an outpost in my native county.

In mid-June, I packed a bag, rented a car, turned up the satellite

radio, and headed for Wichita, moving toward a reality I'd been pursuing, in one form or another, for at least twenty-five years. Or maybe it
had been pursuing me. Hate groups across the country were up more
than 50 percent and white supremacists were reuniting with a renewed
sense of purpose. The new American civil war, which appeared to have
faded for a few weeks after Barack Obama had become president, was
in full force.

Driving through western Kansas, I saw a billboard showing a huge
image of Jesus rising out of a wheat field, holding stalks of grain in his
hand and trying to recruit for Christianity. Numerous signs along I-70
held messages like "Abortion Kills What God Created." The billboard
and signs made me uncomfortable, as they had every previous time I'd
driven this road back to my hometown. They were a part of where I was
from, a part of me I couldn't escape, a part of the war that was affecting
countless Americans. With the Grateful Dead playing in the background, I drove and thought about President Obama, whose African
father was black and whose white mother, Stanley Ann Dunham, came
from just outside Wichita. Racial discomfort and racism itself were
things the president had known intimately since birth. I wondered if
he, like so many of his countrymen, had learned to live with a divided
heart—with love for his homeland and family, but with shame for the
sins that lay very close to his bones and his blood.

Wichita was just over the next hill.

# ON THE ROAD

# XXXXIV

Twelve days after Tiller's death, Roeder wrote to his ex-wife from jail. He was no longer forced to wear the "skirt" that had restrained his movements inside the cell and was off suicide watch, but his mood wasn't good. Reading his letter, Lindsey wondered if he'd been in a manic phase before and during the murder, but had then crashed, sitting by himself in solitary confinement with nothing but a mattress and a toilet. His confusion and bitterness about marriage and fatherhood were festering again, and he'd selected his target of blame.

He'd heard "from secondhand sources" about Lindsey's interviews with the media following the shooting and this had further angered him. If she was willing "to share with the world" her views about Tiller's demise, Roeder wrote, would she let him know what she'd said? He surmised that he'd never hear back from her about this request— "because that would keep in character with being the grown up spoiled brat that you are," the same character he accused her of displaying hundreds of times in the past when she'd hung up on him.

But his real concern was with Nick, who'd also turned into a spoiled brat. During their marriage, he'd taught their son "basic things in life LIKE SAYING THANK YOU," but Nicholas never thanked him for taking him out to dinner or to a movie or after Roeder had given him money. At the end of their evenings together, Nick would just say good-bye, and Roeder was particularly rankled that he'd lately given the young man "a fairly decent knife," but received no gratitude in return.

"I'm sorry to say," he wrote Lindsey, "but it looks like you've done a very poor job of raising Nicholas after our divorce."

Along with the letter, Roeder had sent Lindsey and his son very graphic photos and some writings he'd received from Iowa's Dan Holman, of the anti-abortion group Missionaries to the Preborn. The material included the infamous biblical passage from Genesis 9:6, "Whosoever sheds man's blood, by man his blood shall be shed." Following the killing in Wichita, Holman had told CNN that "all abortionists are deserving of death, and they are not the only ones. There are politicians and judges, and others who support this murder are also deserving of death."

When asked about the assassination of Dr. Tiller, Holman replied, "I was cheered by it."

Roeder fired off another angry letter to Troy Newman, after learning that the head of Operation Rescue had publicly stated that the inmate was "not a friend, not a contributor, not a volunteer" to OR. During a jailhouse interview, Roeder told *The Kansas City Star* what he'd been telling others since the shooting: he'd donated at least a thousand dollars to Operation Rescue and had the paperwork to prove it. To the *Star*, he claimed that he'd written Newman, "You better get your story straight because my lawyer said it'd be good for me to show that I was supporting a pro-life organization."

Operation Rescue had larger concerns than Roeder's pointed remarks to Newman. For years it had thrived financially by having a visible enemy like Tiller to stir up passion and inspire its members to keep sending in money; with him gone, the impact was quick and severe. During the summer of 2009, the organization told supporters that it faced a "major financial crisis" and might shut down entirely unless help arrived soon. It also reported that since Tiller's demise, it had received a number of death threats.

While Operation Rescue, Kansans for Life, and other anti-abortion

groups had immediately distanced themselves from Roeder, the extremists in the movement rallied around the inmate. They were still
talking about pooling their funds and hiring a private attorney for the
defendant to fight the first-degree murder charge with a legal strategy
called the "necessity defense" or "defending those who cannot defend
themselves." One was justified in committing a murder, went this argument, in order to stop a greater evil. The tack had been tried before
in the case of Paul Hill, and it had failed.

Donald Spitz, the sponsor of the Army of God Web site, sent Roeder
seven anti-abortion pamphlets, which the prisoner distributed to others
through the mail. He got more support from two anti-abortionists in
the Kansas City area, Anthony Leake and Eugene Frye, and Leake in particular saw him as a new hero of their movement. Roeder had the backing of the activist Michael Bray, author of *A Time to Kill*, and of Dave
Leach of Des Moines, Iowa. In 1996, Leach had interviewed Roeder for
his *Uncle Ed Show* on Des Moines's public access cable, giving Roeder the
chance to explain his Freeman philosophy. In the mid-1990s, Roeder
had visited Shelley Shannon in a Topeka jail, and she now sent him money
from her cell in Minnesota, where she was still serving time for her anti-
abortion crimes. Bray, Leach, and Spitz had all signed the 1993 declaration advocating the use of force against abortion providers, distributed by
Paul Hill before he'd killed Dr. John Britton. Following Tiller's murder,
Leach created a homemade video, available on the Internet. It featured
two very young girls, one black and one white, who stood next to some
stuffed animals and posed questions.

"Can a pro-lifer," the white girl asked, "shoot an abortionist and still
get a trial . . . by jury?"

Leach answered this by saying that "most lawyers" did not expect
Roeder to get "what average citizens would call a trial by jury. I'm trying to help him get one." To this end, Leach began composing a detailed and legally sophisticated motion that would run to more than a
hundred pages and eventually be submitted to the judge in Roeder's case.
Leach would emerge as the defendant's most significant anti-abortion

ally and his document would play a role in the upcoming trial—a role that some found outrageous.

As Roeder communicated with the fringes, U.S. Attorney General Eric Holder spoke to the Washington Lawyers Committee for Civil Rights and Urban Affairs. The recent killings in Wichita, at the Holocaust Museum, and elsewhere in America, he said, showed the need for a tougher U.S. hate crimes law to stop "violence masquerading as political activism . . . Over the last several weeks, we have witnessed brazen acts of violence, committed in places that many would have considered unthinkable." He urged Congress to pass an updated version of the current hate crimes legislation, allowing for more effective prosecution of those who attacked people based on gender, disability, or sexual orientation. Holder also issued a directive to all U.S. Attorneys' Offices to coordinate with the FBI, the U.S. Marshal's Service, ATF, local law enforcement officials, and reproductive health care service providers to assess the current level of threats and take any and all measures to ensure that criminal conduct would be prosecuted.

The most intriguing official question following the death in Wichita was whether or not the Department of Justice would take Dr. Hern's suggestion and open a larger probe into those who for years had openly called for the murder of abortion doctors. Did Roeder's activist friends have any culpability in Tiller's murder? Did they come under the umbrella of abetting a hate crime? Had they supported Roeder financially in a way that might have aided the shooting? And would the government go after suspects who'd advocated this kind of domestic terrorism, as they had in the Alan Berg case? That investigation had focused on all twenty-four members of the Order who'd either pled guilty or were successfully prosecuted under the federal RICO (Racketeer Influenced and Corrupt Organizations) statute. Would the feds employ it again, or conclude that Roeder was a "lone wolf" who'd acted by himself?

The murder of Dr. Tiller was the most publicized hate crime in years, and the first of its magnitude since President Obama had taken office. How the government responded would help define the new administration.

In June 2009, Dr. Hern became the target of an anti-abortionist and three months later a Denver grand jury indicted Donald Hertz, a seventy-year-old retired real estate broker from Spokane, Washington. He was charged with calling Hern's Boulder office and threatening to kill his family.

Over the summer, *The O'Reilly Factor* contacted Hern, as he'd anticipated, and asked him to appear on the show. He expressed interest in doing this—*if* he could fly to New York and go on the program with his lawyer, and *if* his interview would be aired as it had been recorded and not subjected to a lot of editing. In the aftermath of Tiller's murder and his own recent threat, Hern was ready for Fox.

"O'Reilly," he says, "is a bully and a paid thug. I wasn't going to duck him or to take any of his shit on the air. I wanted to do this for George because he never wanted to defend himself against these people. We have to confront them and call them what they are."

According to Hern, he gave an O'Reilly producer several conditions under which he would be on the program and several dates that worked for him to make an appearance. He didn't hear back with a confirmation.

"Mr. O'Reilly," Hern says, "knew that he was not going to have a very pleasant experience with me. So they backed down. I guess they want to wait and have me on their show after *another* abortion doctor gets murdered."

# XXXXV

On a July Sunday afternoon, Lindsey drove around suburban Kansas City, retracing her ex-husband's steps leading up to the murder.

"I feared Scott for a period of time," she'd once written, "and was constantly afraid he would kidnap Nick—but down deep inside him somewhere was that funny sweet carefree guy I married. Scott not only killed Dr. Tiller. He killed Nick's dad and any remnants of the man I knew."

Both Lindsey and Jeanne Tiller had lost their spouses in this new American war, with one man facing possible life imprisonment and the other dead. Neither woman had been able to keep her husband from pursuing the things that moved him most passionately, but each had reacted very differently to the tragedy, at least in public. Lindsey wanted and needed to talk; she had decades of backed-up feelings, and the more she confronted them, the more she was able to give expression to her anger and hurt. It seemed to have a cathartic effect. She'd never bargained for marrying or living with a terrorist.

Jeanne Tiller had apparently turned down all interview requests, withdrawing within her family and closest friends, while preparing for the legal ordeal that lay ahead. Nick Roeder had done the same thing, despite Lindsey's encouraging him to open up about his dad. He wasn't yet able to say anything to his father, let alone to the rest of the world.

What was Jeanne Tiller's life like now, as a mother of four and grandmother of ten, with no one to send off to work in the morning and worry about until he was safely home at night inside their gated community? She and her family were survivors of a battle that hadn't existed when she'd married the promising young doctor; she also hadn't bargained for marrying a man who became a pariah in his own hometown. How had *she* coped since the mid-1970s being intimately connected to the target of people's rage and hatred? What had this cost her, even before Tiller had died? In March 2009, she'd sat in a courtroom next to Scott Roeder, not knowing who he was or how he felt about her husband. Now she'd be in court with him again, just a few feet away from the man who'd killed the love of her life. How would she cope with that?

And what about the nameless and faceless thousands of mothers, daughters, and sisters, the unknown brothers, sons, and fathers, the cousins and extended families and friends of those who'd been shot to death at work or inside a church, a school, a hospital, or a business because they'd walked into the wrong location on the wrong day? And then there were the shamed families of the killers who were living with a different kind of pain. More than a decade passed before Susan Klebold, the mother of the Columbine shooter Dylan Klebold, offered a few public comments about what her son had done in April 1999. When had we turned into a society so filled with "random violence" that it hardly seemed random at all?

The overwhelming difference in the United States between 1984, when Alan Berg was shot in an act of domestic terrorism, and 2009 was that extremism was no longer extreme. The sense of victimization that had once fueled the Order was now broadcast twenty-four hours a day on talk radio, on cable television, and was encouraged in countless other respectable venues. Public outrage was still all the rage, and still just as unexamined. Why were highly successful adults behaving in ways children on playgrounds were commanded not to? What were we fighting about? When had the need to be right overriden every other concern? How could such an unhealthy environment *not* produce violence? What if the problems were less political than behavioral?

# XXXXVI

Roeder's preliminary hearing was set for July 28, as the country heated up with "tea parties," town hall meetings, and other demonstrations against the Obama administration, a steadily rising volume of anger and inflamed rhetoric. At one gathering, a speaker said that the Democratic Party's proposed health care reform would bring about waves of physician-assisted suicide.

"Adolf Hitler," another protester declared, "issued six million end-of-life orders—he called his program the final solution. I kind of wonder what we're going to call ours."

Five years earlier, Americans for Prosperity, the organization founded by the Wichita native David Koch, had debuted as a conservative activist organization. Its critics saw it as a front for the petroleum and petrochemical industries, after it had circulated a pledge to federal, state, and local officials asking them to oppose any climate change legislation leading to an increase in government revenue. Nearly 150 lawmakers and candidates signed the pledge. By 2009, AFP had evolved into a leading anti-health-care-reform group. In the past few years, millions of Americans had seen their health insurance premiums double or triple, and for many families the cost of basic medical care was becoming prohibitive, but these were not issues for David Koch. He lived in Manhattan and was reportedly New York City's second-wealthiest resident, behind Mayor Michael Bloomberg. In 2008, Koch had pledged $110 million to renovate the New York State Theater at Lincoln Center, renamed the David H. Koch Theater. Two years earlier, he'd given $20 million to the American Museum of Natural History, creating the David H. Koch Dinosaur Wing.

Americans for Prosperity received funding from a Koch family foundation, and its opposition to health care reform was uncompromising. One of its projects was called "Patients First," and 220,000 Americans quickly signed its online petition.

"Congress," it read, "should oppose any legislation that imposes greater government control over my health care that would mean fewer choices for me and my family . . ."


In Wichita, Nola Foulston, the Sedgwick County district attorney, would be prosecuting Roeder herself, along with two assistant DAs, Kim Parker and Ann Swegle. The preliminary hearing was in the same downtown courthouse where Tiller had gone on trial last March, just three floors higher. Now Roeder was the defendant and facing both Gary Hoepner, who'd watched him shoot the doctor in the forehead in May, and Keith Martin, who'd chased him across the church parking lot and thrown coffee on him as he was speeding away. The two Reformation Lutheran ushers were still shaken by what they'd seen that Sunday morning, and Hoepner stopped his testimony several times to get himself under control.

In a white shirt and red tie, Roeder looked on from the defense table with his public defenders, Steve Osburn and Mark Rudy. The scuttlebutt around the courthouse was that while the anti-abortionists were still trying to find the defendant a private attorney, the best candidate had wanted a $60,000 retainer and the price tag was too high. Osburn and Rudy were experienced, dedicated lawyers, but their client had continued talking with the press and virtually admitted to certain reporters his role in the crime. His legal team didn't appear to dispute that Roeder had killed Dr. Tiller, but were contesting the two aggravated-assault charges that came from the defendant pointing his gun at Hoepner and Martin. Roeder had said that if his lawyers could get the lesser charges dropped, he might come up for parole in twenty years or so and not die in prison.

His shackled feet never stopped jumping beneath the defense table. He was hyper, constantly on the edge of his chair, shifting around and glancing over his shoulder at three people in the gallery. One was the Kansas City activist Eugene Frye and another was Jennifer McCoy of Wichita, who'd done time for two abortion clinic arsons in Virginia. The other, a handsome, gray-haired, middle-aged man, conjured up an aging tennis pro or a fashion photographer, except for his worn-looking fingers and meaty forearms, which belonged on a farmer or a butcher. Dressed casually in blue jeans and loafers, he carried a worn Bible and kept it open to the New Testament Epistles that Paul had written to the Ephesians when he was imprisoned in Rome in A.D. 62 or 63. As the testimony unfolded, the man went over certain passages again and again, underlining them and then tracing the underline with the tip of a pen as he read the ancient words. He seemed far more interested in absorbing this two-thousand-year-old text than in anything taking place in the courtroom. If he did not convey the impression of being a radical, that impression was false.

He was Tony Leake, who for years, according to *The Kansas City Star*, had "vocally supported the killing of abortion doctors."

Following Tiller's death, reporters had sought him out and he'd been interviewed by the *The Wichita Eagle*.

"I support the shooting of George Tiller as justifiable homicide," he'd told the paper. "I only wish it had happened in 1973, before he was able to murder his first child."

When Judge Warren Wilbert ordered the lunch recess, Leake took the elevator downstairs to the lobby.

With obvious pride, he talked of having edited Paul Hill's book.

"I'll get you a copy this afternoon," he promised a journalist.

Wearing a menacing grin, Leake said, "Tiller had nine lives and he'd used them all up. I wasn't sorry to see him stopped."

After nearly a full day of testimony, Judge Wilbert bound Roeder over for trial on the first-degree murder charge and two counts of aggravated assault. Jury selection was set for less than two months away, on September 21, which satisfied the defendant's desire to go to trial as soon as possible.

# XXXXVII

That evening Roeder greeted me as exuberantly in the jail visiting area as when we'd first met, a few weeks earlier. His spirits were high following the hearing and his good mood lasted until I mentioned that portions of the letters he'd written to his son during the past fifteen years had appeared on the front page of that day's *Eagle*. Glaring through the smudged glass wall between us, he dropped the receiver, shot out of his chair, and began pacing in the tiny, enclosed room, barely large enough to hold him.

"How did that happen?" he shouted. "Who did that?"

I shook my head, not telling him that Lindsey had recently given me copies of the same letters.

"Why did they put my private thoughts to my son in the paper? How can anyone do that?"

The good ol' boy mask he usually wore was gone and anger radiated off him as he paced and asked more questions. He cared more about Nick than anyone else and had been reaching out to the young man ever since the murder, hoping to salvage a connection there. His son wanted nothing to do with him and Roeder still didn't realize that he'd been an embarrassment to Nick for years and was now something far beyond that. The inmate had a kind of naïveté or ingrained innocence, even now, even after the murder, which made him all the more frightening. What had it been like for Nick to have him as a dad at Cub Scout meetings and elementary school gatherings, where he'd harangued other parents about abortion and bad government and not paying income taxes? What was it like for Nick today?

Roeder sat down and grabbed the phone. His cheeks, which incarceration had turned pale, were burning pink.

"Why did you come back to see me again?" he demanded. "Why are so you interested in this subject?"

I hesitated, uncertain how to respond. Like most reporters, I was much more comfortable interviewing others than being asked my own views.

I threw a question back at him about being in the courtroom at Dr. Tiller's trial last March and he unleashed a broadside against the prosecutor Barry Disney.

"He did nothing to stop the steamroller that was happening every day at Tiller's clinic," Roeder replied. "Operation Rescue said we'd be able to get his license lifted through the courts, but I'd been hearing that for years. If they couldn't convict him in court on these charges, how could they ever pull his license? That wasn't going to happen."

When asked about the conditions at the detention facility, he didn't complain as much as before. His cell was warmer now, he'd settled into the routine of being a prisoner and had adjusted to the food. Lindsey had half-jokingly told me that he might actually like being locked up, because he didn't have to hold down a job: "He has nothing to do all day but lie around, be served three meals, and have someone else do his laundry."

Looking back, what did Roeder remember most vividly about last May 31?

"I had relief running out of that church, man," he said. "Lots of relief. I'd gone in there with a pretty good idea of what Tiller looked like, but I had to pick him out from the other people and ushers. I was fairly sure it was him. After leaving the church, I got on those open roads to Kansas City and it was a really beautiful day for a drive. Sunny and warm and calm. I drove and drove and wondered what was going on back in Wichita. When the police finally pulled me over, I just sat there for a moment and thought, 'This is it.'"

He paused and said softly, "I've never considered myself a murderer."

Roeder had a gentleness that went in and out of focus almost minute by minute. His political and religious rage wasn't obvious and he wasn't a stereotypically angry white man, like the neo-Nazis I'd met earlier in my life. He wasn't macho and didn't subtly threaten me or try to test me. He seemed genuinely happy to have a visitor and genuinely pleased with what he'd done; he wanted me to be too. Tiller's death, it was obvious, meant nothing to him; he'd never mentioned anything about the doctor's family or what Jeanne Tiller and her children had been experiencing since the murder. It was the opposite of remorse; he saw himself as a modern-day Saint Paul, locked up for fighting a society gone wrong.

As with Randall Terry and other anti-abortion leaders, women simply did not figure into his equations. If all the abortion providers were dead, the problem would be solved, and he'd never have to think about those who sought to end their pregnancies through illegal or dangerous means.

Before coming to Kansas, I'd contacted a local clinical psychologist. In 1975, Dr. Howard Brodsky had moved to Wichita and for the next decade was chief psychologist for Sedgwick County Mental Health, before going into private practice. With a special interest in forensics, he'd been an expert witness at legal proceedings throughout the state, often testifying about a defendant's competency to stand trial. Following BTK's arrest, he'd become a national media commentator and was known for being incisive and somewhat irreverent.

"For a long time," he liked to say, "I've been the go-to guy in town for analyzing all the weird and disgusting stuff that people do."

Dr. Tiller's murder had occurred a few miles from Brodsky's office and when I brought up the alleged killer, he immediately said, "Roeder's a loser. He couldn't hold on to anything—not his wife or his son or even a place to live. He drove a fifteen-year-old Taurus. He couldn't stay employed at a McDonald's."

I'd always disliked terms like "loser" because they told me nothing that I wanted to know about a person. Yet when reading about the history of the anti-abortion movement, I'd kept running into one thing: many of the men who'd spearheaded it had never gone out into the world and learned a skill, a craft, or a profession, something that took years of effort and discipline, something based on actual experience and an accumulation of hard-earned knowledge. They'd had intense religious conversions, emerged from these events "born again," and declared their passionate desire to improve the world or rid it of evil. They'd desperately wanted to do something good for their country and given themselves the job of altering the course of American political, legal, and medical history, without anything approaching expertise in these fields.

What was the most significant change Dr. Brodsky had seen in his patients during the past thirty or forty years?

"That's easy," he said at once. "The incredible growth of narcissism. This wasn't a big problem or trend when I started working. Now it's all I see in my practice. It's everywhere, not just in criminals but throughout the entire culture. It's affected everything and is the underlying condition of our time. Several decades ago, Roeder would have stood out more in his community because of his narcissism, but now he doesn't. He blends in because there are so many other people who share some of these same traits. He thinks that he—and he alone—can very simplistically fight and stop evil. He can end abortion in America by killing Dr. Tiller. The murder will be a hugely transformative event for the country.

"Guess what? There are no transformative events in the sense that he's thinking about. Social change happens, but slowly and gradually. Murdering an abortion doctor is an act of extreme self-indulgence and narcissism on his part. It must have been a great shock for him to realize in the weeks after the murder that not only did everything not change, but that those people he believed were his close allies turned their backs on him. And tens of thousands of women are going to keep getting abortions."

How did Dr. Brodsky define narcissism?

"We all have a choice. We can either try to change ourselves emotionally, which takes real effort, or we can tell ourselves that we're changing the world. This is the fundamental narcissism of our age. People will do *anything* to avoid confronting and changing themselves. So what happens to others when they try to change the world doesn't really matter. Those people don't count. Roeder doesn't even see what he's done as a criminal act."

During his sixth day of incarceration, the inmate had phoned the Associated Press and told a reporter to expect more attacks like the one that had just happened in Wichita, prompting the state to raise his bail from $5 million to $20 million.

Sitting face-to-face with Roeder now, I asked him if he could be more specific. He wanted to open up, he said, but believed that the lines we were talking on were not secure, so he couldn't go into detail. Once he'd been tried, convicted, and transferred to a state prison, we'd be able to speak without using telephones and he'd be freer to divulge what he knew. More acts of terrorism were coming, he implied, and he was in on the plans.

As he'd done in my earlier visit, he bragged about stopping abortion in Wichita, but of course that wasn't the same thing as stopping abortion. According to state health statistics, roughly eighty thousand abortions were done annually in New York City alone. Closer to Kansas, Dr. LeRoy Carhart of Bellevue, Nebraska, had recently hired two people from Tiller's closed office and was using them to train his staff to perform late-term abortions. The sixty-eight-year-old physician had rechristened his business the Abortion and Contraception Clinic of Nebraska, and its new brochure featured a photo of Tiller, stating that "our services to women" were in honor of the slain man.

It wasn't long before Troy Newman showed up in Bellevue to launch Operation Rescue protests against Dr. Carhart and to submit a complaint about the physician to Jon Bruning, Nebraska's attorney general.

"We're trying," Newman told *The New York Times*, "to get criminal charges against him, to get his license revoked, and to get legislators there to look at the law."

Dr. Carhart, a former air force officer, had responded to Operation Rescue by installing a metal detector and security cameras, and bringing in a full-time security consultant. The physician had altered his route to and from work, given up eating in public, and when his daughter got married in the fall of 2009, the ceremony was held at a nearby military base because of the protection it offered.

Others besides Dr. Carhart were stepping in to replace Dr. Tiller and the services he'd provided in Wichita. In early 2010, Curtis Boyd, an Albuquerque physician, announced on his Web site that in response to Tiller's death he'd begun performing third-trimester abortions. The seventy-two-year-old Boyd had also hired two California doctors, Susan Robinson and Shelley Sella, who had worked with Tiller on a rotating basis. An ordained Baptist minister, Boyd explained in a 2008 speech his motives for becoming an abortion provider:

"In my generation, many of the doctors of conscience who chose to provide abortions were moved by the horrors of botched illegal abortions. But that was not what drove me to risk my career and sometimes my life. I was moved by the certain knowledge that women's lives could be ruined when they could not abort a pregnancy."

On the July evening Roeder and I spoke at the jail, Lindsey appeared on *Anderson Cooper 360* and blitzed the inmate in front of a worldwide audience—after the CNN reporter Gary Tuchman asked her what she'd like to say to her ex-husband.

"Scott," she answered, "you had no right to take another person's life. You're not God. You're not a judge. You're not a jury. You say that you are protecting the unborn, that you did it for the children, that you were justified. If you did it for the children, why did I have to fight for years to get child support to care for Nicholas? If you did it for the children—if you did it for the children—why wouldn't you pay for a dentist for Nicholas?"

She began to cry.

Lindsay and Nick both were on the prosecution's witness list, which meant they could be compelled to testify, but that wouldn't happen anytime soon. Roeder's September 21 trial date did not hold and jury selection was rescheduled for January 11, 2010. Since that was nearly six months away, the defendant continued thinking about hiring a private attorney, but he needed funds. His supporters, led by Regina Dinwiddie and Dave Leach, wanted to raise money by holding an eBay auction and selling memorabilia from the anti-abortion movement: an Army of God manual, videotapes of Paul Hill praying, a cookbook written in prison by Shelley Shannon, a copy of Michael Bray's *A Time to Kill*, and a bullhorn autographed by Dinwiddie herself, like the kind she'd used to protest abortion clinics (the originals had all been confiscated by the police). An inmate whom Roeder had befriended at the jail had done some drawings that the alleged killer had autographed and all these products were to be auctioned off—if eBay would permit it.

In a statement after this issue arose, the company said "eBay does not allow listings that promote or glorify violence, hate, racial or religious intolerance, or items that encourage, promote, facilitate or instruct others to engage in illegal activity."

When the Tiller family learned about the auction, it was appalled, and in a very rare public move, Jeanne Tiller had her attorney Lee Thompson send a letter to eBay asking its executives to halt the sale.

"These materials contain hate messages," Thompson wrote, "that glorify violence against abortion doctors who provide constitutionally protected medical services, and instruct on means of violence, including bombing, of abortion clinics. We urge you to deny access to the resources of eBay for this reprehensible and vile 'auction.'"

Lindsey also contacted eBay and asked the company to stop the event.

"I believe that this auction," she wrote in an e-mail, "could incite more violence on abortion doctors and clinics. I do not believe that cancelling this auction will in any way hinder Scott's right to an adequate defense, as he has a good team of public defenders."

The protests worked and eBay denied the auction, telling *The Kansas City Star* that these listings "would violate our policy regarding offensive material."

While this controversy played out on the local stage, the subject of abortion found itself at the heart of the most ambitious political reform in recent American history.

By September 2009, James Pouillon had regularly stood outside a local public high school in Owosso, Michigan, holding up a sign with one side depicting a chubby baby and the word "LIFE," while the other side displayed an image of an aborted fetus and the word "ABORTION." On September 11, the day before the nation's largest anti-Obama demonstration to date, a pickup stopped in front of the school and Harlan James Drake, a thirty-three-year-old local trucker, allegedly opened fire, killing Pouillon before driving on to a gravel pit business and murdering its owner. His motives were not revealed.

The next morning, tens of thousands of people marched to the U.S. Capitol carrying placards that read, "Obamacare Makes Me Sick," and denouncing illegal immigrants, increased taxes, restricted gun rights, and big government. Glenn Beck, whose annual earnings were now estimated at $23 million, had sponsored the rally and it had been organized by Freedomworks, a group headed by the former House Republican leader Dick Armey. Beck had chosen September 12 because it was one day after the eighth anniversary of the September 11 attacks on the United States. He'd started the "9/12 Project" in order to "bring us all back to the place we were on September 12, 2001" when "we were not obsessed with Red States, Blue States or political parties. We were united as Americans, standing together to protect the greatest nation ever created." In almost the exact spot where President Obama had been sworn in eight months earlier, Beck and Armey addressed the angry crowd, which waved posters calling Obama the "parasite in chief" and once again compared him to Hitler. Some of the demonstrators had come out dressed in costume—as Betsy Ross, Patrick Henry, and Death.

"Pelosi has to go!" they chanted, referring to the California representative and Speaker of the House Nancy Pelosi.

"You lie! You lie!" they shouted, echoing what Representative Joe Wilson (Republican of South Carolina) had yelled out three days earlier when interrupting President Obama's congressional address.

America had seen such populist uprisings before, going back to the inauguration of President Andrew Jackson in 1829, when hordes of protesters had stood on the White House lawn and railed against the money interests; in the 1850s, when the Know Nothing movement had sprung up over fears that German and Irish Catholic immigrants were destroying the country's traditional values and religious beliefs, opening the way for the pope to dictate to U.S. politicians; again with the 1890s People's Party, led by Western and Southern farmers ruined by the Panic of 1893; and more recently, in the efforts of the perennial presidential candidate Lyndon Larouche, who in 1988 was sentenced to fifteen years imprisonment for conspiracy to commit mail fraud and tax code violations. At the first national Tea Party convention in Nashville in early 2010, Sarah Palin declared that America was ripe for revolution. Mocking Obama's 2008 campaign slogans, she said, "How's that hope-y, change-y stuff workin' out for you?"

Populism, of course, is in the eye of the beholder. Palin received $100,000 for this nonprofit event.

# XXXXVIII

President Obama had staked his young presidency on health care reform, and by late 2009 abortion was the key issue in this battle. Democratic members of the House, led by Nancy Pelosi, supported a compromise allowing Americans to buy government-subsidized insurance plans covering abortion (as many as 87 percent of employer-based insurance policies currently offered their subscribers similar coverage). If this passed, families of four earning less than $88,000 a year would be eligible for federally subsidized insurance. A large majority of those expected to buy the new policies would pay part of the premium and receive government tax credits for the rest. Abortion foes, not just Republicans but conservative Democrats, vehemently opposed this policy and supported existing law, known as the Hyde amendment, under which government funds could be used for abortions only in cases of rape or incest, or to save the life of the mother. These restrictions also applied to Medicaid, military health care, and the federal employee health plan. In a letter signed by 183 lawmakers and sent to Speaker Pelosi, they wrote, "The U.S. government should not be in the business of promoting abortion as health care. Real health care is about saving and nurturing life, not about taking life."

In early November, as a House vote approached on America's biggest health care overhaul ever, Catholic and evangelical leaders saw an opportunity to accomplish something they couldn't get done during a collective five terms—or two full decades—under President Reagan and both President Bushes. While many Catholics had turned away from the 2004 Democratic Catholic presidential candidate John Kerry, a majority had supported Obama in 2008 and felt they had political leverage with him. In recent years, women's groups had placed less emphasis on abortion rights and the nation's support for abortion had gradually eroded to around 50 percent, from its earlier height of 75 percent. Now, with health care reform as *the* primary Democratic issue, both Republicans and the Catholic Church smelled vulnerability.

After Senator Ted Kennedy died in August 2009, Boston's Cardinal Sean O'Malley approached the president at the church altar at Kennedy's funeral and appealed to him not to back publicly funded abortions. The United States had 68 million Catholics and Cardinal O'Malley wanted the president to know that although the Church backed health care reform, the Vatican adamantly opposed abortion. It was a moment of great historical context. When running for president in 1960, the Catholic senator John Kennedy had diligently tried to convince Americans that if he won the White House, he wouldn't take orders from Rome. Half a century later, the Vatican was about to weigh in heavily on American politics.

On Friday, November 6, Nancy Pelosi got a call from Cardinal Theodore McCarrick, Washington, D.C.'s, former archbishop, who reiterated the pope's position on the abortion issue. Legally, the Catholic Church could not lobby for political causes and continue to maintain its tax-exempt status, but this kind of pressure was not technically considered lobbying (many Americans disagreed with this interpretation of the law and felt it should be changed). Ever since Cardinal O'Malley had gently muscled President Obama at Kennedy's funeral, Catholic officials across America had been talking with worshippers and local church officials about supporting health care reform—but opposing any public funding of abortion. The U.S. Conference of Bishops, the Church's Washington-based advocacy group, was staffed by 350 members who maintained close contact with Washington lawmakers. The organization sent out flyers to every parish in the country, asking Catholics to pray for restrictions on abortion and to phone their representatives and ask them to "fix these bills with pro-life amendments."

Evangelicals kept just as busy working their constituents. Since 1935, the highly secretive Washington Christian fellowship known as the Family had built a membership including scores of U.S. senators, congressmen, White House officials, military officers, corporate executives, and other politicians and ambassadors outside the United States. The Family was widely regarded as the best-connected fundamentalist Christian organization in the nation, if not the world. Its resident headquarters on Washington's C Street had twelve bedrooms, nine bathrooms, five living rooms, four dining rooms, three offices, a kitchen, and a small chapel. Rooms were rented out to those in Congress for a reported $600 a month for room and board. The Family's core purpose, according to its leader, Douglas Coe, was to offer public officials a place for Bible study, prayer meetings, and worship services, or to have a forum in which to share their personal troubles (in 2009, two Family members, Senator John Ensign of Nevada and Governor Mark Sanford of South Carolina, became embroiled in sex scandals). The group sponsored the National Prayer Breakfast, attended by every sitting U.S. president since 1953.

Coe also talked about the need to make a personal commitment to Jesus Christ. In a 1989 lecture, he proclaimed, "Jesus said, 'You have to put me before other people. And you have to put me before yourself.' Hitler—that was the demand to be in the Nazi party. You have to put the Nazi party and its objectives ahead of your own life and ahead of other people."

Coe saw parallels between Jesus' demands and those of the Red Guard during the Chinese Cultural Revolution: "I've seen pictures of young men in the Red Guard of China . . . They would bring in this young man's mother and father, lay her on the table with a basket on the end, he would take an axe and cut her head off. . . . They have to put the purposes of the Red Guard ahead of the mother-father-brother-sister—their own life! That was a covenant. A pledge. That was what Jesus said."

Two Family members were the longtime Pennsylvania Republican congressman Joe Pitts and Representative Bart Stupak, a Michigan Democrat. On November 6, after Speaker Pelosi got the call from Cardinal McCarrick, Stupak told her that if she wanted to get her health reform bill through Congress, she should meet with the Catholic bishop's staff, now assembled down the hall in his office. She took his advice and spoke with the group for three hours.

Congressmen Stupak and Pitts then introduced the Stupak-Pitts amendment, barring the use of federal funds for abortion coverage, except in cases involving rape, incest, or danger to the mother's life. If women wanted abortion coverage, they'd have to buy it separately. The amendment blindsided House Democrats. Stupak knew that virtually no Republicans were going to vote for the health reform bill in its present form and forty to sixty conservative Democrats would vote against it unless the amendment was accepted. He had Pelosi boxed in.

She then met with leaders of the 190-member Pro-Choice Caucus, explaining to them that without the Stupak amendment the bill was dead. Shouting matches and tears erupted in her office, with many in the caucus feeling betrayed by their leader. As Pelosi frantically tried to keep the reform bill on track, the word went out from America's Catholic hierarchy to announce "at all Masses" that priests and parishioners should tell House members: "Please support the Stupak Amendment that addresses essential pro-life concerns . . . If these serious concerns are not addressed, the final bill should be opposed."

Outside on the streets of Washington, abortion protesters stood next to the U.S. Capitol, carrying signs showing piles of bodies at the German concentration camp Dachau. The signs' caption read, "National Socialist Healthcare." Other placards displayed grisly photos identified as aborted fetuses.

On Saturday, November 7, with the vote coming that evening, Democrats launched a counterattack. If the bill passed, said Congresswoman Diana DeGette of Colorado, it would amount to the broadest "restriction of a woman's right to choose" in her lifetime. Representative Rosa DeLauro, a Connecticut Democrat, told *The New York Times* that "abortion is a matter of conscience on both sides of the debate. This amendment takes away that same freedom of conscience from America's women. It prohibits them from access to an abortion even if they pay for it with their own money. It invades women's personal decisions."

That night the House voted and sixty-four Democrats favored the Stupak-Pitts amendment, which passed 240–194, sending tremors through the Democratic Party's national leadership. The House's health reform bill, with the Stupak-Pitts amendment included, passed 220–215, gutting public funding for abortion. Exactly one Republican, Congressman Anh "Joseph" Cao of Louisiana, had voted for the bill. Representative DeGette now promised to kill this legislation if the Stupak-Pitts amendment wasn't stripped from the final version.

Feminist and women's rights groups immediately launched a public relations battle against the amendment:

"Stop Abortion Coverage Ban!" read an online solicitation from NARAL Pro-Choice America, which warned that women could lose the right to use "their own personal, private funds to purchase an insurance plan with abortion coverage in the new health system."

"Stop Stupak!" read the headline of an online petition doubling as a fund-raiser for Emily's List, which solicited contributions for female candidates who supported abortion rights.

President Obama had called for the health reform bill to be on his desk for his signature by Christmas 2009. He hoped to talk about the passage of this historic legislation at his State of the Union speech in January 2010. But the fight over abortion would threaten to take away the Democratic majorities in both houses of Congress and to weaken Obama's presidency.

The battle over sex and reproduction was intensifying not just nationally, but globally.


Within weeks of the emergence of the Stupak-Pitts amendment, Cardinal Javier Lozano Barragán of Mexico, recently retired as the Vatican's chief spokesman on health care, declared to a magazine in Rome that homosexuals and transgendered people would not get into heaven.

On the Web site Pontifex, he said that taking a "morning-after pill" to prevent pregnancy was comparable to "an assassination" and that every abortion was a crime that "merits punishment." Like Scott Roeder, he backed up his assertions with quotations from Saint Paul, referring to the first chapter of his Letter to the Romans, in which Paul chastened those who'd turned against God through erotic behavior:

"Their females exchanged natural relations for unnatural, and the males likewise gave up natural relations with females and burned with lust for one another. Males did shameful things with males and thus received in their own persons the due penalty for their perversity."

People who rebuffed God were "filled with every form of wickedness, evil, greed, and malice; full of envy, murder, rivalry, treachery, and spite. They are insolent, haughty, boastful, ingenious in their wickedness, and rebellious toward their parents. They are senseless, faithless, heartless, ruthless."

On November 20, more than 150 Christian leaders issued a statement reaffirming their opposition to abortion and gay marriage. The 4,700-word document, called "The Manhattan Declaration: A Call of Christian Conscience," admitted that "Christians and our institutions have too often scandalously failed to uphold the institution of marriage," but rejected same-sex marriage. Allowing gay marriage would open the way for "polyamorous partnerships, polygamous households, even adult brothers, sisters, or brothers and sisters living in incestuous relationships."

The document said that President Obama's desire to reduce the need for abortion is "a commendable goal," but his health care reforms would likely increase the number of elective abortions. "The present administration is led and staffed by those who want to make abortions legal at any stage of fetal development, and who want to provide abortions at taxpayer expense."

Signees of the Manhattan Declaration included fifteen Roman Catholic bishops, including Archbishop Timothy Dolan of New York and Archbishop Donald Wuerl of Washington; Focus on the Family's founder, James Dobson; the National Association of Evangelicals president, Leith Anderson; and seminary leaders, professors, and pastors.

Not even a member of the nation's most famous Catholic family was spared the Church's wrath for backing women's rights and the laws of the United States. The Rhode Island Roman Catholic bishop Thomas Tobin banned U.S. Representative Patrick Kennedy, son of the late Senator Edward Kennedy, from receiving communion in his state because of the congressman's support for abortion rights. The war over abortion had extended to Rome, and was deepening in the American south.

In Atlanta, anti-abortion groups erected sixty-five alarmist billboards proclaiming that "Black children are an endangered species." Georgia Right to Life, in partnership with the Radiance Foundation, sponsored the billboards, featuring a worried-looking African-American boy and suggesting that Georgia's black women had a disproportionately high number of abortions. In 2006, according to the Centers for Disease Control (CDC), nearly 58 percent of Georgia's abortions were performed on black women, even though blacks made up about 30 percent of the population. Only New York and Texas reported a higher number of abortions performed on black women, but this didn't appear to endanger black children as a group. Based on CDC numbers, the fertility rate among black women, or births per thousand females of childbearing age, remained higher than the national average and had increased in recent years.

In early 2010 in Utah, Governor Gary Herbert signed a controversial law stating that women who sought illegal abortions could be charged with criminal homicide. The push for the new bill came after a seventeen-year-old paid a man $150 to beat her in the stomach in an effort to end her pregnancy.

That May, Sister Margaret McBride, a member of a Phoenix Catholic hospital's ethics committee, was excommunicated for her role in allowing an abortion to take place at St. Joseph's Hospital and Medical Center. Both the nun and the surgery, considered necessary to save the life of a critically ill patient, were condemned by Bishop Thomas J. Olmsted, head of the Phoenix diocese.

"The Catholic Church," said Bishop Olmsted, "will continue to defend life and proclaim the evil of abortion without compromise, and must act to correct even her own members if they fail in this duty."

# XXXXIX

The inside of Dr. Warren Hern's Boulder office held the slightly acrid scent of medicine being practiced and the sense of being in a near-total female environment, women coming and going in the halls carrying files, women employees consulting with women patients about reproductive questions, women eating sandwiches with women over lunch in a back room and talking about women's issues. The walls were lined with artistic photographs Dr. Hern had taken on his travels around the globe, many from impoverished Third World countries with little or no medical care. The quiet, gentle atmosphere within the office stood in sharp contrast to the locked doors, bulletproof glass, and barred windows that had turned the exterior of this abortion clinic into a fortress. One Monday in early November 2009, as the health care struggle intensified two thousand miles to the east in Washington, I drove to Boulder to meet with Dr. Hern. Since Tiller's death, he'd become more of a focal point for abortion foes. Protesters had just camped outside his office for forty days and nights, and as we spoke in one of his waiting rooms, Hern said that he couldn't walk out the clinic's front door because "I'm afraid they'll shoot me." He also couldn't walk across the street to another medical facility to get paperwork on some of his patients. He couldn't drive his car into the lot next to his office, where visitors parked, because "that's how they shot George the first time, when he was behind the wheel."

He led me out a back door and through a security gate. Walking with him in the streets of Boulder, I was keenly aware that until last May only three high-profile, late-term abortion doctors remained in the United States—Drs. Tiller, Hern, and Carhart—and only two were left. As we passed through a crosswalk, he warily looked in all directions and over his shoulder.

"A local Catholic church," he said, "supports the protesters who came to my office during those forty days. They should lose their tax-exempt status for harassing me."

We went to a nearby restaurant with an open-air patio and he wanted to sit outside on this warm, magnificent Indian summer afternoon. Facing the street, he ordered a glass of wine, as he had little planned for the rest of the afternoon, and we both took in the towering view of Boulder's renowned Flatiron Mountains, rising majestically reddish in the perfectly clean autumn sunlight. Dr. Hern looked as if he needed to unwind from the recent siege at his office—if not the past thirty-six years.

Like Tiller, he'd never intended to be involved with reproductive medicine or abortion, but after helping a few pregnant women early in his career and experiencing the enormity of their relief and gratitude, he'd been drawn into the field. When Boulder decided to open a clinic soon after *Roe v. Wade*, he was the natural choice to run it and had been doing this work ever since. Now seventy and an avid skier, he was fit and tanned, with a powerful-looking torso and arms, but his strongest feature was his face. He had sad eyes, a hawk's nose, grayish hair flopping down across his forehead, and cheekbones worthy of the American pioneers who'd come west and survived endless summers and winters on the prairie. Born in Kansas, he'd moved to Colorado at age three and made it his home.

Raising his glass of wine, he recalled how he and Tiller had talked on the phone every week and skied together in the Rockies, building a friendship despite the very different ways they saw the world. With an irreverent smile, Hern said that when his own tightly knit group of physicians got together, they liked to tell stories about prominent Republican anti-abortion politicians who secretly paid for their wives or mistresses to end their pregnancies.

"We're in a position to know about these things," he said, "but George never did this with us. Gossip wasn't his style. He was committed to helping people, even those who totally opposed him. He was much more tolerant than I am. Battle with me and I'll fight back. George was a very polite and considerate man, the model of Christian forbearance."

A few years ago, Gail and Robert Anderson, a devout Catholic couple in Baton Rouge, Louisiana, had learned that cystic masses were covering their unborn baby's left lung and building up pressure on the undeveloped heart. Gail was twenty-seven weeks pregnant and would have to deliver her child through a C-section. Under the very best scenarios, the infant would be on life-support machines for months until the suffocated heart had been repaired and the masses removed from the lung. Women from Gail's parish, with whom she'd regularly protested outside an abortion clinic in Metairie, Louisiana, came to the Andersons and tried to talk them into keeping their baby. After great prayer and anguish, they decided not to and contacted Dr. Tiller. The car ride from Baton Rouge to Wichita was the longest of their lives.

When they arrived in Kansas, Tiller prayed with them about their decision and explained how, if they chose to go forward with him, they could memorialize their child. The compassion they'd hoped to find at their church and among Gail's women friends was offered them by the Wichita physician. On the morning of the operation at WHCS, they were surrounded by adult protesters who begged Gail not to get an abortion, and by children holding a model of a fetus. The demonstrators approached the Andersons and called them murderers, declaring that God would not save their souls.

"*Roe v. Wade* threatened our patriarchal society at the deepest cultural levels," Dr. Hern said over lunch, "and set off a reaction that's never stopped. In terms of biology, we're hard-wired to protect young, vulnerable creatures, like babies and small animals. Abortion hooks into this wiring and creates certain feelings and they've been used to great effect by the Republican Party. It started with Reagan's election as president in 1980, when the GOP realized this was the issue that could bring together the political right and the religious right. They've used it ever since to get people to the polls and to get political power. That's what the fight over abortion is all about."

His cell phone rang and he answered it. While he listened, he looked across the table at me and raised his index finger, as if he were hearing something relevant to our discussion.

A reporter from Wichita was calling to say that Roeder had just contacted the Associated Press and admitted on the record that he'd shot Tiller inside his church.

"There is a distinction between killing and murdering," Roeder told the AP. "I don't like the accusation of murder whatsoever, because when you protect innocent life, that's not murder."

After giving the journalist a few quotes about Roeder's confession, Hern hung up and told me that the man accused of threatening his own family last June had entered a guilty plea and would soon have a sentencing hearing.

"I'll speak at this hearing," he said, "and tell him exactly what I think of him."

He was silent for a while. The call from Wichita had visibly affected him and he stared past me, up toward the mountains.

"George's murder," he said, "is the worst thing that's ever happened to the pro-choice movement."

He fell silent again and I asked him how he dealt with his own sense of vulnerability, especially since Tiller's death.

He set his glass on the table, raised his hands to his cheeks, and lowered his head. Tears were forming in the wings of his eyes and his shoulders slumped forward, as if being pressed on by a considerable weight. For a while, I thought he wasn't going to respond.

"What can I say?" he asked. "I have a lot of things left to do and so much I want to do. I just want them to stop bothering me, but they won't. It ruins your life. For a long time, I felt that these people had irrevocably ruined my life. The purpose of what they do is to create terror in others, and they're very effective at this. They create terror in me. For a decade I was depressed because I couldn't have a normal life. Why would any woman want to be with me when I was under all these threats?"

The tears were falling and choking off his words. He covered his face and sobbed, determined to keep talking.

"Meeting my wife . . . in recent years . . . has made . . . a tremendous difference. It's made me . . . feel part of . . . the human family again."

I glanced around at the people passing by, wondering who they were and if they were watching Dr. Hern.

His crying subsided and he lowered his hands back to the table.

"Our body politic," he said, "is like a rotting corpse—repugnant, but still interesting. We're setting ourselves back so far from where we could be. Health care reform is something that can actually help people, the citizens of our country. Isn't that what government is supposed to do? Isn't that the goal?"

I didn't answer, because I knew he wasn't finished.

He wiped at his eyes with a napkin. "From O'Reilly on down, it's the same horseshit. When you deny reality, people get hurt."

# THE NECESSITY
# DEFENSE

L

One of Roeder's attorneys, Steve Osburn, the chief public defender of Sedgwick County, was stunned to learn of his client's confession to the Associated Press and said he'd have to speak with the defendant about this (Osburn was even more stunned that the inmate had been the one getting in touch with the media). Roeder then did something just as confounding by announcing that his other lawyer, Mark Rudy, had given him the "green light" to speak about these matters to the press. Both attorneys were scrambling to respond to Roeder's actions and to hold their case together. During the prisoner's call to the AP, he said that he hoped to use the "necessity defense" at trial to argue that by shooting Dr. Tiller he was serving the greater good of protecting un-born children. One provision of this defense was that when taking such a step, a killer had to be facing an "imminent threat." What imminent threat, many wondered, did Tiller pose to Roeder that morning as an usher inside his church?

The day the defendant phoned the AP, November 9, 2009, a group of twenty-one anti-abortionists nationwide, including Roeder himself, released a new "Defensive Action Statement."

"We, the undersigned," it read, "declare the justice of taking all godly action necessary to defend innocent human life including the use of force."

The statement was signed by Eric Rudolph, James Kopp, and Shelley Shannon, all in prison for targeting abortion doctors. On November 10, Osburn surprised his client by telling *The Wichita Eagle* that there was no such thing as a necessity defense under Kansas law—or American law, as far as he knew; he and Rudy would be using a regular first-degree-murder defense in this case, whatever that might be now that Roeder had publicly taken credit for gunning down Dr. Tiller at his church. Osburn did, however, want the judge to move the trial out of Wichita because of all the local publicity, and a change-of-venue hearing was scheduled for December.

Following Roeder's confession, the National Organization for Women again asked the Obama administration and the Justice Department to treat his assassination of Tiller as domestic terrorism, to employ all available anti-terrorism laws to prosecute the killer, and to broaden the investigation to those who might have aided or financed him. NOW also commented on the legal strategy Roeder was promoting in the media.

"The absurdity of his defense is insulting and dangerous to women," said NOW's president, Terry O'Neill, "but it also reveals his terrorist methodology using murder to accomplish his political goals. It is precisely this unrepentant domestic terrorism—and those who fund it—that must be stopped or else we will see more clinic violence and people will be killed. We urge the administration to freeze the assets of people or organizations, domestic and international, who helped fund and supported Roeder's anti-choice activities."

With these issues playing out behind closed doors at the Department of Justice, the foundation was being laid for an all-out legal battle in Wichita.

After Roeder had confessed, the DA's office filed court papers seeking to ban his use of the necessity defense. Osburn then changed course and filed his own documents stating that his client had the "absolute right" to present his case that the murder was justified to stop abortion. As part of its strategy, the defense sought Tiller's appointment books, records of scheduled abortion procedures, and related documents for the period May 1 to June 30, 2009, with the apparent idea of putting the doctor on trial posthumously for the operations he'd planned during these two months. The defense, in spite of Roeder's penchant for sabotaging his case by talking with the media, was finding its voice.

"For the Court to grant the State's motion to prohibit 'any evidence' in support of the necessity defense would be premature, and contrary to Kansas law," the public defenders wrote to Judge Wilbert. The state's motion was "nothing more than an attempt to force the defense to reveal their defense strategy and forgo what may be a valid defense."

The prosecution had cited a criminal trespass case at an abortion clinic, in which the Kansas Supreme Court ruled that to allow personal beliefs to justify criminal activity and interrupt services at the clinic would "not only lead to chaos but would be tantamount to sanctioning anarchy."

The defense contended that Roeder's situation was different because trespassing at a clinic, unlike murder, did not actually stop the practice of abortion.

"It is inconclusive whether the lives of the unborn were spared as a result of the act of criminal trespass," they wrote. But in Roeder's case, "the result of the alleged murder resulted in the termination of abortions being performed in the City of Wichita by the victim, Dr. George Tiller."

In ruling on the trespassing case, the state Supreme Court had sidestepped the fundamental legal issue by saying that whether or not "the necessity defense should be adopted or recognized in Kansas may best be left for another day."

That day had now arrived, as a critical judicial decision loomed ahead, and Judge Wilbert would have to confront the necessity-defense question straight on in his courtroom. This made him the most important figure at the trial, since the facts were not in dispute: Roeder had killed Dr. Tiller to end abortion in Wichita. But what were the judge's own views on abortion? A practicing Catholic, a Republican, and a married father of two, he'd been appointed to the bench in 1995, but had faced no opposition in his first three elections. In 2008, he was finally opposed and won by only 471 votes out of almost 166,000 cast. That year he sought the endorsement of Kansans for Life, and the KFL political action committee supported him in the race, but didn't directly contribute to his campaign. In September 2008, Wilbert paid KFL seventy-five dollars for his name to be listed in an ad in its quarterly newsletter, containing articles entitled "Update on Tiller Charges" and "Planned Parenthood—a Snake in the Grass!" The ad holding Wilbert's name read, "The Kansans for Life PAC urges you to vote for, work for and pray for the following pro-life candidates." As a member of Wichita's St. Thomas Aquinas Church, Judge Wilbert was also a lay minister.

He'd never tried a case this high-profile before and was facing some very sticky legal issues. Should a jury be allowed to consider that Roeder's actions were justified based on the necessity defense or was this a first-degree murder trial like any other? Should prospective jurors' views on abortion be central to their ability to serve, or not serve, at this trial? To what extent should the lawyers be able to interrogate potential jurors about their religious or political convictions, and was it a given that every juror would tell them the truth? And what if, at the end of testimony, they decided to vote for Roeder's acquittal regardless of the evidence, a practice known as jury nullification?

If Steve Osburn had initially seemed lukewarm about representing Roeder, his and Rudy's involvement was growing stronger and more committed as the trial approached.

Maybe they could win, after all.

# LI

On November 11, two days after Roeder confessed, Lindsey went to work as usual and came home that evening to take care of her ailing father. In addition to keeping up with her regular duties at school and with her family, she had many other things to manage now. For worse and for better, Dr. Tiller's death had opened up a new life for her, a more visible and outspoken life that was more in line with how she really thought and felt. She'd played a role in keeping eBay from auctioning items whose sale was intended to pay for her ex-husband's expenses. She'd had extensive communication with Susan and Mark Archer of Pennsylvania, after the news broke that Mark had warned the FBI last April about Roeder, in an effort to keep him from boarding a plane and coming to visit his biological daughter, Olivia. Lindsey had been very distressed when someone satirically suggested on the Internet that Nick be tortured in front of his father by smashing his testicles, until Roeder told the police who else was involved in the murder.

NBC had aired an episode of its long-running hit series *Law and Order* with a plot about a man who went into a church in New York City and shot to death an abortion doctor. In this fictional story, the son of the killer tries to help his father after the crime. The program infuriated Nick, who'd never done anything to assist his dad since the crime, and Lindsey shared the sentiment.

"It was really quite outrageous," she says. "It had everything Scott would have wanted, except for the verdict in the case. The only thing good about the show," Lindsey grimly joked, "was that the killer's ex-wife was depicted as skinny."

Since Tiller's death, Nick had been struggling with his feelings for his father and the effect of the murder on his own life. Those feelings got rawer after the nasty June 2009 letter Roeder wrote Lindsey and Nick from jail, calling them spoiled brats. When Nick was a boy, his dad had told him that he'd blow up an abortion clinic late at night because that wouldn't hurt anyone, and the youngster had held on to this as something separating his father from a terrorist like Timothy McVeigh. As he'd gotten older, Nick had more and more strongly disagreed with his dad's beliefs, but at least Roeder hadn't shed anyone's blood. That was no longer true and Nick could no longer remain silent.

On October 30, five months after Tiller was murdered, he sat down, composed an angry letter, and sent it to his father. Until now, he wrote, he'd kept an open mind about the existence of God, had thought about different religious paths, and had nurtured an idea of developing his own spiritual base as he came into adulthood. He'd wanted to connect with something larger within himself and beyond, but his father's actions at Reformation Lutheran last May had ended his search. His dad was a killer and God was an illusion. There was no point in being a seeker. Of all the things he might have written to the prisoner, this was likely the most devastating.

"Given Scott's religious convictions," says Lindsey, "this had to be very, very hard for him to read."


As Lindsey did chores around the house at 6:30 p.m. on November 11, the phone rang and she answered it.

"Will you accept a collect call," the operator said, "from an inmate at the Sedgwick County Detention Facility?"

She was caught off guard, but understood that for the first time since Roeder's arrest, he was calling her. Like Nick, she'd also been thinking since May 31 about what to tell Scott if she ever got another chance. She'd also been thinking about the ugly letter he'd written them after his arrest, but now that he was actually calling, she didn't want to say anything, or wasn't ready to, especially if she had to listen to him complain about being in jail and had to pay for this, so she hung up. A minute later, the phone rang again. The operator asked her the same question and she hung up once more.

As she stared at the receiver, the shock of what had just happened subsided a little and she reminded herself that two days ago her ex-husband had confessed to the Associated Press. Roeder was, in all likelihood, never going to get out of prison or pose a threat to her, Nick, or her father. He'd be locked up for the rest of his life, where he belonged, and the fear she'd felt in the man's presence for nearly two decades was no longer necessary. Her family seemed safe for the first time in a very long time, yet there still *were* lingering fears working inside her. If she wanted to be truly free of Roeder, she needed to do something.

The phone rang again and she grabbed it, telling the operator that she'd put twenty-five dollars on her credit card for the next twenty minutes. Scott came on the line and they awkwardly mumbled hello. She said that three days after the murder his former girlfriend had come to her front stoop and knocked, but Lindsey had shut the door in her face. Throughout the past five months, she'd wondered if Scott had sent her there on a mission and what it might have been (one of the many rumors following the murder, which Lindsey and the Archers had kicked around together, was that the woman had aborted Roeder's baby in the mid-1990s and that this had enraged him ever since, ultimately driving him to kill). She asked him about the visit and if he'd fathered a child with her. None of this was true, he insisted. She'd become pregnant with her husband's baby and given birth to the child; and he'd had nothing to do with her visit to Lindsey's home last June. By the time they'd hashed this out over the phone, the twenty minutes had all but disappeared.

She asked if he'd received Nick's angry letter and he said he had, but didn't want to talk about that with her. He was calling to speak with his son and to tell him he loved him, but Nick wasn't available. Their time was up and the call abruptly ended, with Lindsey having more to say.

Using a few clues she'd gathered from Roeder during their conversation, she spent the next day tracking down the woman, determined to know why she'd come to her house following the murder. After hours of legwork, Lindsey finally located her. The ex-girlfriend had shown up on Lindsey's doorstep because she'd wanted to apologize for her behavior all those years ago in front of the five-year-old Nick. She spoke frankly and Lindsey accepted her apology, giving her one piece of closure—but she needed another. It was a small thing perhaps in the eyes of the world, but not for her. Her marriage would never really be finished until she'd gotten something out.

That evening, the phone rang and she told the operator that she'd accept the charges. Roeder began grilling her about what she'd said about him to the media. Had she ever described him as racist? Had she told any reporters that he'd had a copy of the anti-Semitic novel *The Turner Diaries* in his possession? He was concerned with his public image, especially around the issue of race, and it was important to him that she hadn't.

When he'd finished and there was a pause, she closed her eyes, took a deep breath, and mustered all of her resolve. She was never going to take another call from him, so as far as she was concerned this was the last interaction they'd ever have. She'd rehearsed this speech many times before in the privacy of her mind, and once she started it, the words came tumbling out.

"I just want you to understand," she said, "that I'm a card-carrying, pro-choice, Obama Democrat."

No response.

"And a member of the Feminist Majority Foundation."

Still nothing.

"And I don't believe in anything you've done, Scott. I think it's totally wrong."

The line remained silent.

"And that's who I am."

Very quietly, and to her surprise, he said, "I know."

This had to be a lie—he didn't know who she was or what she believed or how she felt about his assassination of Dr. Tiller, or so many other things, because he'd never bothered to ask, but had labeled her ignorant. He hadn't just terrorized doctors or women seeking abortions, but her own family.

"If you ever need anything from me," he said, "just let me know."

"I don't need anything from you, ever again."

She hung up, with a growing sense of relief. Walking around the house that evening, reliving their discussion and thinking about his silence on the phone, she'd never felt so powerful or so free.

# LII

On December 22, Judge Wilbert scheduled arguments on the defense's change-of-venue motion and several other matters, as the courtroom battle Roeder had been waiting for was about to commence. Half a continent away, a different kind of struggle was unfolding in the nation's capital.

Shortly after one a.m. on Monday, December 21, following an interminable debate and with Washington snowbound from a weekend blizzard, Senate Democrats held a procedural vote on the 2,700-page health care reform bill. The Senate voted strictly along party lines, and by a count of 60–40 the majority party ended Republican filibustering efforts, seeming to lock in the margin needed to overhaul the nation's health care system and cover 30 million Americans previously without such care. Costing an estimated $871 billion over the next decade, the bill was expected to reshape one-sixth of the national economy. Democrats hailed the vote as a step closer to completing a reform process that had begun with President Truman nearly six decades earlier. Republicans bitterly denounced it, declaring that the bill had been fashioned in secret and rammed through the Senate in a snowstorm in the middle of the night in the days leading up to Christmas, when Congress was normally out of town. The Republican senator Lamar

Alexander of Tennessee called it "a historic mistake," while others labeled it a historic compromise.

The last Democratic senator to vote for the bill was the abortion opponent Ben Nelson of Nebraska. He accepted the legislation only after the Democratic leadership agreed to permit individual states to prohibit abortion coverage in the insurance markets where most new health plans would be sold. Subscribers to these plans would have to make two separate monthly premium payments: one for all insurance coverage except abortion, the other for abortion coverage. Planned Parenthood, NOW, Pro-Choice America, and the National Women's Law Center instantly denounced the compromise. It was just as aggressively decried, for exactly the opposite reasons, by the United States Conference of Catholic Bishops and the National Right to Life Committee. The president, however, was pleased.

"The United States Senate . . ." he said, "scored a big victory for the American people."

Nelson's deciding vote had come with a significant—some said corrupt—price tag. While the Senate bill imposed tough new restrictions on referrals of Medicare patients by doctors to hospitals in which the physicians had financial interests, the bill provided an exemption to a few such hospitals, including the Bellevue Medical Center in Bellevue, Nebraska. According to the Congressional Budget Office, the cost of this provision benefiting Massachusetts, Vermont, and Nebraska was "approximately $1.2 billion over the 2010–2019 period." And in Nebraska, the federal government would indefinitely pay the full cost of covering low-income people added to Medicaid rolls. The Republicans called this the "Cornhusker kickback." The outgoing California governor, Arnold Schwarzenegger, went further, urging his state's national representatives to vote against the health care reform legislation—unless California could wrangle the same benefits Senator Nelson had just won for Nebraska.

Schwarzenegger called the bill a "trough of bribes, deals and loopholes . . . While I enthusiastically supported health care reform, it is not reform to push more costs onto states that are already struggling while other states are getting sweetheart deals. California's congressional delegation should either vote against this bill that is a disaster for California or get in there and fight for the same sweetheart deal that Senator Nelson of Nebraska got for the Cornhusker State."

Nebraska, the governor said, "got the corn and we got the husk."

The American Medical Association quickly endorsed the bill, and unexpectedly the Catholic Health Association (CHA) and an umbrella group for nuns, the Leadership Conference of Women Religious (LCWR), also backed the legislation. The CHA represented hundreds of Catholic hospitals across the country, which stood to gain financially by reducing their number of uninsured patients. The LCWR said that it was "increasingly confident" that the new bill "can achieve the objective of no federal funding for abortion," while the U.S. Conference of Catholic Bishops called the bill "morally unacceptable" and Catholic scholars said the bishops had reached this conclusion by applying the Church's teaching against "cooperation with evil."

The Republican U.S. representative Todd Tiahrt, whose congressional district included Wichita, endorsed a move by local lawmakers to exempt Kansas from national health care. Tiahrt believed it was unconstitutional for the federal government to tax citizens or threaten to send them to jail for not buying health insurance. In Topeka, a group of state legislators began their latest and strongest push to tighten restrictions on late-term abortion procedures, the same legislation that Governor Sebelius had vetoed the year before. The group wanted doctors carrying out late-term procedures to be forced to report more information to the medical authorities—and to face the possibilities of more lawsuits—even though no physicians were left in Kansas to perform these kinds of abortions.


On December 22, Judge Wilbert rejected a change of venue for Roeder's trial and jury selection remained on schedule for January 11. That same day Steve Osburn and Mark Rudy fought for the necessity defense and told the judge that under certain conditions the taking of human life could be justified. They wanted Judge Wilbert to allow them to present this argument to the jury.

"This is certainly not a position I want to be in," Wilbert told the attorneys, "because I am not God."

The judge, after due consideration, ruled against the necessity defense, since neither Roeder nor anyone else had been in "imminent danger" when he'd killed Dr. Tiller. Using this rationalization for murder, the judge added, would be to "sanction anarchy."

Some defense lawyers responded to this by wondering if Roeder would have had a much better legal argument if he'd shot Tiller not at his church, but on his way into his clinic to perform an abortion. The defense might have then been able to say that an unborn baby's life was, in fact, in imminent danger.

"I recognize," Judge Wilbert said on the twenty-second, "that we all have our own individual personal views, religious views, moral and ethical views. But the United States Supreme Court has come down many, many years ago in *Roe v. Wade* that an abortion is a legal and constitutionally protected decision by the mother and . . . the health care providers."

The matter was not yet settled. Surprisingly—and shockingly to abortion rights supporters and DA Nola Foulston—Wilbert decided to "leave the door open" for the defense to present evidence that Roeder had shot Dr. Tiller because of his conviction that the murder was justified to stop a greater evil. If this was not the necessity defense per se, it was a close relative. The judge's decision created the possibility that Roeder's lawyers could ask the jury to convict him not of first-degree murder but of voluntary manslaughter, defined under Kansas law as the "unreasonable but honest belief that circumstances existed that justified deadly force." A voluntary-manslaughter conviction carried a four-to-six-year sentence. Roeder could be back on the street by 2015.

The DA's office, led by Foulston, was apoplectic. She and her two assistant DAs quickly launched a counterargument against this so-called "imperfect self-defense." It could not apply in this case because Tiller had been gunned down at his church, where he was a threat to no one. The only question the jury had to answer, prosecutors said, was if the shooting was premeditated, and they felt confident they could prove this at trial. These issues, the judge now made clear, wouldn't be fully re-solved until the jury and His Honor had heard all the testimony, but before the lawyers presented their closing statements. The DA wasn't mollified.

Following the December 22 hearing, Mark Rudy sharply criticized the judge, saying that Wilbert was trying to muzzle the defense—an obvious attempt to influence potential jurors before the trial got started. By early January, three hundred Sedgwick County citizens had been mailed summonses to appear at the courthouse on the eleventh of the month. An initial pool of forty-two women and men would be se-lected and the lawyers would whittle them down to the final fourteen: twelve jurors and two alternates. People could not be eliminated from serving because of their feelings about abortion. The judge took the unusual step of closing the jury selection process to the press, so those being questioned would, he hoped, be more candid (after media law-yers appealed this decision to the Kansas Supreme Court, Wilbert relented and made the final part of jury selection public).

"Potential jurors," he said about this process, "were asked very per-sonal and sensitive questions regarding their religious beliefs . . . their knowledge of George Tiller and any pretrial publicity regarding the defendant, Scott Roeder."

One example of the jury inquiry was question number 86: "What are your personal opinions on abortion?"

For Wilbert and the fourteen jurors ultimately selected, the case would not unfold in a vacuum, but against the backdrop of their own experience in Wichita and thirty-five years of anti-abortion demon-strations in the city. Jurors would be expected to ignore the 1986 bombing at Tiller's clinic and Shelley Shannon's wounding of the physi-cian at WHCS seven years later. They were supposed to set aside their views of the mass arrests and chaos that had filled the streets during the Summer of Mercy in 1991; to dismiss the 1,846 straight days abortion foes had gathered at the clinic leading up to the murder; to disregard the trial and acquittal of the doctor in March 2009; and to forget about the closing of his office after he was killed. The jury's job, according to the prosecution, was simply to focus on the testimony of the ushers in Tiller's church last May 31 and on the state's other evidence. The DA had a witness list holding 230 names, including Lindsey and Nick Roeder, while the defense had subpoenaed, among others, Phill Kline.

Wichita law enforcement was on heightened alert and courthouse security was about to get beefed up by bomb-sniffing dogs provided by the Bureau of Alcohol, Tobacco, Firearms and Explosives. They were preparing for the worst.

# LIII

Awaiting trial, Roeder had deepened his relationship with the anti-abortionist Dave Leach of Des Moines, Iowa. If Randall Terry had for decades represented the flamboyant, media-grabbing wing of the pro-life movement, the aging Leach was less intrusive and more scholarly, but every bit as committed to stopping abortion. With his wife, he ran a music store in Des Moines and instructed children on various instruments, but nowadays he needed Social Security to keep up with his bills. He was curious and a good listener, but his extremism regarding abortion wasn't far below the surface. Once Tiller was dead, Leach had begun studying how to use the killing as a vehicle to bring the necessity defense into the courtroom in a serious way, during a high-profile case, in order to get crucial issues in front of a judge, a jury, and the national press. He wanted the Roeder trial to become a publicized legal forum on abortion. While not an attorney himself, he was a dedicated student of the law and had finished his 104-page motion, written on behalf of Roeder and submitted to Judge Wilbert in the weeks preceding jury selection.

Like others in his movement, Leach drew parallels between the fight to stop abortion at the start of the twenty-first century and the battle to end slavery in the years leading up to the start of the Civil War in 1861. The anti-abortionists liked to cite the infamous 1857 Dred Scott

U.S. Supreme Court decision, which ruled that people of African descent imported into the United States and held as slaves—and their descendants—were not protected by the Constitution and could never become American citizens. Further, Congress could not prohibit slavery in federal territories, slaves could not sue in court, and they could not be removed from their owners without due process. The failure of the legal system to remedy slavery had fed the momentum that created the War Between the States. When abortion opponents brought up the Dred Scott decision, one implication was that because the U.S. Supreme Court had made abortion legal under *Roe v. Wade*, the only option left to prevent the killing of the unborn was violence against abortion providers.

With Roeder having sacrificed his freedom in order to make this point, Leach saw his chance to have an impact on the trial and possibly on setting legal precedents. He'd taken the writing of his motion very solemnly, citing case law and quoting the Bible, but then presented the document as if Roeder had penned it himself.

"Every defendant," the motion began, "has the right to present his theory of his defense . . ."

While Roeder appreciated the efforts of his attorneys, Steve Osburn and Mark Rudy, the letter said, "they have publicly given mixed signals about their willingness to represent me on the central theory of my defense, which is the only reason I maintain my innocence and demand a trial by jury, and is the only reason I took the action which got me here . . . American justice embodies the vision of the freedom of defendants to at least raise their defense high enough to be shot down in a public forum after all sides are heard . . . The facts and arguments motivating defendant are not the exclusive fabrications of wild-eyed fringe kook radical fanatics, but are established by American leaders who include Congressmen, presidents, and Supreme Court justices . . ."

As the document unfolded under the guise of the defendant, Leach delivered his own subtle warnings and threats:

"Courts simply have failed to squarely address questions about the legality of abortion to the satisfaction of even a majority of Americans.

This case presents the court an opportunity to resolve these lingering disputes and heal America, which will end the violence. It is America Herself which will suffer, if Courts gloss over these unanswered questions one more time. Conscience's cry for justice will continue to press for satisfaction outside legal channels, as long as legitimate questions cannot be addressed *through* legal channels . . .

"Defendant desires the violence to stop. On both sides. Defendant offers the rest of his life for the lives of the unborn whose murders he prevented . . . Kansas law will not help a hero who saves thousands of lives if the cruel and unusual slaying of these human souls is legal . . . what really made me despair [was] the law could not or would not touch him [Dr. Tiller]."

To support his argument, Leach mentioned another famous American criminal trial: hadn't the deceased unborn Connor Peterson been legally regarded as a person and a homicide victim, along with his mother, Laci, in the notorious 2005 Scott Peterson double murder case? Therefore, shouldn't *all* unborn fetuses be viewed the same way in the courtroom? Since 2005, Leach wrote, the "entire legality of abortion has been reversed," even though this may not yet appear to be true because of current inconsistencies in case law.

"The only mechanism for resolving this is a case that requires those inconsistencies to be resolved. This is that case."

Leach ended with a flourish, evoking the cultural war that had pervaded the United States since the 1960s. Woven into his words was the same impassioned rhetoric about a changed and changing America used by the men in the Order a quarter century earlier. They'd hated what their country had become and saw no alternative but to blame others for the massiveness and complexity of that change.

"I pray," Leach wrote, "along with God's spiritual army that the terrible natural consequences prophesied for crimes so great as America's need not fall any harder than they already have. I pray America will turn from kicking the roses barefooted (Acts 9:5) to cradling the bruised but still fragrant roses, allowing the bloodshed to stop on all sides. What suffering has been the natural consequences of hearts hard enough to slay 50 million of our own offspring! Unfaithfulness. Divorce. Domestic violence. Child abuse. Crime. An economic black hole at hand, created by political corruption added to a depleted work force from abortion and the turning away of immigrant labor. Are we bloody enough yet to stop kicking?

"It is not my vision that America's judiciary will walk still in the dark footsteps of *Dred Scott* until reversed by a civil war, carrying this scar until America ceases as a nation, but that this time courts will reverse the evil which they initiated and lead our nation in righteousness. Scott Roeder."

The motion claimed that the trial would be a "charade" unless the defendant could argue that his actions were needed to save unborn children.

"This is not," Judge Wilbert had said, "going to become a trial over the abortion issue. It will be limited to his [Roeder's] beliefs and how he came to form those beliefs . . ."

After the judge had received the 104 pages, he cracked open still more legal doors on January 8, saying that he could imagine "the very real possibility evidence could come from the defendant alone that would give me a duty to instruct the jury on voluntary manslaughter." And that one instruction could change the entire course of the trial, and its verdict.

This handful of words angered abortion rights supporters across the country, and by sundown of the eighth, Katherine Spillar, executive vice president of the Feminist Majority Foundation, prepared a statement in response to Judge Wilbert's ruling.

"Today's perplexing decision," she said, "is effectively back-door permission for admitted killer Scott Roeder to use a 'justifiable homicide' defense that is both unjustifiable and unconscionable. Allowing an argument that this cold-blooded, premeditated murder could be voluntary manslaughter will embolden anti-abortion extremists and could result in 'open season' on doctors across the country . . ."

In Boulder, Dr. Hern characterized the judge's ruling as a death sentence for those physicians trying to help women. In Kansas City, Lindsey was in complete shock, thinking about the possibility of her ex-husband being freed within the next few years. At Harvard Law School, Professor Alan Dershowitz told *Slate* that Wilbert's ruling was "an absurd approach to the law that would open the door to the most dangerous extension of the defense of imperfect necessity."

On January 11, the prosecution filed a last-minute motion asking the judge not to give the jury the option of convicting on voluntary manslaughter charges. Roeder couldn't seek this legal outcome, the DA said, because that required the presence of an imminent threat by Dr. Tiller, and he wasn't at his clinic performing an abortion when he was killed.

"The State," prosecutors wrote, "encourages this Court to not be the first to enable a defendant to justify premeditated murder because of an emotionally charged political belief. Such a ruling has far reaching consequences and would be contrary to Kansas law . . . Taken to its logical extreme, this line of thinking would allow anyone to commit premeditated murder but only be guilty of manslaughter, simply because the victim holds a different set of moral and political beliefs than the attacker."

This would further "allow an attacker to choose the time and place of the murder, regardless of whether the victim was engaged in threatening conduct at the time of the killing."

Judge Wilbert delayed the start of jury selection for two days to hear the lawyers argue the issue in front of him. Because his latest ruling had given so much hope to the anti-abortion movement, the activist Donald Spitz and other Army of God members announced they were coming to Wichita for the trial. While some of his colleagues hadn't killed abortion doctors in the past because of their fear of life imprisonment or the death penalty, Spitz told the AP, they might be more willing to take that risk now.

On Tuesday, January 12, the defense filed a new motion stating that when Roeder had committed the crime he'd in fact believed that Tiller was an "imminent threat" to the unborn. The physician was not a threat "based on character, or exchange of words, or provocation of physical

self defense, but instead based on abortion procedures that have resulted in deaths and been reported to the state of Kansas . . .

"The imminence of danger was greater than mere fear of future
harm. There was a state licensed facility operating in Sedgwick County
to perform abortions. It had staff. It had a practitioner. It had a budget.
It had clientele. It assumedly had a schedule of pending abortion procedures. In the mind of Mr. Roeder, the victim presented a clear danger
to unborn children."

It was up to the jurors and not the judge, the defense said, to decide
what charge Roeder was guilty of. That afternoon, Judge Wilbert
agreed with this position, saying it was improper for him to rule out
the voluntary-manslaughter defense before a jury was even seated.

"We don't fast-forward," he said. "We don't jump to conclusions, and
we don't arrive at the end of the process without a full and complete—
and hopefully impartial—hearing."

The prosecutor Kim Parker tried to salvage a partial victory by asking
Judge Wilbert to prohibit the defense from commenting on Roeder's
beliefs about protecting the unborn during jury selection and opening
statements.

Mark Rudy objected.

"The state," he said, "is trying to script the trial, and trials aren't
scripted. This trial is going to be on television [with national coverage
provided by TruTV], but it's not a TV trial. It is a real trial."

On Wednesday afternoon, January 13, the whittling down of the
jury pool began in earnest. By Friday evening, only twenty-five potential jurors had been questioned and then came a three-day weekend, followed by several more days of jury vetting. The trial was finally set to
start on January 22—thirty-seven years to the day since *Roe v. Wade*
had been handed down by the U.S. Supreme Court. People on both
ends of the abortion issue saw this as a providential sign that their side
was about to triumph in the courtroom. That same evening abortion
foes and supporters planned rallies in Wichita and Topeka to com-
memorate the anniversary.

# WICHITA DIVIDED

# LIV

In mid-January, Wichita was frigid, foggy, drizzly, and snowbound, its downtown streets covered with sleet and ice. Tree branches were brittle enough to snap and you often couldn't see more than two blocks in any direction, during what became the coldest winter in the city since 1888, when they began keeping records. The single-digit temperatures and the hardships of bad weather seemed to add to the gravity of what was about to take place at the Sedgwick County Courthouse. Regardless of how one felt about abortion, life-and-death issues were in play in Judge Wilbert's courtroom and the assembled press corps, which could be incredibly snarky during murder trials, would be respectful at this one. Media from around the nation, including both coasts, had flown in for the event, and like the public they were subject to extremely tight security measures. Bomb-detecting canines and ATF officers patrolled the ninth-floor hallways and Judge Wilbert's crowded courtroom. They were assisted at all times by at least nine hefty (some would say overweight), blue-clad, heavily armed Sedgwick County sheriff's deputies.

"Not exactly," one journalist noted while studying the cops, "a thin blue line."

The same bailiff who'd presided over the Tiller trial was in charge of this one. Once again, Jeanne Tiller, this time accompanied by her four grown children, would be in the courtroom with Scott Roeder, seated just a few feet to the right rear of the defendant. He'd make no eye contact with them or acknowledge their presence; as he was about to tell Dave Leach, to him Mrs. Tiller was no different from the wife of a Mafia killer. The Tiller family and friends were kept isolated from all other spectators and placed just in back of the three female prosecutors: DA Foulston, Kim Parker, and Ann Swegle. At the defense table, Roeder sat between Osburn and Rudy, and behind them was a row of reporters. Behind the journalists were two rows holding women's rights activists, led by Kathy Spillar of the Feminist Majority Foundation, and a representative of the Department of Justice, on hand to see if there was fodder for a federal prosecution of Roeder or other anti-abortion extremists.

Jammed together with Spillar and the federal government rep was a who's who of the radical wing of the anti-abortion movement—in town to make a show of force and solidarity for the defendant. They included Michael Bray, a former U.S. Naval Academy midshipman who'd been convicted in 1985 of two counts of conspiracy and one count of possessing unregistered explosive devices in connection with ten bombings of women's health clinics and offices of liberal advocacy groups. He'd served forty-six months in prison between 1985 and 1989, and in 1994, according to a confidential teletype sent out to all fifty-six FBI field offices, the feds suspected him and others of developing "a conspiracy that endeavors to achieve political or social change through activities that involve force or violence." Throughout Roeder's trial, Bray, who was still considered a terrorist by the National Memorial Institute for the Prevention of Terrorism, was upbeat, friendly, and accessible to reporters. He liked to remind journalists that just because Scott Roeder had murdered one abortion provider didn't mean that if he were acquitted and released from prison, he'd ever harm anyone again. Wasn't Bray himself proof of that?

Also present was Regina Dinwiddie, the Kansas City activist who'd protested at clinics with the defendant. Her red lipstick and red hair stood out as she described walking the streets of Wichita with a "defense action petition" that attempted to justify Roeder's actions; according to her, scores of local people had signed it. Joshua Graff, another trial attendee, had spent three years in prison for a 1993 clinic arson in the Houston area. From her cell in Minnesota, Shelley Shannon lent her support to Roeder in an e-mail she'd sent to Dave Leach. Dr. Tiller, she wrote, had "needed to be killed for the sake of justice . . . Whatever happens in the Kansas courtroom, justice was done on May 31, AD 2009." Jennifer McCoy of Wichita, who'd done time for two clinic arsons in Virginia, was in the gallery and pregnant with her tenth child. For two decades she'd demonstrated at WHCS and had visited Roeder in the local jail.

Donna Holman was the wife of Dan Holman of the Iowa anti-abortion group Missionaries to the Preborn. He'd sent the defendant some graphic photos and writings since his arrest. Donna had come down from Iowa in a "truth van" with pictures of aborted fetuses on its side panels, like the ones Operation Rescue drove around Wichita (neither Operation Rescue nor its Truth Trucks nor its leader, Troy Newman, were to be seen during the trial, as Newman did everything possible to distance himself and his organization from Roeder). Donna had parked the vehicle in front of the courthouse and in full view of the press. Her husband had not been able to make the trip to Kansas because he was awaiting sentencing in Michigan for an aggravated-assault charge for a road rage incident involving the same truck.

Dave Leach was at the trial and the rumor was that Randall Terry was about to arrive and do what he did best—make the biggest media splash of all. A few days later, he showed up looking dapper in a long winter coat, a tweed hat, and a pair of expensive-looking square-toed alligator boots. He smiled at everyone and was eager to make contact with any journalist he could find. He'd brought with him several colleagues, who also seemed to function as bodyguards, and before the trial began each morning, they stood in front of the courthouse in the biting cold and held up a sign accusing Dr. Tiller of killing tens of thousands of babies. Like Leach, Terry was using the trial to draw comparisons between the defendant's situation and the start of the Civil War.

"We are not coming to condone or condemn Scott Roeder's actions," read a handout Terry had prepared for reporters and the public. "That decision will soon rest with the jury. However, there are those who want to pretend that this trial has nothing to do with child-killing by abortion; that is a farce. It's like saying that the trials of Nat Turner and John Brown had nothing to do with slavery . . . George Tiller murdered 60,000 babies by his own hand. Scott Roeder knew this. How can Mr. Roeder receive a fair trial if this data is kept from the jury?"

Had Judge Wilbert prevented the defendant from getting a fair trial by "having a jury questionnaire that was geared to identify Christians and pro-lifers, and thereby exclude them? In other words, has His Honor denied Mr. Roeder a fair trial by a **jury of his peers**?" Terry called some inquiries on the jury questionnaire "patently offensive and discriminatory:

- What is your religious affiliation/denomination, if any?
- Do you attend a place of worship, i.e., Church, Temple, etc.? It yes, state where and how often?
- If applicable, does your place of worship and/or particular denomination take an official stand on the practice of abortion?
- How would you rate the importance of your religious beliefs in your day to day life? Utmost important. Very important. Somewhat important. Not important at all.
- Do you have any principles based on religious or ethical teaching or dogma that would affect your ability to serve as a fair and impartial juror? If yes, please explain.

Living up to his reputation, Terry had become the focal point of the anti-abortion protests as soon as he'd hit town.

The only thing perhaps more unusual than the tension in the gallery was Roeder's legal position. He was not disputing that he'd "killed" Dr. Tiller. The defendant not only agreed with nearly every aspect of the state's case against him, but was about to provide some new details that made him look even guiltier of the premeditated destruction of the physician. He revealed, for example, that he'd thought about cutting off Tiller's hands. Roeder's goal, like Leach's and Terry's, was to make the trial about abortion and to give the jury the opportunity to consider his beliefs and motives in killing the doctor. If just one juror among the eight men and four women agreed with his views and felt that he'd stopped a greater evil in Wichita, he or she might vote for his acquittal. If the judge gave the jury the instruction that they could find the defendant guilty of voluntary manslaughter, instead of murder, this might make casting that vote much easier. Across the country, but especially in Boulder and Bellevue, Nebraska, abortion doctors were watching the trial closely (in late January, the pro-choice movement would lose another champion when Tiller's ex-colleague Dr. Susan Hill of North Carolina died of breast cancer). Wichita was on edge.

# LV

Nola Foulston had a feisty personality, not a bad thing when prosecuting people such as BTK and other noted Sedgwick County killers. She was outspoken in the courtroom, fierce in her legal arguments, tightly controlled in what she said to the press, quick to let people know that she was in charge and they needed to stand back. If one heard grumblings about her managerial style and penchant for drama, one also heard a lot of praise and respect thrown her way. She relished prosecuting the biggest cases and taking on the defendants accused of the most heinous offenses. She'd gone after the self-confessed sexual predator Leroy Hendricks, who became the first person confined under Kansas's 1994 Sexually Violent Predator Act—not because of a specific crime of which he'd been found guilty but because he had mental problems that predisposed him "to commit sexually violent offenses." The case went to the U.S. Supreme Court and Foulston won a precedent-setting victory. In 2003, she was selected the state's "Prosecutor of the Year."

When describing the roots of her professional tenacity, she liked telling people, "I'm an Italian from New York."

Her father, Dominick "Teddy" Tedesco, was one of seven children of immigrant parents from southern Italy. Born in America, Teddy left New York's Manhattan College in the 1930s to enroll at Fort Hays

State College in Hays, Kansas, and a couple of his friends followed him out west. One was an aspiring young writer named Mickey Spillane, who gained international fame through his legendary fictional character, Mike Hammer. After returning to New York, marrying a dance artist, and having children, Teddy regaled his offspring with stories about Midwestern values and virtues. Nola Foulston graduated from Fort Hays State and Topeka's Washburn University School of Law. In 1976, she was hired as an assistant district attorney in Sedgwick County and by 1989 she'd become the DA, with a special interest in reducing crimes against women and children. That year she was diagnosed with multiple sclerosis, which had no effect on her ability to function as district attorney or her fire for the job.

In special cases, and there was no doubt in Wichita that the murder of George Tiller was special to the DA's office—given Foulston's involvement in the doctor's prior legal scuffles—she was going to run the show. On the day the trial opened, she arrived in court wearing a black sweater, a long black velvet skirt, and black boots with tassels, a gold chain dangling around her neck—drama indeed. A well-coiffed, dark-haired, attractive middle-aged woman, she had a presence that was larger than her size. For a defendant facing a first-degree murder charge, she might have conjured up Darth Vader or the Grim Reaper herself. In the minutes just before Judge Wilbert called the proceeding to order, and in what could be seen as a display of cooperation among the many law enforcement agencies at the trial, Nola was down on the courtroom floor rubbing the belly of the ATF's bomb-sniffing dog.

With the Tiller family shoulder-to-shoulder and the pro-choice and anti-abortion forces mingled together in the gallery, the DA laid out the state's case, emphasizing something that the prosecution would raise again and again: Roeder had used the openness of Reformation Lutheran Church and the friendliness of its worshippers to gain access to the doctor in an unguarded moment and kill him in front of his congregation. Men, women, and children who'd come there to pray had all been exposed to the aftermath of the homicide. Throughout the four days that the state presented testimony, photos of Tiller lying dead on the carpet of the church foyer, blood pooling around his head and his frail-looking glasses knocked off to one side, would be shown again and again on a large video screen. The first time this occurred, an abortion opponent made an approving sound and the judge delivered a fearsome admonition—if anyone did anything like that throughout the remainder of the trial, the offender would be permanently removed from the courtroom. It never happened again.

Whenever the image was introduced into evidence, the Tiller children, along with one of the pastors from Reformation Lutheran, leaned in closer to Jeanne and held her hand or rubbed her back. The picture was never put up without at least one of the Tillers giving in to tears. It likely did not escape the jurors that the dead man's son, Maury, looked a lot like a younger version of the victim. Nor could one avoid the fact that three forceful women—Foulston, Ann Swegle, and Kim Parker— were taking turns prosecuting Roeder and in effect standing up for Tiller's right to have performed abortions for female patients under the laws of Kansas and the United States. The three men sitting at the opposite table were trying just as diligently to show that the defendant's actions against the doctor were justified.

"Tragic" is the only word for the impact the shooting had left on Jeanne Tiller's lean, lined face. She was determined to attend the trial and sit through the graphic testimony, but her features had become a mask, at times almost a death mask, that no outsider could penetrate. She had short, frosted hair, a down-turned mouth, and wary damp eyes, and came to court each day elegantly dressed in long gray or blue outfits, accompanied by strings of pearls. They did not conceal her grief. Watching her brought back the memory of ten months earlier, when she and her life partner had celebrated their victory in this courthouse on a snowy late March afternoon, hoping that their legal ordeals were finally at an end. Now she and her children were staring at the back of the head of the man who'd killed their husband and father.

Following the closing of the clinic, Jeanne had taken Tiller's staff to dinner and had the doctor's armored vehicle broken down and sold for scrap parts. She'd collected ten thousand medical files from his office, including some of those Phill Kline had tried so hard to gain access to when he was attorney general, and had them shipped off to storage in a 650-foot-deep salt mine in Hutchinson, Kansas. The location would help preserve them intact for decades, maybe centuries. The moving of the files had brought a piece of closure to her husband's life and death, but nothing would really be resolved until and unless Roeder was found guilty.

Whenever there was a recess, four or five policemen jumped up and formed a wall between the Tiller family and the anti-abortion spectators just to their left. The Tillers were always allowed to depart the courtroom first, and on her way out, Jeanne repeatedly shot nasty looks at those who supported the killing, but no one made any sounds or gestures toward her or her children. The family then hurried away, using a rear exit that was off-limits to others. Because of all the police officers on the premises displaying multiple guns and wearing body armor, the pro- and anti-abortion sides were forced to be polite to each other in the courthouse hallways. You couldn't go anywhere in the building without running into a cop and being given a once-over to determine if you looked at risk of becoming violent. Security outside the courthouse was just as tight. Each morning, officers used a mirror to inspect the underside of the van bringing in the jurors to see if a bomb had been planted there. The civility that hadn't existed over most of the past thirty-seven years of the abortion struggle was forced into existence at the trial.

On the final day the state presented its case, Sedgwick County's chief medical examiner, Dr. Jaime Oeberst, took the stand, and without warning the prosecution showed a close-up of Tiller taken during the autopsy. It was shocking to the point of having one's entire body flinch. Reading about mass murder is one thing, but seeing the damage done by a single round fired into a man's forehead, the gun barrel placed against the skin as the trigger was pulled, is an entirely different matter. How the Tillers endured watching this was unfathomable. The doctor's face was contorted by the impact, which had left bullet fragments embedded in the back of his skull. Blood was everywhere and he no longer looked human.

As the state prepared to rest on Wednesday afternoon, January 27, and with the jurors out of the courtroom, the polite and pleasant-looking Mark Rudy tried to persuade the judge that both Barry Disney and Phill Kline should be allowed to testify for the defense. They should be able to tell the jury about the AG's office bringing a case against Dr. Tiller in March 2009, and about Kline's conviction that when performing late-term abortions at his clinic, the physician was in violation of the law. Kline's actions against Tiller, Rudy argued, went to the essence of what had motivated Roeder to kill. If the head legal official in Kansas was convinced that Tiller was breaking the law, wasn't it reasonable for a Kansas citizen like Roeder to draw the same conclusion? And if the state's top law enforcement official could not halt Tiller's illegal operations through legal means, by successfully prosecuting him, then how could he be stopped? Having Phill Kline state his beliefs about Tiller in front of the jury might very well add credibility to Roeder's case.

The Inquisition, or at least its residue, was still alive in Wichita, and the DA was not pleased.

Until now, Foulston hadn't publicly given in to her contempt for the defense's strategies throughout the past few months. It was bad enough for Roeder to have shot Dr. Tiller in cold blood inside his church; even worse, she felt, for his legal team to say that he'd done this because the physician had represented an "imminent threat" to the defendant or anyone else. If Foulston and her two assistant DAs needed any more motivation for seeing Roeder found guilty of first-degree murder, they'd gotten it during the past four days by being several feet away from the Tiller family and listening to them cry during the testimony. Now that they'd made their case with ironclad forensic and DNA evidence, Rudy was, in her estimation, trying to drag Disney and Kline into the proceedings just to muddy the legal issues.

With the jury out of earshot, Foulston let fly a tirade against the public defenders, calling their logic "psychotically circuitous." Rudy, his normally reddish skin growing more inflamed as he spoke, fought back in the best tradition of defense lawyers everywhere, even though his client had told the world that he was a killer. Rudy paced and argued, seeming to grope for the words to support his position, which Foluston did not have to do; she'd been waiting patiently to tell the court exactly what she thought of Roeder's defense. The two attorneys went head to head in front of the judge and the gallery, and for those who enjoyed heated, high-stakes lawyering, it was a moment to savor.

More than once, Rudy's voice rose so high that it broke. Scott Roeder, he contended, had formed his deepest feelings about abortion based upon watching the ex–attorney general go after the Wichita doctor. Because of this, it was imperative that the jury hear about Kline and Disney's "good faith" prosecution of Tiller.

But the defendant, the judge countered, "can't corroborate his own beliefs by bringing in Barry Disney or Phill Kline. You could call a member of his Bible study group to corroborate his beliefs . . ."

Judge Wilbert then emphasized once again what he'd been saying to the lawyers for weeks: "We are not going to make this a referendum on abortion."

Foulston stood to address the court.

"The state," she said, "does not believe any of this mishmash. These allegations are totally outrageous . . . and this is not the direction this trial should be going in."

After Rudy had passionately restated his arguments, Foulston did the same.

"This is outrageous," she repeated, "and the state continues to ask this court to make a clear ruling about presenting evidence."

Judge Wilbert, who had a twang reminiscent of President Clinton's, had to hustle to keep the peace in his courtroom. Throughout the debate, Rudy's friendly persona had remained intact, but the DA was ready to blow. She hadn't waited eight months since the murder to see her case derailed by the very same Phill Kline who in late December

2006 had filed charges against Dr. Tiller through Don "the Dingo" McKinney on Kline's way out the door as AG. She hadn't devoted the past four days to painstakingly showing *how* Roeder had killed the physician so that the defense could now turn the trial into the issue of *why* he'd done it. The law wasn't about why, she argued, but about due process, forensic evidence, and sworn testimony. She talked so fast that her throat dried out and she grabbed a bottle of water from the prosecutors' table and took a swig, before launching another salvo.

The judge, who looked more and more uncomfortable as the arguments grew more intense, reminded the DA that none of the conflict at the heart of the trial was his fault. In 1992 the Kansas legislature had enacted a new law declaring that a defendant could have an "honest but unreasonable belief" when committing a crime. This law might leave a judge no choice in a case like the present one but to offer a jury the option of a voluntary-manslaughter conviction. Wilbert's concern was clearly with the appeals court above him.

"If I don't allow the defendant to present his defense," he told the DA, "this verdict will be overturned in a minute."

"This," Foulston shot back, "is irrelevant and immaterial, Judge."

As the three parties plunged deeper into the legalities, Jeanne Tiller held her head in her hands and stared at the floor, her children massaging her back and shoulders. Two rows of abortion protesters looked on, silently urging the judge to let Kline testify. After an hour of nonstop debate, Judge Wilbert reached a decision.

He would follow the same middle ground that he had during most of the case. He'd keep Disney out of the courtroom, but allow Kline to take the stand—with conditions. The former AG could offer his opinions about Tiller and his work at WHCS, but not in front of the jury. Kline's testimony would become part of the judicial record but not, in effect, part of the actual trial. If Roeder chose to testify, the judge said, he promised to give the defendant "fairly wide latitude" to tell the jury what he believed and why he'd taken this course of action, but not permit him to talk about the details of late-term abortion or other things beyond his expertise. When court was adjourned for the day, Rudy smiled at his opposition, but Foulston looked ready to go a few more rounds.

A major overnight storm was rolling into Wichita, and if the snow got deep enough, it could stop the trial and postpone it indefinitely. Nobody wanted a delay and everyone was relieved on Thursday after only four inches of snow and ice had landed on the city, instead of the predicted eight to twelve. That morning the jurors were able to make it to the courthouse by nine, and Kline entered the courtroom shortly thereafter, looking as confident as ever, although he'd brought two lawyers with him as backup. He was sworn in, laid out his credentials, and began his testimony, unleashing echoes of the Inquisition, the 2,600 pages of documents his investigation had left behind at the Kansas Supreme Court, and Bill O'Reilly. He told the judge, the lawyers, the media, and the gallery, but not the jury, that in his view 75 percent of the women coming to Kansas to see Dr. Tiller were having abortions on viable fetuses (a contention that Assistant DA Ann Swegle immediately took issue with, saying that Kline's presentation was filled with "historical and factual inaccuracies").

Kline said that criminal charges were filed against Tiller on December 21, 2006, once a judge had found probable cause to support this complaint.

"After we filed the complaint," he said, "I got an e-mail from the DA . . . It said that I did not have jurisdiction to file this case and it was dismissed. The case never moved forward."

The unnamed DA was Nola Foulston.

Kline wound up his testimony by stating that although he'd come to the conclusion that Tiller "was performing unlawful abortions," killing the doctor was not justified or reasonable.

"Withering" is too soft a term to describe Jeanne Tiller's expression as the witness left the stand and prepared to return to his teaching position at Jerry Falwell's Liberty University.

Her day wasn't going to get any easier.

# LVI

The defense began its case with Steve Osburn delivering a modest opening statement, and then Mark Rudy called Roeder to the stand. The defendant, his face pasty after nearly eight months in prison, was remarkably composed under oath. This was his chance to explain himself to the jury and the world, via live television coverage, and he seemed to have been readying himself for this moment not just since the previous May 31, but for years prior to that. With unshakable calm and in a tone that was alarming because it was so matter-of-fact, he told the jury what he'd been telling reporters and other visitors to the jail since last June—how he'd thought about killing Tiller for as long as a decade and then carefully planned and carried out the execution. His clarity and absolute certainty about the rightness of what he'd done never wavered. If the DA didn't want to hear about the why behind the homicide, or to give the defendant a nationwide audience and a legal platform from which to denounce abortion, she'd lost that battle.

"Did protests stop Dr. Tiller?" Rudy asked his client.

"No."

"Did Shelley Shannon stop him?"

"No."

"Did the 1986 bombing?"

"No."

"Did you think the law would stop Dr. Tiller?"

"Yes . . . I followed this as close as I could and he—"

Foulston was out of her chair and in front of the judge.

"These answers are being fed to the witness," she said.

Wilbert told Rudy to take another tack and he did, with Roeder now repeating many of the same points Kline had just made about unlawful abortions in Kansas. He remained on the stand throughout the morning, giving a step-by-step account of the crime, gaining momentum as he spoke and obviously proud of what he'd done. Of all the things revealed at the trial, one of the most unsettling for Lindsey and Nick, as they watched the proceedings in Kansas City, was a detail about the weekend leading up to the shooting. His first choice for his last Friday night of freedom was not to spend it with his son at dinner and a movie. Instead, he'd hoped to be at his brother's home outside Topeka on May 29, taking target practice with his new gun, but this hadn't worked out, because David Roeder had been busy. Seeing Nick that night was his back-up plan, but the young man and his mother hadn't known that until now. Despite all they'd learned about their father and ex-husband, both Nick and Lindsey were further hurt and angered by this revelation.

Nick's reaction to the piece of information, Lindsey wrote in an e-mail, "can be shared with anyone—I want people to know Scott was an uncaring *&%*%*$(#."

During breaks in Roeder's testimony, the anti-abortion group clustered together in one corner of the ninth-floor hallways or in the main-floor lobby or in the basement cafeteria, while the pro-choice forces gathered near the Feminist Majority Foundation's Kathy Spillar and talked among themselves. The media drifted from one side to the other, looking for quotes on the unfolding trial. The two factions never spoke to one another.

The war that had divided Wichita and America for nearly four decades was alive inside the courthouse—in every chance encounter between enemies during an elevator ride and every trip to the small restrooms. It was on the faces and in the furtive eyes of those who could not quite bring themselves to look at their opponents. It was in the sorrow embedded in Jeanne Tiller's face, in the silent glee that some in the courtroom took from her husband's death, and in the haunting feeling that the doctor's career should have ended some other way. An ineffable pain had filtered into the halls and the courtroom, getting stronger as the trial unwound.

Randall Terry let no opportunity pass to call an impromptu press conference and surround himself with journalists, telling them and passersby that Roeder could not get a fair trial and that George Tiller had been a mass murderer. Terry was a natural-born entertainer who loved the spotlight, as outgoing and boisterous as Dave Leach was quiet, polite, and meek. Usually accompanied by two gray-haired women, Leach liked to hang back from the crowd, lean against a wall, and let others come to him. One of the women usually carried a copy of Sarah Palin's book *Going Rogue*.

Asked during a break in Roeder's testimony whether the shooting of Tiller was justified, he said "Yes," without hesitation.

Were the lives of the people who'd died in Vietnam or Iraq as sacred as the lives of the unborn? Did he ever protest the violence of war as he did abortion? He shook his head and gave a patronizing smile, his eyes twinkling, saying that those two things had nothing to do with each other.

"If we hadn't invaded Vietnam," he added, "many more lives would have been lost."

When the trial resumed, Roeder told the jurors why he'd gone into Reformation Lutheran Church last May 31 with a loaded .22 handgun.

"There was nothing being done," he said, "and the legal process had been exhausted and these babies were dying every day. If someone didn't do something, he was going to continue aborting children and I needed to act for these children . . . The lives of these children were in imminent danger if someone did not stop him."

"Do you regret this?" Rudy asked.

"No, I don't."

The defense attorney nodded at his client and sat down.

For her cross-examination, Foulston walked to a lectern positioned near the jury, faced the witness, and began peppering him with one clipped question after another, revealing more of her contempt.

If the defendant had never wanted to hurt anyone except Dr. Tiller, why hadn't he told law enforcement right after his arrest that he'd left a loaded handgun in a dirt pile in a parking lot in Burlington, Kansas?

Unfazed, Roeder replied that because he'd hid it in a remote, safe location it wasn't a danger to anyone.

What had happened in the foyer the morning of the shooting?

Tiller had never seen him coming, Roeder said, so he'd been able to get very close. After he'd fired the gun, the doctor seemed to have stood in front of him for quite some time without moving, perhaps for several seconds, before toppling over onto the floor.

Was he nervous pulling the trigger?

"I was a little nervous. I wasn't overly excited."

How did he feel afterward?

"I got gas and pizza. I was hungry."

The DA appeared disgusted.

Unable to look at the defendant as he testified, Jeanne Tiller had dropped her forehead all the way down to her knees, her fingers gripping a Kleenex, her shoulders heaving.

"If he was gonna be stopped," Roeder told Foulston, "someone had to do it."

"Do you feel," the DA asked, "that you've successfully completed your mission?"

"He's been stopped."

Foulston glanced at the jury, took her seat, and the defense rested. The jurors left the courtroom, the gallery emptied out, and now that the testimony was finished the judge was left alone to decide the most important question of the trial—whether or not to give the jury the option of convicting Roeder of voluntary manslaughter. For the next several hours, the issue remained unresolved as Judge Wilbert gave the matter due diligence and other legal duties were being pursued elsewhere.

That morning, for the first time ever, Mark Rudy had told the DA and the WPD what had become of the gun Roeder had used. Two Wichita police officers immediately took off for Burlington in the hope of retrieving the firearm where it had been buried. They questioned the town's police department and the local newspaper, but the lot had long since been paved over and the dirt hauled away.

# LVII

By nightfall, the judge had made his decision: the voluntary-manslaughter option was dead. The defendant was either going to be found guilty of first-degree murder and two counts of aggravated assault—or set free.

On Friday morning, the snowfall had nearly stopped, the constant clouds that had hung over Wichita for the two weeks of the trial were thinning, and the fog had dissipated. For her closing argument, Ann Swegle dispassionately reiterated the state's case. Mark Rudy then did about everything he could think of to try to help his client, alluding in his final argument to the Magna Carta, habeas corpus, trial by jury, the Stalinist purges, the Holocaust, the relocation of Native Americans, and Martin Luther King. It was a noble effort, delivered with grace and grit, but had a ring of desperation.

"Scott," he told the jury in summation, "proved that he killed Dr. Tiller, but only you can determine if he murdered Dr. Tiller. We'll ask you to acquit Scott Roeder of first-degree murder."

Kim Parker then crossed the courtroom, stood behind the lectern, and spoke last for the DA's office.

"On May 31, 2009," she said, "Wichita changed from a community celebrating the Sabbath to a terrorized city. Scott Roeder said he had the right to invade that church and hide behind its welcoming arms . . . While [the usher] Charles Scott greeted him at the open door of the sanctuary with an open heart and mind . . . Roeder was calculating his intent [with] feigned piousness and a murderous heart . . . While Jeanne Tiller sang in the choir, Scott Roeder put a bullet in the head of her husband . . ."

Grouped closer together and holding hands and arms, the Tiller family looked on, wearing "Attitude Is Everything" buttons today in honor of the victim, as they had at his funeral.

"While Dr. Ryding," Parker said, "tried to suck the blood out of Dr. Tiller's mouth and save his life, Roeder wondered if he'd shot the right man . . . As WPD responded to the church, he was eating a pizza . . . He claims justification but these are not the acts of a justified man. These acts are cowardly. A justified man does not have to hide inside a church . . . or hide his gun . . . or take his victim unawares . . . or need to run. Roeder is not justified. He is only and simply guilty of the crimes he's been charged with. I ask you as citizens of this community and this state and the United States of America to hold him fully ac-countable and find him guilty of first-degree murder and two counts of aggravated assault."


By ten a.m., the judge had instructed the jurors about the charges and sent them off to deliberate. In the lobby, crowded with cops and full of activity, Dave Leach stood by himself taking in the movement around him, as the spectators clustered in their usual groups and talked on cell phones. He was joined by Randall Terry, who'd been loitering nearby. Throughout the morning, Terry had been passing out a three-page flyer about what was wrong with the anti-abortion movement and how it needed to make a stronger commitment to its goals and take bolder steps. Seizing the opportunity to talk with Leach, because he was now accompanied by a journalist, Terry strode up in his striking alligator boots and introduced himself to the reporter. The conversation had only begun when a uniformed deputy approached.

"You better get up to the ninth floor," he said.

"The verdict is already in?"

He nodded. "Get up there."

The trio went to the bay of elevators and stepped into an open one, Terry complaining that he couldn't believe that less than forty-five minutes (thirty-seven, actually) had passed since the judge had given the case to the jury. Leach was silent, but a little smile played around the corner of his mouth, as it often did, his purpose never as obvious as Terry's. The day before, Leach had said that bringing national attention to the Roeder trial, and getting the public to think about violence being justified to stop an abortion doctor, and motivating a judge to consider the necessity defense and the voluntary-manslaughter charge in these circumstances were all victories. He didn't seem to take the situation nearly as personally as Terry.

"This case can be the start of a new process," he had said. "And no matter what anyone says, the trial was about abortion."

Within minutes, the jury and the legal parties had all gathered in the courtroom and the judge called the proceedings to order. As the Tiller family looked on, one or two of them were clearly praying. The gallery fell still, the scene echoing the Tiller trial ten months earlier, when on March 27, 2009, with a blizzard about to slam into Wichita, six jurors had taken roughly twenty-five minutes to reach their conclusion and acquit the physician.

While he sat at the defense table and glanced around the room, Roeder's face colored just slightly, no longer looking quite so calm. He'd set himself up for martyrdom but then tried to find a legal way out of that fate. Maybe he was questioning his decisions or maybe, as Lindsey had suggested throughout the trial, he was having trouble sleeping. No one knew him better than she did or cared more about his health, even now. She and Nick had watched every moment of the trial and were awaiting the denouement, as Lindsey offered up her own hope that Roeder would never again be free to show up at their front door.

The judge cleared his throat and Jeanne Tiller held her hands over her eyes. Wilbert thanked the jury and asked them for their verdict, which came in swiftly and without fanfare, surrounded by near-total silence: guilty on one count of first-degree murder and two counts of aggravated assault. No one in the gallery made a sound. Roeder would be sentenced in two months, but before the judge could adjourn one last time and everyone dispersed, Nola Foulston stood and made a point of saying that she was going to ask the court for the maximum sentence of a "Hard 50." If the judge agreed with this, the fifty-one-year-old Roeder could not become eligible for parole for five more decades—the DA's parting shot at the convicted murderer, as he lowered his eyes and walked out of the room with two guards, his steps a little uncertain as he made his way back to his cell. He'd soon be headed up the road thirty miles to the state correctional facility at El Dorado, the most dangerous prison in Kansas.

From her own cell in Minnesota, Shelley Shannon commented on the jury's decision in an e-mail to Dave Leach. Her message, which found its way to the Associated Press, was that because of the trial's outcome, America could expect more violence.

"Abortionists are killed," she wrote, "because they are serial murderers of innocent children who must be stopped, and they will continue to be stopped, even though Scott didn't get a fair trial. May God bless Scott for his faithfulness and brave actions and stand."

"Other doctors," said Kathy Spillar in the courthouse lobby right after the verdict, "remain under threat. There are substantial questions left to answer about other people's involvement in this case and with Scott Roeder. We've given information about these matters to the Justice Department and all of it needs to be investigated further."

"My son and I," Lindsey said, "are relieved and gratified that a verdict of guilty was decided. We are anxious to put this behind us and move forward. Our prayers are with the Tiller family, who showed great strength and also show my son and I what unity of a family truly means. We do not expect or ask that the Tiller family find closure. We pray that they feel a sense of justice.

"We understand that the gaping hole where their husband, father, and grandfather once was will never close but we hope and pray that over time with love of family, church, and community those jagged edges will heal. We humbly ask their forgiveness for any part we may have played to increase their pain and suffering. Sincerely, Lindsey and Nicholas Roeder."

Outside the courthouse, Randall Terry protested the verdict and said, "The blood of these babies slain by Tiller is crying for vengeance."

A few miles east of downtown, Reformation Lutheran Church issued its own statement, wishing to thank people for their "many prayers and thoughts of encouragement during these difficult months following the murder of Reformation member Dr. George Tiller . . . As a guilty verdict was handed down today in the case against Scott Roeder, we are grateful that the state presented the facts clearly, the witnesses boldly told what they knew to be true, the judge led with clarity, and the jury discerned and acted in regard to the law.

"While these proceedings will obviously not bring George back, we trust in the promise of the resurrection and move forward in that hope. We pray that all places of worship will be sanctuaries—places of reconciliation, peace, and hope, setting the pace for a fractured world that so desperately seeks unity with God and one another . . . Pastor Lowell Michelson and Pastor Kristin Neitzel."

Donald Spitz, who ran the Army of God Web site, ominously told the Associated Press that "there is not a lot of good feeling out there. Everybody is pretty angry . . . Times change. People are not as passive as they have been. They are more assertive."

The National Organization for Women responded to the verdict by urging "the Department of Justice to investigate this network of anti-abortion terrorists. NOW leadership and our dedicated grassroots activists across the country have been tracking these terrorists at work for decades. Some of our own members have survived harassment and assault. NOW would be happy to share with the Justice Department any relevant evidence we might have that would help shut down this conspiracy to deny women their fundamental right to abortion through violence and the threat of violence."

"Once again," wrote the Tiller family, "a Sedgwick County jury has reached a just verdict. We also want to thank George's countless friends and supporters in Wichita and around the country who have offered their comfort. At this time we hope that George can be remembered for his legacy of service to women, the help he provided for those who needed it and the love and happiness he provided us as a husband, father and grandfather."

A few days later, Dave Leach recorded a long prison interview with Roeder via telephone and put it up on YouTube. He gave the inmate the time and opportunity to say for the public all the graphic things about abortion that the judge had not allowed him to say in court. He reemphasized his lack of sympathy for Jeanne Tiller and again compared her to a woman who'd been married to a hit man.

# EPILOGUE

With my own courtroom vigil now over and the sun attempting to break through the clouds on Friday afternoon, I turned away from the courthouse and began walking in the snow back to my downtown hotel, my final image of the event being Randall Terry standing outside in the bitter cold hunting for one more reporter to speak to. I was eager to be alone with my thoughts and to feel the peculiar emptiness that comes at the end of a murder trial, especially one that had generated this much anticipation and attention. The media would move on to a new story, the Sedgwick County Courthouse would become less crowded, and the bomb-sniffing dogs would be given another mission at another venue, but this verdict signified a larger ending than that. The life and death of Dr. Tiller had not concluded until the jury had heard the facts of the case and reached its own judgment about Scott Roeder.

The national abortion wars would continue, but for thirty-five years they'd been centered in Wichita, on a street corner in a modest-looking neighborhood, around one figure who'd never given an inch to those who hated him the most. Kansas had once again played a crucial role in a divided America, but the battle would have to find a new focal point and other targets in other places, because there was no one left in Wichita to demonstrate against. The streets felt emptier than ever, but the pain and uncertainty were still in the air. Things had ended, but nothing had been resolved.

Nineteen days after the verdict, on February 17, Joseph Stack of Texas sent his own anti-government message by flying a small plane into a federal building in Austin to protest the IRS and the tax laws of America. Before setting his house on fire, loading his plane with an extra gas tank, and slamming it into a structure holding IRS offices, killing the tax employee Vernon Hunter and Stack himself, he'd posted an online manifesto.

"I would only hope," he wrote, "that by striking a nerve that stimulates the inevitable double standard, knee-jerk government reaction that results in more stupid draconian restrictions people wake up and begin to see the pompous political thugs and their mindless minions for what they are. Well, Mr. Big Brother IRS man, let's try something different; take my pound of flesh and sleep well."

His suicide mission generated numerous supporters in cyberspace, including Facebook groups such as "The Philosophy of Joe Stack," which quickly had two thousand fans. Tributes to the dead man showed up on Web sites and then came a video game challenging players to burn down a house and fly a plane into a building.

Two weeks later, on March 4, John Patrick Bedell of California opened fire at an entrance to the Pentagon, wounding two police officers before he was fatally gunned down. Bedell had been diagnosed as bipolar and been in and out of treatment programs for years. His parents reported him missing on January 4, one day after a Texas Highway Patrol officer stopped him for speeding in Texarkana. He returned to his parents' home, but the next time he went missing he showed up with a 9-millimeter pistol in D.C. and began shooting outside the Pentagon.

As spring approached, with President Obama's health care reform on hold and tragedies such as those in Austin and Washington dominating the news, the United States struck more people than Joseph Stack or John Patrick Bedell as not merely unmanageable, but ungovernable. According to a Pew Research poll conducted March 11–21,

2010, trust in the U.S. government had reached an all-time low. Only about one in five registered voters believed they could rely on the federal government to do the right thing "just about always" or most of the time, while an overwhelming majority said it will do the right thing only some of the time—or never. The survey attributed this negative view to a "perfect storm of conditions associated with distrust of government—a dismal economy, an unhappy public, bitter partisan-based backlash, and epic discontent with Congress and elected officials."

Heading back to Denver following the trial, I recalled the previous June, two weeks after Dr. Tiller had been murdered, when I'd visited my hometown. The summer heat had only begun to gather on the plains and build up throughout the long hours before dusk brought some relief. One sweltering afternoon I'd walked over to the small swimming pool near my old school—a form of recreation and escape from the scorching air that hadn't existed in the community when I was a child. Standing outside the pool and looking in through a chain-link fence, I hoped that the water could steer local teens away from the drinking and drugs so rampant when I was their age. Watching the boys and girls swim, I saw a black youngster, maybe ten or eleven, paddling un-self-consciously next to the white children, all of them splashing around in the sunlight, grabbing each other's arms and legs and laughing in the high-pitched squeals of kids everywhere having fun in a pool on a hot summer day.

When I was ten or eleven black people had been banned inside the city limits of our town after sundown. In those years, tens of millions of Americans had railed against integration, declaring that it would destroy the country and erode our democratic foundations. The mixing of the races was unnatural and against what God had intended—it would undermine the fabric of society and leave the United States vulnerable at home and abroad. Seeing beads of water slide off the black youngster's shoulders and onto the skin of the white children beside him, I felt a knot rise in my throat and I lowered my head, turning away from the pool and continuing my walk. America had proven itself more resilient and flexible than some had ever imagined. The center had held during the Civil War, during integration, and again during the controversy surrounding the death of George Tiller. The country wasn't yet finished with its evolving and its becoming, and something *was* about to be resolved through the processes of government.

On Saturday, March 20, 2010, thousands of opponents of President Obama's health care legislation encircled the Capitol in Washington, waving signs and chanting, "Kill the bill!" They threw racial slurs at three black Democratic lawmakers—Representatives André Carson of Indiana, Emanuel Cleaver II of Missouri, and John Lewis of Georgia— and a protester spat at Cleaver as the trio walked toward the Capitol for a vote. Other demonstrators hurled anti-homosexual remarks at Representative Barney Frank, Democrat of Massachusetts, who's openly gay. The man who spat at Congressman Cleaver was arrested, but Cleaver decided not to press charges.

The legislator's office then released this statement:

"This is not the first time the Congressman has been called the 'n' word and certainly not the worst assault he has endured in his years fighting for equal rights for all Americans. That being said, he is disappointed that in the 21st century our national discourse has devolved to the point of name calling and spitting. He looks forward to taking a historic vote on health care reform legislation tomorrow . . . Our nation has a history of struggling each time we expand rights. Today's protests are no different, but the Congressman believes this is worth fighting for."

At eleven o'clock the following night, the House was finally ready to vote on the measure, which offered policies to tens of millions of uninsured Americans, covered others who had pre-existing medical conditions, and lowered the cost of drugs for senior citizens. The vote came after a compromise had been reached on the most difficult issue surrounding the new bill: President Obama had agreed to sign an executive order affirming that the legislation would prevent any federal monies from being used for abortions. Representative Bart Stupak of

Michigan, who'd vehemently opposed the reform bill last November, was satisfied with the order and decided to support the president.

"Make no doubt about it," Stupak said that Sunday evening. "There will be no public funds for abortion."

During Stupak's speech on the House floor leading up to the vote, Representative Randy Neugebauer, a third-term Texas Republican, cried out "baby killer."

Congress approved health care reform by a vote of 219–212 and the president signed the legislation into law two days later. At least ten Democrats who'd voted for the bill, including Stupak, had their offices vandalized or received death threats.

Between January and June 2010, eleven states passed laws regulating or restricting abortion, while four other states put forth similar bills that had made it through at least one legislative house. Governor Haley Barbour of Mississippi signed a bill barring insurers from covering abortion under the new health care reform act, and the Oklahoma legislature overrode a gubernatorial veto of a bill requiring abortion doctors to answer thirty-eight questions about each procedure. Thirteen other states had now introduced or passed similar legislation.


On April 1, 2010, Judge Wilbert held a sentencing hearing for the convicted man, the last opportunity for Roeder to address the court, the media covering the event, and the national viewing public. The proceeding, which many expected to take an hour or two, ran from nine a.m. until six p.m. before the judge exhaustedly brought it to a conclusion. At one point, he threatened to toss Roeder from the courtroom for the killer's outbursts against the legal system that had tried and found him guilty. The only issue before the judge was whether he'd make Roeder eligible for parole after serving twenty-five years or give him the Hard 50 and prevent the fifty-two-year-old from coming before the Kansas parole board for half a century—a certain life sentence. The prosecution, led by Nola Foulston and Ann Swegle, and the Tiller family, represented by their attorney Lee Thompson, both delivered statements that echoed each other. Their words were clearly intended to place the murder in a larger context by repeatedly using the terms "hate crime," "domestic terrorism," "anarchist," and "political assassination."

"The impact of this crime," said Thompson, "is felt on the medical profession far beyond Wichita. He [Dr. Tiller] gave his life for the rights of women . . . His legacy cannot be diminished by the act of a single terrorist."

Stalking was one of the aggravating factors in ruling on the Hard 50 sentence, and Foulston emphasized just how long Roeder had tracked the physician before murdering him. He'd first gone to Reformation Lutheran Church in 2002 to develop a strategy to kill the man at his place of worship.

The defense presented four character witnesses, including Eugene Frye, Dave Leach, and Regina Dinwiddie, who testified about how religiously committed and well mannered Roeder had been around them. The psychologist George Hough, who'd examined the defendant for ten hours in the summer of 2009, told the court that Roeder had chosen to obey God's laws, not man's, but he was mentally competent to stand trial.

The judge spoke at length for the first time since the case had started and part of his decision today depended on whether he felt that this crime was especially "heinous, atrocious, and cruel." Roeder's actions fell into that category, Wilbert said, because he'd shot Dr. Tiller not at his home or office or even in the parking lot of Reformation Lutheran but inside the church itself—designed to provide "asylum or sanctuary in our society . . . the very place that abhors violence."

In late afternoon, Roeder himself addressed the court and read extensively from the writings of Paul Hill, who'd killed Dr. John Britton and James Barrett in July 1994. As most everyone who'd spoken with Roeder had discovered, he could appear quite normal for the first ten minutes or so of a conversation, but then his fanaticism over abortion surfaced, along with his rage against government, a feeling that was spreading across America. Four days before the hearing, a federal grand jury in Detroit had indicted nine suspected members of a Christian militia group, the Hutaree, and charged them with plotting to kill local, state, and national law enforcement officials. Three days later, the FBI and Department of Homeland Security warned that another outfit, the Guardians of the Free Republics, wanted to "restore America" by dismantling parts of the government. They'd sent more than thirty governors letters saying that if they didn't leave office within three days, they'd be "removed."

"How is it," Roeder asked the judge, while complaining about his treatment since his arrest, "that a man can speak openly and freely at his sentencing, but not at his trial? This court stifled my testimony . . . The blame for George Tiller's death lies more with the state of Kansas than with me. You may sentence me to twenty-five or fifty years in prison but it does not serve justice in any way . . . I agree with Paul Hill wholeheartedly. God will avenge every drop of blood that stains Kansas grass . . . Give me liberty to defend the unborn or give me death."

For more than half an hour, the judge let him ramble without interruption, until he began attacking the district attorney, sitting a few feet from Roeder. Then Wilbert stepped in.

"You killed Dr. Tiller," he said. "You're not going to politically assassinate Nola Foulston. I'm going to draw the line there."

Roeder was undeterred.

"If you would follow a higher power," he told the judge, "you would acquit me."

"If you think," Wilbert replied, "you're going to convince me with some last-minute plea, you're wasting your time . . . I'm not going to provide you with an all-night political forum."

After forty-five minutes of listening to Roeder speechify, the judge delivered his ruling, giving the killer fifty years plus two more for threatening Gary Hoepner and Keith Martin at the church on the day of the murder.

The proceeding was finished, but not Scott Roeder.

As he was being ushered out of the courtroom by the beefy guards for the final time, he tried to turn back toward the prosecutors' table, but was restrained.

"The blood of babies," he yelled, "is on your hands, Nola Foulston and Ann Swegle!"

Later, outside the courthouse, the DA summed up her experience by saying, "This was a difficult case [and] the difficulty was apparent from the emotion that rang across the courtroom . . . across our community, and across the world." A few weeks later, as the one-year anniversary of the murder approached, the Senate majority leader, Harry Reid of Nevada, spoke about the physician on the floor of Congress: "He was murdered by an unrepentant assassin who took a life in the name of protecting life. It was an indefensible crime and an incomprehensible excuse."

The Reverend Dr. Carlton Veazey, president of Washington, D.C.'s Religious Coalition for Reproductive Choice, which had held a memorial for Dr. Tiller in June 2009, also honored the occasion. "Today," Reverend Veazey said: "we call on all who value life to join with us in recommitting ourselves to creating the kind of society that George Tiller sought—in his words, where 'every pregnancy is an invited guest in the woman's body and a welcome addition to her family.' In such a society, women would be trusted to make decisions about pregnancy, doctors would provide health care without fear, and conscience and religious beliefs about reproductive choice would be respected. We pray that the compassion, wisdom, and courage of Dr. George Tiller will be carried forward in creating this world."

Around the first anniversary of Dr. Tiller's murder, Lindsey drove down to Wichita for the first time since the killing, determined to visit the sites her ex-husband had made famous and notorious. The FBI had been speaking with her lately, indicating that the federal investigation of Roeder was not finished. Pulling up in front of Reformation Lutheran Church and staring at the large redbrick structure, she couldn't make herself go inside and look at the foyer where the physician had died. Leaving the crime scene, she found the office building that had long been Dr. Tiller's clinic and stepped out of her car, walking up to the fence surrounding the structure and tucking a bouquet of white silk lilies above a "No Trespassing" sign, her belated tribute to the man. She went by the cheap motel where Scott had stayed the night before the shooting and felt something she'd felt at the other locations: everything was smaller than it had appeared on television, yet being here in person added an emotional dimension to the tragedy that TV couldn't convey.

She'd come nearer to a sense of closure than before, but that would remain elusive as long as her former husband kept sending letters to her son. Nick refused to read them but asked his mother to, and one that had arrived on May 27, 2010, tried to justify Roeder's actions through what Lindsey called "Scott's usual blackmail."

If you don't respond to this letter, the inmate had written the young man, "Then I will know that you agree with me."

In an e-mail she sent out after receiving the letter, Lindsey said, "I would think he would learn that does not work on us anymore—we are safe from him."


That evening in June 2009 in my hometown, I drove out into the countryside, turning up the car's CD player and letting out the music of Muddy Waters and B.B. King, so loud that it rattled the dashboard and flushed some crows from the branches of a cottonwood tree. I stuck my head out the window and felt the breeze on my cheeks—shivering with the memory of what I'd seen a few hours earlier at the swimming pool, an everyday event but also a reminder of the progress our country had witnessed in the past half century. The acceptance of a new skin color in my hometown was as significant, in the context of my upbringing, as the arrival of a black face in charge of the White House.

As the music blared and the sun went down and the western horizon became golden pink, I allowed myself to feel that my generation—despite the talk show madness, the endless narcissism, and the constant violence against ourselves and our children—had accomplished something in my lifetime. Our job, unlike my father's, had never been to go abroad and defeat an enemy as obvious as the Nazis, or to bring down the Vietnamese or the Soviet Union with our unlimited bullets and bombs. It had always been to confront ourselves and our deepest prejudices and angers, our terror of change and our most secret and damaging ghosts. And to find a new way to live with them or to let them go.

America had survived its first civil war, and we'd come a distance in the second one, still searching for that more perfect union. This afternoon I'd glimpsed where we were going and what we were capable of, and it had constricted my throat and lifted my heart once more. Riding over the dusty gravel roads of my birthplace, returning to the blue notes and steady 4/4 beat that had always given me the greatest joy and deepest hope, and always pushed away the fear and ignorance, I sensed that despite our current troubles we were never turning back.

In recent times a lot had been written about what was the matter with Kansas, and that subject didn't resound any deeper with anyone than it did with me. A lot had also been written about what had been lost since the good old days in the Sunflower State, but I'd just seen and felt what had been gained—and there was no comparison. Both Kansas and America were more creative and more unpredictable than any nostalgia could suggest. We'd survived historical messes and tragedies before and might just do so now, if we leaned on the foundation of law, equality, and self-rule we were given at birth. These had been won through blood, worth every drop, and we undermined or attacked them at our peril. It was indeed time to wake up. So I rolled down all the windows and plunged farther into the countryside, cranking up the music again, letting it ride the wind and shake the darkening sky.

# ACKNOWLEDGMENTS

Several hours after Dr. George Tiller was assassinated in Wichita on May 31, 2009, I began the process of making contact with Charlie Spicer at St. Martin's Press. I knew that Charlie, like me, had a deep interest in books about crimes, especially ones with large social implications. The murder had occurred in Kansas, where I grew up, and I knew people involved in the situation unfolding that day in Wichita, as the police hunted for the killer. Beyond that, I'd begun writing about domestic terrorism twenty-five years earlier and instinctively felt that this story would lead in that direction. In recent years, nothing had struck me as more important than how fear, rage, and a sense of being victimized by the outside world had moved from the edges of our culture into the mainstream. What used to be clearly on the margins was now packaged and sold as prime-time entertainment. I was very pleased that Charlie was interested in this subject, and a few weeks later I was sitting in a Wichita jail cell with Dr. Tiller's assassin, Scott Roeder. His Kansas roots were just a few miles from mine and he was more than willing to share with me the thinking behind his own brand of terrorism. In a way that was almost eerie, his crime led me straight back to my first book, *Talked to Death*, about the 1984 neo-Nazi murder of the Denver talk-show host Alan Berg. The death of Dr. Tiller seemed like a natural sequel to that story. All the elements were in place, but

I'd yet to meet the most important figure, from my perspective, in the building of the book.

The first time I sat down with the killer's ex-wife, Lindsey, we were in the basement of her church and she talked for three hours straight, describing how she'd met Roeder and married him in 1986, and how their union had gradually disintegrated and ended in 1996. As I got to know her and we spoke on other occasions, I realized that I was hearing what it was like to fall in love with a man, have a child with him, and then watch him turn into an American terrorist. In recent decades, as I'd observed the normalization of hatred and demonization in our politics, media, and religion, this was the subject I most wanted to write about, but I hoped to find the human side, and the human cost, of this evolution. Lindsey had lived it.

When I got together with her in June 2009, it was as if she'd been waiting for years to tell someone about her wrenching experience with Scott Roeder. She knew the timeline of events and the people involved, and could recall details of the distant past. Learning that her ex-husband had gunned down Dr. Tiller unleashed her own need and desire to tell her family's story, and her courage and honesty are at the core of this book. I've often been asked about writing long pieces of nonfiction and my answer is always the same: in order to do this kind of book justice, you need at least one person who's critically important to the events, is ready to talk, and is willing to tell the truth. In this instance, it was Lindsey, which is why I've dedicated the book to her.

I'd like to thank Dr. Warren Hern of Boulder for speaking with me on numerous occasions and sharing his writings about the abortion conflict. This extremely busy physician always found the time to help make this a better and more complete story. Photos were provided by Dr. Hern, the Feminist Majority Foundation, the Religious Coalition for Reproductive Choice and Marjorie Signer, by Georgia Cole of Wichita's Eighteenth Judicial District, the Kansas attorney general's office, Lindsey Roeder, and the Kansas Historical Society. Thanks to all of them. My understanding of this topic was assisted throughout the past year by studying *The Wrath of Angels*, the excellent history of

America's abortion wars written by Judy L. Thomas and James Risen. I also want to thank my agent, Mel Berger of William Morris, for working with Charlie Spicer to make this book a reality.

A special note of gratitude goes out to my mother, Mary, my wife, Joyce, and to my lifelong friend Bob Haight for his inspiration and stream of provocative questions and thoughts during the course of researching and writing *The Wichita Divide*. He was there when it counted. Last, and perhaps most important, my editor, Yaniv Soha, deserves praise for his distinct gift for focusing a story and moving it forward. His critical eye, his deft touch with handling a first-person narrative, and his understanding that every word should serve the story and nothing but the story are behind all of these pages.

The best part of covering any nonfiction subject is when you get in your car for the first time, fill up the gas tank, and begin driving in search of something new, uncertain where you're headed but sensing that a story out there is ready to be told. Then the right people seem to show up and start talking and take you into realities that are richer than you could have imagined—as if everything had been prepared for your arrival and all you really needed to do was trust your instincts and start the engine.